HYMNS AND THE FAITH

By the same Author
HYMNS AND HUMAN LIFE

HYMNS AND
THE FAITH

ERIK ROUTLEY

B.D., D.Phil.

★

WILLIAM B. EERDMANS PUBLISHING COMPANY
GRAND RAPIDS, MICHIGAN

To
ARTHUR HENRY WALTON STARKEY,

3 - 88

First U.S.A. edition, March 1968
Printed in the United States of America
Library of Congress Catalog Card Number: 68-20583

Contents

v

Preface

IN order to tell the truth about anything, it is necessary to attend not only to its origin but also to its end. There is now a considerable literature on the origins of our hymns, to which I have myself ventured to contribute. But ever since the publication of my *Hymns and Human Life* I have had this on my conscience, that that book contributed nothing to the redress of what I believe to be a certain lack of balance in our interest in hymns. Hymnology, the study of sources and history in this field, is all very well, provided it be not pursued at the expense of the contents of the hymns themselves.

In this present book, then, I have attempted a commentary on a series of popular hymns with a view to re-creating their atmosphere and re-telling the spiritual story of each. At one stage I had intended to exclude from the text all names of authors and all dates, to write a book about hymns which needed neither indexes nor footnotes. But that would perhaps have been pedantic, and there are places where a literal adherence to such a rule would have been a positive disadvantage. Where possible, therefore, some reference is made to the circumstances in which the hymn under review was written ; it may, of course, be surprising to some that in so many cases we know nothing reliable about the circumstances surrounding the composition of some well-known hymn, but then hymn-writers are a modest race, not on the whole given to autobiography, and where we do not know for certain we had better not guess. The principle, however, is to discuss each hymn with the chief emphasis on what it says, to elucidate the occasional obscurity, and, by reference to scripture and the Church's teaching, to throw light on our traditional Christian beliefs as they are adorned by traditional Christian songs.

For the selection of this series of ' popular hymns ' I have not relied on my own judgment. The basis of the selection is the list set out on pages 288 and 289 of *Hymns and Human Life*, which list was deduced from certain observations which I undertook in the year 1951 in order to find out what were the popular hymns of English Protestantism. But I have not quite kept to that list. It contains, for one thing, two harvest hymns which I think perhaps I ought to have omitted, since no other seasonal hymns were included in it. One hymn (but the really exciting thing is that in this list of well-known hymns there is only *one*) I honestly hold to be too thin in content to bear any weight of commentary. I sacrificed an evening hymn and a psalm-version for two hymns on the Holy Spirit, one of which is popular enough to have gone into the original list, the other of such august associations that I thought it ought to have a place.

But here is the point which I cannot forbear to stress. It will be found that the papers that follow form a con-spectus of Christian belief which, although I am sure it is neither profoundly expressed nor adequately celebrated here, none the less covers the whole of the credal country. Without straining the texts by an inch it has been possible to say something about all the cardinal doctrines of the Church. That is to say, our normal canon of popular hymns does really provide a popular commentary on the creeds of Christendom. It has been the rewarding thing about this present piece of work that I have found that the popular hymns provide a much better-balanced view of the Christian faith than you would have got from any collection of my own favourites. I believe that to be of the greatest importance. It has been a labour of love to examine again the hymns that everybody knows, what we often call the ' good old hymns ' and find in them so much to respect and rejoice in. It is only too easy for anybody who has done much work on hymnology to come to think that the best hymns are those which hardly anybody knows. Now I do not privately think that the hymns here set out are the forty-nine best hymns in the world ; they are not my forty-nine favourites. A glance at the last few pages of *Hymns and Human Life* will tell anybody who wants to know what hymns I personally most value and why. That is not the

point here at all.   The richness of the experience of putting
these pages together has been the rediscovery of what I had
thought almost too familiar to notice ; and although I have
made it a rule to make virtually no reference to the defects
of any of these hymns, the rule has turned out to be a
thoroughly cheerful discipline.

Some variety of treatment has been, of course, necessary.
Some of our best-loved hymns are some of the most profound
in theological penetration ; others are simple folk-songs of
the Christian traveller.   I have thought it best to go where
the hymn seemed to lead me, whether into the deep waters
or into the common ways of life.

I have said that I have renounced footnotes.   But I cannot let it be thought that what is set down here represents
any original invention of mine.   I do not want to make
anybody else responsible for my errors, but I think it could
be fairly well proved that anything of interest that I have
been able to write I owe to somebody else.   It would be
well, then, to provide a short list of citations in case any
reader is attracted by some thought I have clearly borrowed
from another.   For the rest, I must simply record here my
inestimable debt to all those who by personal kindness have
made me free of their wisdom.   It will be obvious to many,
for example, that some of these pages could not have been
written by anybody who had not had some contact with the
fertile and generous wisdom of two Principals of Mansfield
College, Dr Nathaniel Micklem and Dr John Marsh.   I
particularly recall sermons by Dr Norman Goodall and the
Reverend John Huxtable which have fertilized my own
thinking to some extent.   These and other good friends
will probably not recognize themselves here, and almost
certainly I have misrepresented them.   But for what I have
received I am truly thankful.

As to the versions of the hymns given here, I have generally used that version which appears in the majority of
current hymn-books, which means, in practice, a leaning
in the direction of the customs of the Church of England.
I have allowed this consideration to override any obligation
to print either the author's original or what I myself think

to be the best contemporary version. In one or two cases hymns have been deliberately shortened in order to save space ; but this has not been done in any case where the omission of verses would do violence to the general sense of the hymn. For the convenience of any who wish to recall the historical background of the hymns, a reference to the pages of *Hymns and Human Life* in which the reader may find information about their authors and associations is appended to the text of each hymn.

ERIK ROUTLEY

Oxford
November, 1954

1

Anon. (1796). *Psalm* 148

Praise the Lord ! ye heavens, adore him ;
  Praise him, angels in the height ;
Sun and moon, rejoice before him ;
  Praise him, all ye stars and light.
Praise the Lord, for he hath spoken ;
  Worlds his mighty voice obeyed ;
Laws, which never shall be broken,
  For their guidance hath he made.

Praise the Lord, for he is glorious ;
  Never shall his promise fail ;
God hath made his saints victorious ;
  Sin and death shall not prevail.
Praise the God of our salvation ;
  Hosts on high, his power proclaim ;
Heaven and earth and all creation,
  Laud and magnify his name.

H.H.L. 80

Praise

IT cannot be an accident that the word for ' Praise ' in any language is always a fine word for singing. ' Praise the Lord—Louez Dieu—Lobe den Herren—Laudate Dominum—Eulogeite Theon—Hallelujah ! '—no matter what the language, all words for ' praise ' are words that it is impossible to sing badly. They are words of full vowels and strong consonants, words that exercise the muscles of the mouth and throat, and the strength of piety, to their utmost. This, I say, cannot be an accident, for praise is the foundation of all hymnody—you may say, indeed, of all singing.

It is at least possible to suppose that men sang before they spoke. The nightingale has never learned to speak, but it can sing ; and the biological origin of song is a well-being, a happiness which cannot be contained in silent peace, and must emerge in some form of noise. When a man is happy he always wants to put his happiness outside himself so that he can look at it and share it with his neighbour. Music is his primitive way of doing that—of putting himself outside himself, or, to use a stale modern phrase, of expressing himself.

Some might wish to leave it there, and say that all the sound in the world, all mortal and animal music, is simply a number of finite beings expressing themselves. But why do they do this ? Who put the music there in the first place ? Who, if anybody, is listening to the music ? If you are willing to answer that God made them, that God put the music there, that God listens to it, you have already described the activity of praise. For praise is the expression of pleasure in the presence of him who gave the pleasure. Praise is the returning to God of a gift he gave in the first place. That is the Christian view of praise, and of that activity hymn-singing is a familiar example.

In Scotland all hymn-singing is referred to as ' praise ' ;

but the usage is older than that. For in the Hebrew the title of the Book of Psalms is ' Praises ', and the word there used for ' Praises ' is the one Hebrew word every Christian knows, for it appears in the word ' Hallelujah ' (*hallélu—* praise : *jah—*the Lord). In the ancient tradition of Israel, then, as well as in that of Reformed Scotland, singing hymns to God was compendiously called ' praise ', even though many of the songs (and psalms) were not what we call in the narrower sense ' praise '.

In modern speech ' praise '—not a very common word in ordinary English speech—means little more than the opposite of blame ; it means approval and the expression of approval. But between the modern and the ancient uses of the word its meaning broadens out like an enormous crescendo-mark, so that you find it embracing such meanings as ' speak well of ', ' rejoice in ' and ' make a conspicuous demonstration about '. Praising God is enjoying him and sharing your joy with your neighbours. Praise is fundamental to religious life ; religious life begins there, and it is proper that our hymn-singing, and where possible even our hymn-books, should begin there.

Now just as a Scottish hymn-book, though called a Book of Praise, will contain hymns whose subject matter is penitence or prayer, so does the Psalter. Conversely (and again like the modern hymn-books), the Psalter contains certain hymns which it distinguishes as hymns of praise (the same word again—*hallels*). Just which psalms were so distinguished in different editions of the Psalter is not our business here ; but one which was always marked as a ' hymn of praise ' in this special sense was Psalm 148 ; and Psalm 148 is the basis of the hymn, ' Praise the Lord ! ye heavens, adore Him '.

Psalm 148 is in a sense the most primitive and universal of all the praise-psalms, because it calls on all nature to join in praising and enjoying God. The hymn is much shorter than the psalm, but it gathers up all its points ; the brevity of the hymn, indeed, is one of the precious things about it. It was written originally for children—that is what we must suppose from its having been first printed in a collection of hymns used at the Foundling Hospital, London. Foundling Hospitals, Orphanages, Magdalen Hospitals and similar institutions were one of the consequences of the Evangelical Revival in our great cities, pre-eminently London, and their children's choirs became famous for their music-making. ' Praise the Lord ' is perhaps the finest of all children's hymns, even if we have long forgotten its origin. It was written, moreover, to carry the tune AUSTRIA, recently composed by Haydn, and, as a consequence of the popularity of the hymn, soon to become a treasured possession of English hymn-singers. And what subject could be better for children than Psalm 148, whose assumption is that all things, living and inanimate, have their ways of giving glory to God in sound or in visible grandeur ?

But if that were all the psalm or hymn had to say, perhaps both could be dismissed as romantic or animistic or simply childish. That is to say, a man could say either ' if you like to believe in talking rabbits and singing trees, you are welcome, but don't ask me to join you ' ; or he could say, ' our woad-wearing ancestors believed in animals and plants all having souls, but surely we have grown out of that.' But Christian doctrine, and that Hebrew teaching which prepares its way in the Old Testament, have a way of putting back on the right lines beliefs of that kind which show signs of going astray ; and towards the end of Psalm 148 we read this :

He shall exalt the horn of his people : all his saints shall praise him,
Even the children of Israel, even the people that serveth him.

Now the man who wants to find romance or animism or anything so easy-going as that in Scripture may well be perplexed and even irritated by this incursion of tribal and local lore. Does it not, after all, show a singular lack of taste and proportion ?

Our hymn helps us, as it happens, in answering that question as regards this particular psalm. Half the hymn paraphrases the first twelve verses of the psalm, the other

half is concerned only with that last verse of the psalm.
That is at least a clue ; and the truth is that the psalmist
introduces this tribal note because he knows no other way
of establishing the personal relation that exists between this
creating God and what he has created. The mystery of
all this was not as clear to the psalmist as it is to us who have
the revelation of Christ to guide us ; but both he and we
know that God not only made all this, but loves it. God
did not stop loving it when he had finished making it.
That is where God's creating acts soar above human anal-
ogies. Men love what they are making while they are
making it; thereafter they turn to something else. Not so
the God of Israel and the God of Christ.

The psalmist's way of saying this is to say that God gives
victory to his people (' exalteth the horn '), that, as Moffatt
translated that last verse, ' to praise him is for all his faithful,
for Israel, the people *near to him*'. While inanimate and
insensate nature praises God, as it were, involuntarily, the
praises of men are a response to that in God which mankind
alone knows ; for man alone can understand and receive
and respond to (or reject) the love of God. Once you have
grasped that, you can see how man projects that back over
nature, how he can think of the birds singing and the waterfalls crashing out God's praise as though they meant it as
men would mean it. The more man thinks of that, the
richer the idea becomes, for naturally he begins then to
think how much better it would be if his own praise were
as enduring as the hills and as inexhaustible as the waterfalls
and as innocent as the birds and as effortless as the wind.
The man who is at one with God tends to be at one with
nature ; and the man who rebels against God tends to find
nature intractable and rapacious.

That last verse is the heart of the psalm, and the second
verse is the heart of the hymn. For in the hymn the second
verse æsthetically balances the first. The first tells of
creation, the second of redemption. ' God hath made his
saints victorious ; Sin and death shall not prevail '—then
that great word ' salvation ', of which more in its place.
It all amounts to this—that now that Christ has come we

see things in a new proportion and with a new clarity. The personal contact between God and what he has made is most fully expressed at that point where God copes with the rebellion of what he has made. The greatest of all the confusions attendant on the impatience of man with God is in the area of sin and death. The promise to us, which corresponds with the ancient tribal promise of victory, is the promise of Easter, that we shall know, beyond any kind of question, that the love of God is powerful enough to destroy all its enemies, that it is deep enough to probe right through and behind and under the impatience and rebellion of man. *That*, the ugliness and disorder which suffocates praise, *that* will not prevail. So much was proved at Easter. And therefore—for reasons which the psalmist had to guess at but which Christians know fully—

> Heaven and earth, and all creation
> Laud and magnify his name.

2

Sir R. Grant (1833).   *Psalm* 104

O worship the King all-glorious above ;
O gratefully sing his power and his love ;
Our shield and defender, the ancient of days,
Pavilion'd in splendour, and girded with praise.

O tell of his might, O sing of his grace,
Whose robe is the light, whose canopy space ;
His chariots of wrath the deep thunder clouds form,
And dark is his path on the wings of the storm.

The earth with its store of wonders untold,
Almighty, thy power hath founded of old ;
Hath stablish'd it fast by a changeless decree,
And round it hath cast, like a mantle, the sea.

Thy bountiful care what tongue can recite ?
It breathes in the air, it shines in the light ;
It streams from the hills, it descends to the plain,
And sweetly distils in the dew and the rain.

Frail children of dust, and feeble as frail,
In thee do we trust, nor find thee to fail ;
Thy mercies how tender ! how firm to the end !
Our maker, defender, redeemer, and friend.

O measureless might, ineffable love,
While angels delight to hymn thee above,
Thy ransom'd creation, though feeble their lays,
With true adoration shall sing to thy praise.
                                        H.H.L. 189

Creation

FOR sheer literary grace and beauty this may be one of the six finest hymns in the language. We all love it for its combination of effortless energy, high-spirited innocence, and the occasional touch of superb dignity. Almost every word in it is a word in the common man's vocabulary—the vocabulary both of its own day (one hundred and twenty-five years ago) and of ours. Yet in the first and last verses there rise two towering lines, built in the monolithic style, which give a grand sweep of structure to the whole—

> Pavilion'd in splendour, and girded with praise . . .
> O measureless might, ineffable love.

This highly wrought and eloquent simplicity gives the whole hymn a texture which very happily reflects that of the psalm on which it is founded.

For the 104th Psalm is, even among the psalms, an astonishing piece of writing. There is about it an ecstatic innocence and exotic splendour that give it a colour which no other psalm shares. Compare it with the other great psalm of Creation, the 147th, and you cannot fail to observe the difference. We said ' exotic ', and it was the right word to use in this context, because it is more than possible that the psalm was written in imitation, or under the influence, of a creation-hymn from an alien land and a foreign faith ; it is rather as if to-day a man were to write a Christian hymn using the imagery and the style of thought (not the doctrine) of an Indian or Chinese lyric. But there is more than that in it, if this literary point be a true one ; for the foreign country with which this psalm provides a link is Egypt. And Egypt, in the days of the psalms, was not the luxurious Egypt of *Antony and Cleopatra* so much as the age-old and implacable enemy of Israel. In some sense it is almost as though a man had baptized for Christian use

8

a Marxist song—if there had ever been, or could be, a Marxist song of such generosity and nobility as the barbaric original of Psalm 104.

It is well to distinguish between hymns which are metrical versions of psalms, and hymns which, using psalms (or other passages of Scripture) as a starting-point, move away from the original into new country. This hymn is an unusual blend of both techniques, in that its first three verses are a careful paraphrase of the opening verses of Psalm 104, while the other three are developments of the thought of the psalm rather than a version of the rest of it. The whole is made homogeneous by the uninterrupted poetic style ; but the last three verses elaborate the theme of God's care, love and faithfulness towards his creatures. The total message of the hymn is that all that is set down in Psalm 104 is a pageant not merely of God's power but also of his love. This takes us to the heart of the Christian teaching on creation.

Dr Karl Barth, lecturing in the ruins of Berlin in 1946 on the doctrines of the Creed, has a pregnant paragraph or two on the subject of ' God Almighty '.[1] What he says there amounts to this, that to think of God as wielding irresponsible and absolute power is dangerously to misrepresent him. For (he says), the late Adolf Hitler was well content to speak of God as ' the Almighty '. ' And ', he goes on, ' " The Almighty " is bad, as " power in itself " is bad. " The Almighty " means chaos, evil, the Devil. . . . This intoxicating thought of power is chaos . . . which God in his creation has left behind him, which he rejected when he created heaven and earth. That is the *opposite* of God. That is the danger by which the world that God created is continually threatened. . . . " Power in itself " is bad, is the end of all things.'

Dr Barth goes on to make profound applications of that principle, to one of which we shall come back on a later page. Here we may apply it to the Creation. For the great question about creation is this, ' Why did God create anything at all ? ' And the answer presupposed in the

[1] Karl Barth, *Dogmatics in Outline* (S.C.M., 1949), p. 48.

hymn, ' O worship the King ', is that the reason is that God is love. ' O measureless might, ineffable love ! '

The analogy with human creation will take us part of the way, even though (as we said under No. 1) it has at one point at least to be abruptly abandoned. But consider an artist creating a piece of music or a piece of furniture or a picture. We will not here discuss how far an artist is creating and how far he is bringing to our attention something that was there all the time ; we will think of him in as much as he is (in our common speech) a creator. Why does he begin to do it ? What makes him enter on his work in the first place ? He enters on it because he feels in himself an irresistible compulsion to *make*. And he knows in part at the beginning, and he comes to know more fully as the work progresses, that in answering this compulsion he is taking on himself a great responsibility.

Suppose he is making a chair. Two things are true about that chair ; one, that it will in a greater or less degree have in it the ' imprint ' of the maker, so that you will be able, to some extent, to make some such comment as ' only Hepplewhite could have made that '. The other is that when it is made it must be a good and serviceable chair that will stand up and carry weight. The extent to which these two truths are made manifest is the extent to which we can call the finished article a ' creation ' as well as an ' object '. Mass-production and the debasement of labour by artificial and external means is the enemy of the former aim, shoddy and careless work of the latter.

That can be put in another way by saying that the ' maker ' is occupied with the good of two things outside himself—the person who uses the chair or enjoys and understands the symphony, and the chair or the symphony *in itself.*

Now we cannot say in any very reasonable sense that God made the Creation for somebody else to enjoy or use ; that is where the analogy does not help us. But we can say, and shall be greatly helped if we often say, that God in making the world committed himself to considering the good of the world in itself. He did not make it just for his own amusement, any more than you can justly say that Beethoven wrote symphonies 'just for his own amusement '. The carpenter with his chair and the musician with his symphony share this sacred obligation to the thing that they are making, that once they have begun the work they must subject themselves to the good of the work. The carpenter must follow the grain, the musician must bow to the logic and form of the music ; if the carpenter adds a decoration, or the musician slips in a chord, which has nothing to do with the form and logic of what he is making, the result will be, to that extent, a bad table, probably an ugly table, and a bad piece of music.

Now the analogy at this point is a good and sound one. Once God had set his creation in motion, he committed himself to abide by those laws which were for the good of that creation ; and one of the fundamental laws which emerged in the process of creation, and by which the Maker always abides, is this, that if man be able to love, he must also be able to sin ; if he be able to enjoy good health he must also be able to suffer bad health ; if he be able to exercise a happy and gracious dominion over the other creatures, he must also be prepared to suffer rebellion from the other creatures. Sin, in fact, in all its forms, was a risk which God took ; suffering was a risk he took ; and he would do nothing to safeguard the world or himself against the risk, because the risk was inseparably involved with the real object of the whole concern—that man should be able to enjoy the supreme felicity of knowing and loving God freely and by choice.

And if we now leave our human analogy on one side, we may say this of God which, because of the difference between man's time-scheme and God's (see 7) we cannot say of man, that although the process of creation is finished, this concern and commitment of the divine Love continues as long as the creation has any being.

So creation and love go hand in hand. God made the world for love—he made it because love must make ; and he made it that it might enjoy love and show love, love between men and love from men to God. He made the

beasts and the flowers and the ancient hills for love.   Love
is never lonely ; love seeks self-denial and submission.   In
God power and love are one.   Absolute power is bad.
Loving power is good. ' O measureless might, ineffable
love ! '

3

F. W. Faber (1814–63)

My God, how wonderful thou art,
  Thy majesty how bright,
How beautiful thy mercy-seat
  In depths of burning light !

How dread are thine eternal years,
  O everlasting Lord !
By prostrate spirits day and night
  Incessantly adored.

How beautiful, how beautiful
  The sight of thee must be,
Thine endless wisdom, boundless power,
  And awful purity.

O how I fear thee, living God !
  With deepest, tenderest fears,
And worship thee with trembling hope
  And penitential tears.

Yet I may love thee too, O Lord,
  Almighty as thou art,
For thou hast stooped to ask of me
  The love of my poor heart.

No earthly father loves like thee,
  No mother half so mild
Bears and forbears, as thou hast done
  With me, thy sinful child.

Father of Jesus, love's reward !
  What rapture will it be,
Prostrate before thy throne to lie,
  And gaze and gaze on thee !

H.H.L. 85, 160

13

Wonder

NOW and again a priest or minister, when he has gained the confidence of his people, will be asked this question by one of the more thoughtful : ' How can I *love* God ? ' To confess to such an intellectual doubt is the act of an honest man, and the question is a great question. It may well be true, moreover, that for every ten people who can understand the notion of God loving man, there may be hardly one who is clear about what is implied by man loving God.

' My God, how wonderful thou art ', a noble and eloquent hymn by a master of Catholic piety who sought (as he himself said) to do for Catholics what Cowper had done for Evangelicals, is one of the very few which provide an answer to that question.

Of course the question about loving God is only another form of the question, ' How can I pray ? ' and indeed the hymn may well be taken as an introduction to prayer. Prayer is the expression of the technique of loving God— you cannot pray to one whom you do not love, or have not loved ; love is part of the definition of prayer ; love is one of the things that make prayer different from superstitious incantation.

In an impressive passage near the beginning of his book, *Prayer and the Service of God*, Mr Daniel Jenkins has written of the two great impediments to prayer that exist in the modern world.[1] His book is written for the special purpose of making prayer relevant to modern life, and he is here putting an ancient and evident truth in contemporary terms. One impediment, the fault of a minority, he calls ' the sin of pride and freedom. These have exaggerated their own individuality over against the world, and have tried to create a private world which has meaning only for themselves, and for the rare spirits whom they find sufficiently

[1] Daniel Jenkins, *Prayer and the Service of God* (Faber, 1944), pp. 15 f.

14

sympathetic to admit into it '—in a word (his word), ' high-browism '. The other, the fault of a majority, is ' the sin of servitude. These find the strain of living on the strenuous level of responsible personal existence too much for them and they give up the very attempt to " attain unto the fullness of the stature of manhood ". They become, as we say, " the masses ", . . . " living and partly living ".' Mr. E. R. Micklem begins his valuable little book, *Heart in Pilgrimage*, from the same ground, saying that people tend not to pray either because they find prayer rationally inde-fensible or because they find it too difficult.[1] To either of these conditions ' My God, how wonderful thou art ' speaks with particular clarity.

For the great and ancient question it puts to the Christian is this, ' When did you last consciously and purposely prac-tise the sacred employment of *wonder* ? ' There is a very familiar, not to say hackneyed, quotation about the useless-ness of a life in which there is no time to stand and stare. That is well said, provided you are staring at something, and that the right thing. (There is not much to be said, as C. S. Lewis says in *The Screwtape Letters*, for staring at a dead fire alone in the small hours.) God has given us a dimension in which we can look at him, a language in which we may speak to him and hear him speaking, the dimension and language of wonder. And wonder is killed by the same things that kill prayer. Communication is broken by the same things. Neither the proud mind nor the servile mind can pray, nor can they wonder. But wonder cannot be commanded, for it is a natural endow-ment of man. It can only be impeded or choked by these habits of mind.

To be able to wonder a man must be without pride but also without anxiety. He must know that that at which he wonders is greater than he, but he must know also that it wishes him no harm. Not that he has nothing to fear—that is something different. A man looking at a mountain may wonder, may rejoice at it ; he may gain great felicity from letting its majesty have its way with his mind and

[1] E. R. Micklem, *Heart in Pilgrimage* (Independent Press, 1942).

affections. To be happy, he must reject all those ways of thought which will minimize the majesty of the mountain and tend to call it trivial. He may also fear—but he will be fearing only the consequences of his own lack of skill and caution. He will not be able to wonder if he really thinks the mountain is his enemy. It is so with God. A man must fear the consequences of his own impatience and lack of reverence for God's word ; but he cannot wonder at God if his mind is filled either with self-love or with grievance. Self-love is the habit of the proud mind and grievance of the servile mind.

Now it has often been thought that this is a hymn of resignation. Its last verse has been widely quoted as a good example of Christian flabbiness and sloth. On the contrary, this is as humble and brave and true a hymn as was ever set on paper. What kind of a Gospel would it be that made out the sight of God to be a negligible or casual thing ? What honest Christian will say he does not want, more than anything, to be near to God and remain near to him, to be as near to him in mind and heart as Mary was when she sat talking with Jesus at Bethany ? The very thought of such an experience, let alone such an eternity, humbles and braces the mind. Prolonged and happy conversation with God, the holder of all secrets, the searcher of all truth, the maker of all things and judge of all men ! There is courage as well as penitence in the thought of that.

Then let us begin our answer to the question, ' How can I love God ? ' along these lines. To love God a man must be a man of humility and a man of honour. He must be great enough and small enough to wonder. The love that goes from man to God cannot be commanded, but it can be impeded. You can hardly tell a man to try to love God ; but you can indeed tell him to stop trying not to love him, to stop closing the avenues of wonder, to stop avoiding every occasion of trusting, every danger of being wrong, every possibility of losing face, every admission that something or somebody is his better. A man will do much, a man will sell his soul, if only he can claim to be master of his fate. A man will renounce everything, a man will seek a solitude more remote than that of the Stylite, if only he can have security. A man will allow his precious and felicitous faculty of wonder and admiration to wither, he will let his love and concern for people rot, rather than be in danger of being ' taken in '. These are (history and experience confirm it) not the happy men or the brave men. They are this world's hermits and slaves, and there is the hermit and the slave in all of us. A verse of the hymn which is not usually in the hymn-books provides the ground of repentance :

> Oh, then, this worse than worthless heart
>   In pity deign to take,
> And make it love thee for thyself
>   And for thy glory's sake.

4

William Kethe (c. 1560). Psalm 100

All people that on earth do dwell,
  Sing to the Lord with cheerful voice;
Him serve with mirth, his praise forth tell,
  Come ye before him, and rejoice.

The Lord, ye know, is God indeed ;
  Without our aid he did us make ;
We are his folk, he doth us feed,
  And for his sheep he doth us take.

Oh enter then his gates with praise,
  Approach with joy his courts unto ;
Praise, laud, and bless his name always,
  For it is seemly so to do.

For why, the Lord our God is good ;
  His mercy is for ever sure ;
His truth at all times firmly stood,
  And shall from age to age endure.

H.H.L. 39

All People

THIS is the oldest among the popular English hymns; some older hymns we sing in translation from other languages; some carols and a few hymns have come down to us from the English Middle Ages. But among the well-known and well-tried hymns of the Englishman's worship, this is by far the most ancient, for we sing it exactly as it was first printed almost four hundred years ago in the first English metrical Psalter.

It has also this to distinguish it among favourite hymns, that while many hymns are founded on psalms, and not a few of those in the present collection faithfully render certain verses of psalms, this alone gives us, in verse, a whole psalm. The 100th Psalm is one of the shortest and one of the greatest in the Psalter. Its words are few but its vision is limitless; and if we except the 23rd, it is, because of this immortal rendering, the most-sung of the psalms, the most universal in its appeal, the most popular expression of world-wide praise.

'All people'—that is the keynote. 'O be joyful in the Lord, all ye lands.' 'Sing to the Lord with cheerful voice : him serve with mirth . . . Serve the Lord with gladness.' We have said (see 1) that praise is the most natural and most cheerful activity of mankind ; it is the gift of which the devil seeks first to dispossess us. Take away a man's capacity for praise and you have him well on the way to hell.

It is, of course, of the essence of the Church's thinking that its reach exceeds its grasp. To call on *all* people, all 2,100 millions of them, to praise God is to ask more than will at any one time be granted yet ; for many have no knowledge of God and many have no love of him. The exalted aims and high purposes of the Church are often taken for hypocrisy, but if the truth about those aims is to be seriously considered, they look more like quixotry. As a matter of fact they are neither, as may be learnt from this hymn.

For one thing there is no better missionary agent than the Christian life of praise. Nothing so penetratingly impressed the early enemies of the Church as the serenity, the almost insolent audacity, and the unshakable happiness of the Christian martyrs. The Pharisees found the gaiety of the disciples of Jesus highly offensive. Any missionary will tell you that more has been done through the spreading of the essential Christian joy and health to turn people to the way of life than through tight-lipped and stern presentations of Christian discipline. St Francis used to call his friends *joculatores dei*, ' God's merry men '. On this ground alone the invitation to all men to praise is based on something more solid than a fantasy or a convention.

But the second verse celebrates the creating love which demands men's praise. ' Without our aid ', it says, and the thought is echoed in the ancient prayer, ' Almighty God, who alone workest great marvels '. God made all things out of nothing ; he made it alone ; he made it because Love cannot live alone. Having made it he now cares for it as a shepherd cares for his sheep. Nothing that a tough, patient, skilful shepherd of the Eastern hills would do for his sheep will God leave undone for his people. We are saying, then, that *all* people are his people, whether they know him or not, whether they love him or not, in the bright days and in the dark days. *We* are his people—not ' some are, some are not his people '. If God has so loved, and so continues to love, it is, in that old homespun word, ' seemly ' to praise and bless him. The tune to which these words are always sung comes from John Calvin's church in Geneva, and John Calvin, commenting on this psalm, writes, ' Seeing then that he ceaseth not to deal in suchwise with us, it were more than a shame for us to be weary in paying him the sacrifice of praise.'

But the heart of the matter is in the last verse. The ground of it all is in this, that God's mercy and truth are everlasting. Mercy and truth are often brought together by the psalmist. ' Mercy and truth are met together ', says

H.F.—C

the 85th Psalm, looking forward to the time when the Messiah will come.   Mercy and truth—for mercy without truth is sentimental and truth without mercy is barren. Mercy and truth are the pillars on which the whole Gospel stands.   In Christ they met, as the psalmist said they would, and met in perfection.   In him was mercy, gentleness, patience, love, submission, obedience ; and in him also was honesty, reality, loyalty and wisdom.   Christ was, to all who encountered him, something of the tender friend and something of the inflexible leader.

> There's a wideness in God's mercy,
>   Like the wideness of the sea ;
> There's a kindness in His justice
>   Which is more than liberty.

And when we read that 85th Psalm we commonly apply it also to that consummation for which we still hope.   ' Mercy and truth are met together,' we say, and in our minds we add, ' How long, O Lord ? '   When that which God has shown has been fully understood by men, when they have fully committed themselves to it, then the prayer of this hymn will be fulfilled.   Then ' All people ' will come unbidden, they will come without argument, they will live and sing and talk their praises, and just as there will be ' no temple therein ', so, no doubt, there will be no hymn-books either.   Mercy and truth, humanity and honesty in parliament, in the United Nations Assembly, in Convocation, in party committee-rooms, in the home.   Mercy and truth !   In sober fact and in strict reason it is possible, given the faith which is demanded and celebrated in the 100th Psalm.

5

Nahum Tate and Nicholas Brady (1696). *Psalm* 34

Through all the changing scenes of life,
  In trouble and in joy,
The praises of my God shall still
  My heart and tongue employ.

Oh magnify the Lord with me,
  With me exalt his name ;
When in distress to him I called,
  He to my rescue came.

The hosts of God encamp around
  The dwellings of the just ;
Deliverance he affords to all
  Who on his succour trust.

Oh make but trial of his love ;
  Experience will decide
How blest are they, and only they,
  Who in his truth confide.

Fear him, ye saints, and you will then
  Have nothing else to fear ;
Make you his service your delight ;
  Your wants shall be his care.

H.H.L. 56

Providence

AS we usually sing it, this hymn paraphrases five verses of Psalm 34: the first, third, seventh, eighth and ninth. This is because modern hymn-books have usually found it best to make a selection from the original, and the original was a close paraphrase of the whole psalm. In the psalm there are twenty-two verses (one for each letter of the Hebrew alphabet: this is rather common in the Psalter), and in the hymn also twenty-two. By making the selection, editors have focused the message of the psalm to a single point—the providence and protection of God.

In the part of the psalm with which the hymn is dealing, the psalmist has a simple and yet challenging thing to say. To say ' I shall always praise the Lord, because he protects me from danger ' sounds simple enough, but the assertion is likely to be attended by a number of shrewd questions, such as ' How do you know? '. No doubt the psalmist has in mind some special experience in which he discovered the protection of God ; but as he sings about it he univers-alizes it, and at the very outset the impact of the great truth on his personal experience strikes a spark : ' I will praise the Lord *at all times.*'

It usually requires some arresting experience, it some-times needs a harrowing experience, to persuade a man that it is not enough to praise the Lord only when praise comes easily. We have said already several times that praise is the highest duty of man, but the common belief is that praise is an emotion or a temperament, that there is a time for praising and a time for withholding praise. (And not even the disgruntled and hard-boiled *Ecclesiastes* ever said quite this.) But when a man has personally realized what the protection of God means, when the arm of the Shepherd has hauled him back from the edge of the precipice, then he may well say that from that time he resolves to praise the Lord ' at all times '.

Another spark is in the second verse of the psalm, which is not included in the selection printed in most hymn-books (though it is in some). ' The humble shall hear thereof and be glad. O magnify the Lord with me, and let us exalt his name together.' The man in this condition wants to share his discovery, to tell his neighbours ; he wants it not that his neighbours may congratulate him, still less that he may make himself out superior to them, but that they may simply ' be glad '. ' This poor man cried, and the Lord heard him, and saved him out of all his troubles,' says the psalmist, and the hymn happily echoes him :

> Behold (say they), behold the man
> Whom Providence relieved ;
> So dang'rously with woes beset,
> So wondrously retriev'd !

Who, then, is entitled to believe that he is ' looked after ' in this fashion by God ? The fifth verse of the hymn provides the answer, which is also a rebuttal of every accusation of spiritual arrogance—' Fear him, ye saints . . . '

It is possible to say, in a general way, that in the Christian life there are no accidents ; but that must not be misunderstood. It would be a dull business if in the Christian life there were no surprises ; it would be a proud man who could say that God could never find him unprepared ; it would be wrong to imply that in life there is no contingency ; and it would be very bad instruction to tell a Christian convert that from the date of his conversion he would be quite safe from all temptations or sufferings. But if we can steer between these rocks and shoals of error, we can still say in a certain sense that in the Christian life there are no accidents ; or at any rate, that the Christian does not pay very much attention to the notion of ' luck '. Consider the things that happen in most lives ; consider especially the dark things that confuse and bedevil them, and the deliverances that illuminate them. The Christian believes that it is not enough simply to categorize these as ' bad luck ' or ' good luck '. He is obliged to see them, as soon as they have happened, as part of a plan which God has for that particular life.

Let us suppose that a man has the grievous misfortune to lose his sight. It would be possible for the afflicted man to say, ' God has bereaved me of my sight. Then I will see to it that the community repays me handsomely.' It is also possible for him to say, ' Now just what is it that God wants me to do that I can do better because of what has happened to me ? What work of charity or word of truth shall I now find it easier to do and speak because of this ? ' The blind man is a good example for us, because as it happens most people know at least one blind person who is a master of heroic Christian courage and cheerfulness. No matter, the choice is always there. Whatever the affliction, the choice must be made between ' I will send in a bill for damages ' and ' I will praise God at all times.'

Or the matter can be looked at from the other end. I heard of a man who missed the 7.31 from Tring on October 8, 1952, a man whose habit it was to travel by that train daily. When I recounted this to another, casually giving the usual secular accent to the story (' What an escape from the carnage at Harrow '), the other replied on the instant, ' He must be needed badly.' There again is the choice of view—either ' what luck ! ' or ' God wants me for something important if he has spared me such a death.'

Of course, once a man has put to himself the right question, he is still not out of spiritual danger. He can close up the whole affair by saying, ' God has spared me. That is because I am a holy man ' ; or even ' Now I know I am a very valuable person.' But the right question at that second stage is this, ' Why, and for what purpose, has God spared me ? '

That is the heart of the Christian belief in Providence as it concerns the individual man. When the hideous thing, or the near-miraculous thing, happens, when a man has just been knocked over by death or by love, it is the first few questions he asks that matter.

One of the most sacred passages in literature to me is an article written by Damon Runyon when he knew he was dying of cancer of the tongue. Runyon (1880–1946) was one of the great heroes of humorous letters, the prince of New York columnists, celebrated, sociable, shrewd and wealthy. The passage I have in mind comes near the end of his collected articles called (in the English edition) *Short Takes*.[1]

' When physical calamity befalls,' he begins, ' the toughest thing for the victim to overcome is the feeling of resentment that it should have happened to him.

' " Why me ? " he keeps asking himself, dazedly. " Of all the millions of people around, why me ? "

' It becomes like a pulse-beat—" Why me ?   Why me ? Why me ? "

' Sometimes he reviews his whole life step by step to see if he can put his finger on some circumstance in which he may have been at such grievous fault as to merit disaster . . . " Why me ?   Why me ?   Why me ? " '

Then Runyon rehearses, in his familiar style, the story of Job. He ends like this (and the italics at the end are his) :

' But when those pals of Job's, Eliphaz, Bildad and Zophar, came to see him he let out quite a beef to them, and in fact cursed the day he was born.   In the end, however, after listening to discourses from his pals of a length that must have made him as tired as the boils, Job humbly confessed that God is omnipotent and omnipresent and repented his former utterances and demeanour " in dust and ashes ", and the Lord made him more prosperous than ever before.

' " Why me ? "

' *Therefore have I uttered that I understood not ; things too wonderful for me, which I knew not.*'

' O fear the Lord, all ye his saints : for they that fear

[1] Damon Runyon, *Short Takes* (Constable, 1948), pp. 255 ff.

him lack nothing.' Fear the Lord ; treat God's plan as relevant and important, and there will be no grievances, no senseless accidents, only at all times grounds for worshipping and praising God.

6

Martin Rinkart (1586–1649)
Trans. Catherine Winkworth (1829–78)

Nun danket alle Gott

Now thank we all our God,
With heart, and hands, and voices,
  Who wondrous things hath done,
In whom his world rejoices ;
  Who from our mother's arms
    Hath blessed us on our way
  With countless gifts of love,
    And still is ours to-day.

Oh may this bounteous God
Through all our life be near us,
  With ever joyful hearts
And blessèd peace to cheer us ;
  And keep us in his grace,
    And guide us when perplexed,
  And free us from all ills
    In this world and the next.

All praise and thanks to God
The Father now be given,
  The Son, and him who reigns
With them in highest heaven,
  The one eternal God,
    Whom earth and heaven adore ;
  For thus it was, is now,
    And shall be evermore.

H.H.L. 43, 222

Gratitude

IF it were possible to wish that the Canon of Scripture had been settled otherwise than the Church finally settled it (which is a barren and vain speculation) there are many who might have welcomed the inclusion in it of the Book of *Ecclesiasticus*. Perhaps it would be better to put it thus, that if a man wishes to read anything apart from the Old and New Testaments, if he would add one spiritual book to those sacred sixty-six, he would be wise to make that book *Ecclesiasticus*; for in that rich and ample treatise there is much deep wisdom, and much that would make a shrewd appeal to any modern reader who came on it for the first time. Not a few will know the passage in the thirty-eighth chapter on the community of labour, and perhaps also the thirty-ninth, on the religious physician; and most people know very well the forty-fourth, which begins 'Let us now praise famous men.'

That forty-fourth chapter begins the final section of the book, which consists of a great pageant of history, rehearsing the glories of the heroes of Israel from Abraham to Nehemiah —like *Hebrews* xi on a larger scale and with a different intention. The pageant closes in the fiftieth chapter with these words (R.V.):

> And now bless ye the God of all,
> Which everywhere doeth great things,
> Which exalteth our days from the womb,
> And dealeth with us according to his mercy.
> May he grant us joyfulness of heart,
> And that peace may be in our days in Israel for the days
>   of eternity;
> To intrust his mercy with us;
> And let him deliver us in his time!

And there, of course, you have the original of ' Now thank we all our God.'

This most famous hymn of thanksgiving is known

throughout the churches of our own country and, in its original German or in other languages, in Europe as well. It is one of the universal hymns. No serious attempt is ever made to sing it to any tune but that which was associated with it almost from the beginning. It has gained and kept its popularity because of its brevity, its simplicity, its commonplace and unpretentious celebration of that brightest of Christian graces, gratitude.

In our country the hymn is usually kept for some occasion which particularly calls for our gratitude—the harvest festival, or the proclamation of peace, or a patronal festival, or some special and impressive deliverance. That is natural ; but the true message of the hymn is not precisely that. Indeed, it is almost a direct contradiction of its intention if we keep it only for the days when we are finding it specially easy to be grateful to God. For it is the mark of the man of faith, not that he distinguishes between that for which he is grateful and that for which he is not grateful, but that he is grateful for all things, distinguishing only between those occasions when gratitude is (to the natural man) a simple pleasure and those when it is a fortifying discipline.

Recall *Ecclesiasticus*. The point there is that God has done mighty things for his people over a period which historians or archæologists may perhaps estimate at a mere two and a half thousand years, but which was, for the author's purposes, the whole of history. Gratitude is always due to God for what he has done through history's heroes, through the Luthers and the Livingstones and the Pasteurs and the Einsteins and the Niemöllers ; through faithful parents and men of God and teachers ; through saints and preachers and doctors. Those achievements of God in history stand as history. Time does not reduce the debt of gratitude. And now more than this, more than all, a man can hardly call himself a man until he is able to feel at least once a day a sense of gratitude to God for Jesus Christ—for his birth and life and Passion and Resurrection : for his skill and patience and courtesy and for the gifts and fruits of the Holy Spirit ; and for the mighty acts which he did and which men have done in his name. ' Who wondrous things hath done : in whom his world rejoices '—gratitude is not a matter of humour or temperament : it is not even a duty which must be performed at stated and conventional times (though to practise it as a duty is better than not to practise it at all) ; gratitude is the very breath of a Christian's life.

But on one essential point let there be no mistake. Gratitude between men and men is one thing, and between men and God quite another. For gratitude at the human level is nearly always something of a burden. Many there are who fly in fear from any condition of ' being under an obligation ' to anybody. ' I don't want your charity,' they cry in desperate defence of their self-respect. And there are some who are far advanced in the art of collecting debts of gratitude from other people, on the strength of which they may throw people into some spiritual counterpart of the Debtor's Prison.

But there is nothing servile about a man's gratitude to God, because the love of God is not smeared with patronage or pride. ' It is a good thing ', said the psalmist, ' to give thanks unto the Lord, yea, a joyful and pleasant thing it is to be thankful.' That is quite literally true. There are some saints on earth of whom you feel that it is a privilege to be grateful to them, not a humiliation. It is so with God. It is a poor act of public worship which contains no prayer of thankfulness, no hymn of praise. It is better that liturgical balance be upset in favour of Praise than against it ; and it is better to have too much gratitude in life than too much caution and calculation.

It is no accident—it is, on the contrary, a great blessing and a great judgment—that this most famous hymn comes from the deep and gross darkness of the Thirty Years War. Its context is not really the country church decorated with corn and flowers and fruit. It is plague and bereavement and slaughter and famine. And they say that the hymn began its life not as a choral hymn for cathedrals but as a Grace to be sung before meat at its author's table. Thanksgiving in the midst of darkness, thanksgiving every day—these are the worship and the joy of Christian folk.

7

Isaac Watts (1674–1748) *Psalm* 90

Our God, our help in ages past,
  Our hope for years to come,
Our shelter from the stormy blast,
  And our eternal home ;

Under the shadow of thy throne
  Thy saints have dwelt secure ;
Sufficient is thine arm alone,
  And our defence is sure.

Before the hills in order stood,
  Or earth received her frame,
From everlasting thou art God,
  To endless years the same.

A thousand ages in thy sight
  Are like an evening gone,
Short as the watch that ends the night
  Before the rising sun.

Time, like an ever-rolling stream,
  Bears all its sons away ;
They fly forgotten, as a dream
  Dies at the opening day.

Our God, our help in ages past,
  Our hope for years to come,
Be thou our guard while troubles last,
  And our eternal home.

H.H.L. 6, 13, 65

Time

'OUR God, our help in ages past' is the gravest and the most universal of English hymns. In our own time it is most commonly associated with occasions of great solemnity, and particularly with occasions of solemn remembrance. Its author, the Independent minister Isaac Watts, who is commonly acknowledged to be the father of modern hymnody, wrote it as a version of the first part of the 90th Psalm; but although it is part of that great labour of love, *The Psalms of David Imitated &c.*, in which almost the whole Psalter is turned into Christian verse, it carries in its text something of the anxiety of the time in which it was written. It is usually thought that it was written in early 1714, just before the death of Queen Anne, and the sorry fact is that had not Queen Anne died unexpectedly in early March of that year the Schism Act would have renewed the dispossession of the nonconformists and brought back all the bitterness which they thought they had left behind twenty-five years before. This is no doubt the origin of that curiously sombre quality in the hymn which has caused it always to be regarded by Englishmen as the indispensable hymn for the day of decision or the day of distress. Its last line but one sounds this note, and nobody who ever heard that last verse sung by itself, in a low key, by the B.B.C. singers at a short service broadcast in the early morning of September 3, 1939, will forget the penetrating impact of the hope and the sorrow which were there expressed.

But the hymn rises above local occasions and is, as we have said, wholly universal. For the 90th Psalm is the profoundest and at the same time the most popular commentary that the Old Testament offers us on the subject of Time.[1] It is the mystery of Time that is really the subject of the hymn—time that passes and brings

[1] On this subject see John Marsh, *The Fulness of Time* (Nisbet, 1952), *passim*.

sorrow and joy, time that is filled by the Christian with
hope, and time that strikes the hour for decision.

Two very different things are meant by the English
word ' time '. First, there is the sense in which ' time '
is frightening. This is when we use the word to mean
the duration or passing of time. ' You have been a long
time,' we say, or ' There is not much time.' As life adds
year to year, a man thinks of how little time is left to him,
and as he looks back he thinks of time wasted. He may
also think, as this hymn leads him to think, of the brevity
of human life in comparison with the life of the ancient
hills and the rich expanse of history and the mysteries of
the far future. Even more, if he pauses to consider it, is
he impressed with the difference between the triviality of
human time and the eternity of God.

But there is another way in which we use this word, as
when we say ' Have a good time,' or ' The train arrived
on time.' When we talk like that we think not of the
duration of a protracted event, but rather of the content
of a moment, or a period, which distinguishes it in importance from other moments or periods. In that sense a man
may say that his life is marked by a series of ' times '
separated by relatively uninteresting periods of ' time '.

Add five years to five years, and ten years to the result,
and then another fifteen years—there you have thirty-five
years, at which age half a man's normal ' lifetime ' is gone.
But then attempt another exercise. Add the time you
first fell in love, the time you were first moved by great
music, the time your first child was born, the time you
first saw Scafell, the time you first knew bereavement,
the time you were in a railway accident, the time you
first knew Christ and the time you first betrayed him, and
what is the result ? It may not be measurable in years
or even in seconds, but it adds up to what you call your
' life ', which you might want to distinguish from your
' existence '.

One consequence of this is the subject of this hymn.
For the fact is that while men live in both kinds of time,
God lives in only one kind of time, and that the second

kind. There are various ways of putting that. You can say that we come and go but God goes on for ever : but that is not particularly helpful, because it does not follow from that that God is our shield and refuge, or that God loves. He could be a dead God or an uninterested God and still 'go on for ever'. Let us rather say that God not merely ' exists ' in a way that you can prove, but ' lives ' in a way that you can personally and by experience *know*. All God's life is like the life which we contrasted just now with ' existence '.

That happens to be just the thing we are trying to recall on those occasions when we sing this hymn. There is much point in the very first word. We address God from the first as ' Our God '. A pity, surely, to address him impersonally, here, as ' O God '. There is the great throne protecting the Kingdom. There is the King who rules it, but who also made it and loves it to the end. ' From everlasting to everlasting, *Thou art God* '—whenever as an organist I have been playing the accompaniment to those words I have wanted to stop just there, to bring out those words with emphasis (any decent organist will tell you that this is shocking technique), because the heart of the matter is there. ' Thou art God '—and with God ' art ' and ' is ' mean everything. The mystery of the being of God is well approached from the thought of what God has done with the verb ' to be '. For human speech that is the most colourless of words, for God the most vital. ' I AM THAT I AM. . . . I AM hath sent thee . . . ' ' To be ', in the sense in which God *is*, contains all the other active verbs of which without sin it is possible to think. But the colour which predominates is the colour of ' love '. God is, and God is love. And so, though a thousand years in his sight are as a day, and a lifetime as the twinkling of an eye, yet God protects and loves and is interested. ' *Our* God, *our* help . . . '

So when we ruefully reflect on the passing of time, on the resistless flood that carries away the saints and the sinners, the brave and the sly, the beautiful and the dowdy, the young and the old, this hymn makes us able to substitute for the preposterous figure of Father Time the gracious figure of him who is our God, our help, and our Father. For him past and present and future are all one, and they all add up to *life*.

And we know what the psalmist did not know and what the author did not therefore express in this hymn—that God shares his kind of life, lived in his kind of time, with any man who will ask for it. The dead pass into it. The living have tasted it. Jesus Christ came to show us, as clearly as Light can show anything to Darkness, the way to it.

I once heard of a minister, whom I know and for this respect above all the heroes, who had to go one day to visit a woman in distress; she had just heard that grievous news which was the heartbreaking commonplace of the two great wars. ' To be cut off at twenty-one ', she cried, ' and some of us spared to grow old.' He found this to say—' That young man *lived* in his twenty-one years as much as I shall have lived if I go on to eighty.' He put it less abruptly, less crudely; and in that moment the truth about God's time and God's life brought comfort. That message of comfort is the message which ' Our God, our help in ages past ' carries wherever it is sung.

8

William Cowper (1731–1800)

God moves in a mysterious way
   His wonders to perform ;
He plants his footsteps in the sea,
   And rides upon the storm.

Deep in unfathomable mines
   Of never-failing skill
He treasures up his bright designs,
   And works his sovereign will.

Ye fearful saints, fresh courage take ;
   The clouds ye so much dread
Are big with mercy, and shall break
   In blessings on your head.

Judge not the Lord by feeble sense,
   But trust him for his grace ;
Behind a frowning providence
   He hides a smiling face.

His purposes will ripen fast,
   Unfolding every hour ;
The bud may have a bitter taste,
   But sweet will be the flower.

Blind unbelief is sure to err,
   And scan his work in vain ;
God is his own interpreter,
   And he will make it plain.

H.H.L. 4, 76

Mystery

THE author of this hymn (the only great classical English poet who was also a great hymn writer) wrote above it ' *St John* xiii. 7 ' ; the reference is to the saying of Jesus, ' What I do thou knowest not now, but thou shalt know hereafter.' This is a hymn of a very rare and gracious kind, a hymn of the mystery of God's being and acts. It runs so smoothly, its lines are so neat and quotable, its thought so familiar, that it is easy to miss the genius of it. But let a man attempt a description of the mystery of God, let him attempt it in prose, let alone in verse, and it is tolerably certain that the statement in the end will be a series of negatives. It is easy and impressive (and there is a grain of truth in it, to be sure) to heap up sonorous adjectives like ' Immortal, Invisible, Unapproachable, Unknowable, Incomprehensible, Uncreated ' and all the rest of them. These are indeed far better than man's trivial attempts to make God in his own image. But they are no help to faith. When a man can present us with the mystery, the ' otherness ' of God, and then put it all so positively that our belief and confidence are strengthened, when such a man can tell us of God's bright designs, his generous mercy, and his grace, then we are in the presence of a true prophet.

There has always been a cast of mind among Christians, usually among the more cultured and sensitive, which leans towards the description of God as the Great Negative. In the second and third centuries this kind of thinking was especially associated with the progressive university city of Alexandria, the Cambridge of the Roman Empire (if we may allow Athens by seniority to be the Oxford). So it has remained. God, the Absolute, the object of devoutly agnostic adoration—this God is in a sense the very God of whom the Old Testament tells us. And yet we may not rob God of that passion and active power which are also his prerogatives. ' God moves in a mysterious way ' is the work of a humble and sensitive man, whose own way became darker as life went on until he fell into total mental night ; but it is a hymn of great and outward-looking faith.

It has, of course, but one thing to say, and it says it over and over again. God's ways are not as our ways, it says, but this we know and can trust, that God is love, and that all his acts are subject to that. Of this the Old Testament is full, especially the second Isaiah. Tracing the workings of God in history, the relation between God's plan and the movements of the great political powers, he cries out ' Verily thou art a God that hidest Thyself ! ' Making a final appeal to men to leave the fashionable frivolity of a prosperous commercial society and return to what can be bought without money and without recourse to the black market, he says, ' My ways are not your ways, saith the Lord, neither are my thoughts your thoughts ' (chapter 55). A lesser man might well have been content to say ' Go to church and all will be well.'

Who will believe in the grace and power of a God who can be reduced to trivial human categories ? Who will be comforted by news of such a God ? Who will be judged and brought to repentence by such an one ? The very mystery of God, the very remoteness and otherness of him, is bound up with his grace. He has promised his protection, his healing, his friendship. ' Seek ye the Lord, for he may be found ; call ye upon him, for he is near ' : yes, indeed, but when you find him, when you know him near, still he is God, and his thoughts are not our thoughts ; he holds the secrets of life and unlocks them at his own discretion, not at our request. ' God is his own interpreter ' ; ' Trust him for his grace.'

The lines were born, we know, of great suffering. They were not written, as some have thought, just after their author has been prevented from committing suicide. They come not from a man emerging from darkness but from a man about to descend into it. They are the more powerful for that. To all who now walk in darkness or fear they bring a message that their author could not, in the end, make his own—that the very darkness, the withholding of light and clear guidance, are a sign of God's grace and power. 'Put your hand into the hand of God'—so runs that passage which the late King George VI made famous for us all during the late war—'Put your hand into the hand of God : that shall be better than a light, and safer than a known way.' Better, and *safer* : for it is safer to trust a God who does not tell you all his plans but promises victory than to some lesser being who has neither the mystery nor the power.

Taken by itself, the hymn may perhaps leave us slightly chilled. Is faith, then, blind ? By what authority can a man say that we know nothing, yet that God is loving and merciful in his purposes ? On what authority may a man trust this kind of proposition when he lies wasting away with an incurable disease, or when bereavement has taken away the light from his house ? The author answers that question in his Scripture-reference, by reminding men of Christ. The love of God made clear and tangible in Christ is the authority. The course of that life and that victory are enough to make an honest man able to believe that the purposes of God are both irresistible and also loving, that God acts in history with a royal gentleness. With the figure of Christ before him, that man can trust the purposes of God.

9

Philip Doddridge (1702–51) *and John Logan* (1748–88)

O God of Bethel, by whose hand
  Thy people still are fed,
Who through this weary pilgrimage
  Hast all our fathers led ;

Our vows, our prayers, we now present
  Before thy throne of grace ;
God of our fathers ! be the God
  Of their succeeding race.

Through each perplexing path of life
  Our wandering footsteps guide ;
Give us each day our daily bread,
  And raiment fit provide.

Oh spread thy covering wings around
  Till all our wanderings cease,
And at our Father's loved abode
  Our souls arrive in peace.

H.H.L. 89

Covenant

THERE is a peculiar kind of magic which a man of letters may work in the human imagination by the dexterous use of the proper name. It is partly in the sound of the word itself, which may be august or may be comic, and partly in the unexpectedness with which the reader, expecting a generality, comes upon the crudely or solemnly particular. This device is most commonly associated with the name of John Milton, and Bernard Manning pointed out in a famous essay to what extent the same device is responsible for the magic of some of the hymns of Charles Wesley and at least one of Isaac Watts. At the other end of the scale, the late G. K. Chesterton could work wonders of wit by writing ' Hoxton ' or ' Hanwell ' where most of us would be content to write ' the suburbs ', and produced his most devastating shaft of satire in that poem in which he stabs the most illustrious barrister of the day, in every other line, with his family name of Smith.

There is no doubt that the hymn ' O God of Bethel ' owes part of its sombre dignity to the colour imparted by that word ' Bethel '. The old name casts a stony shadow over the whole by bringing to mind the vision which Jacob had in that place which, up to that moment, had borne the barren-sounding name of Luz.

Several other hymns have been written on the theme of Bethel ; one of them is in the present series (27). The central theme of this one is the covenanted mercy of God, and it is founded on the last three verses of the passage. These verses run :

And Jacob vowed a vow, saying, If God will be with me, and will keep me in this way that I go, and will give me bread to eat and raiment to put on, so that I come again to my father's house in peace ; then shall the Lord be my God . . . and of all that thou shalt give me I will surely give the tenth unto thee.

44

As it was originally written this hymn followed very closely the form of this passage. It was cast in the form, ' If thou wilt grant certain mercies, then we will worship thee,' and its last verse began

> To Thee, as to our Covenant-God
> We'll our whole selves resign.

The solemn Biblical theme of the covenant was never far from the preaching of Philip Doddridge, author of this original, and he wrote these lines, as he wrote all his hymns, for his congregation to sing immediately after he had preached on the text from which they are derived.

But as we now sing it the hymn has been completely rewritten (the *Bethel* itself is among the inspired improvements). The new version, made forty years after the first, makes the whole into a prayer, and, among other things, spiritualizes and generalizes the ' covenant ' motif which is clearly sounded in that original last verse. (It would be a pity to miss, by the way, the felicitous manner in which our present version spiritualizes the phrase ' so that I come to my father's house in peace ' in the Genesis passage.)

The notion of ' covenant ', then, openly expressed in the original, is diffused through the whole of the later version. It is gathered up in the word ' Bethel ' and in the reference to ' our vows ' in the second verse ; but it underlies the thought of the whole hymn.

' Covenant ' is a word which brings with it all the colourful associations of Old Testament religion. It is a word which has been translated into Christianity by a process not unlike that which transformed the rugged old hymn of Doddridge into the more gracious form in which it is now well known. ' Covenant ' means, of course, ' agreement '. It means a transaction in which two people promise each that he will keep his word, and as a result of which there will be acts on both sides which morally balance each other. The covenant is, so to speak, the fulcrum on which any communal or civilized intercourse turns ; but a covenant is not instinctive or automatic. It is voluntarily made by two responsible persons.

Now this word ' covenant ' has many solemn overtones.
One of these recalls the fact that once you have covenanted
with another person, you stand in a new relation to him
which will never, so long as you live, be wholly eradicated.
You or he may break the terms of the covenant, but it can
never be made as though it had not been. The most
exalted form of human covenant is, of course, marriage.
The covenant in marriage is a promise, externally symbolized in the giving of a ring. There is much more in marriage
than this, but at its heart there stands a voluntary and
responsible promise reciprocally made, a ' loving covenant '.
Those two people can never eradicate the relation in which
they stand after the covenant is made. There may come,
if all goes ill, the sorrow of divorce or the lubricious fiction
of annulment ; much must in law be conceded to the
' hardness of men's hearts '. But those two can never again
meet as strangers, nor (in the ordinary sense) as friends.
The fact of the covenant has done something to them.
They have given something each to the other in the act of
promise which cannot be taken back (even as Jonathan
and David changed clothes as an outward symbol of their
friendship, as a form of covenant which would make something binding and demanding of their friendship).

There are many less exalted, more nearly eradicable
forms of covenant to be met with in common life. But
' covenant ' is, by definition, this kind of enduring and
demanding agreement. And it was the kind of thing, in
family and business matters especially, which the men of
the Old Testament took very seriously indeed.

It was not unnatural that at an early stage men should
look on their relations with God in some similar light.
When the ancient stories came to be set down and interpreted in the books of Genesis and Exodus as we now have
them, this is the axis on which the relations between God
and man always turn. God makes covenants with individual men, and through them with their families, their
tribes, their races, and with all mankind. Each great
experience which answers some primitive question or marks
a new turn in the way along which Everyman is travelling,

is recorded as a covenant. Noah, Abraham, Jacob, and many others had moments when they felt themselves in a special sense close to God, when they had special insights into the purpose of history. Perhaps a modern man in such a position might use a quite different figure ; he might talk of being shown the front of a tapestry of which men normally saw only the back ; perhaps he might say, with Plato, that he had for a moment seen the substance of that which people normally see only in shadow or silhouette : perhaps he would say that for a brief period he had stood with the Captain on the Bridge, or been allowed to over-hear the deliberations of the Cabinet in secret session. The Old Testament mind preferred this other figure, to say that these great occasions were times of covenant.

It naturally came to pass that the greatest event of all, in which all mankind shared, *the* turning-point in Every-man's journey, *the* insight which answers all the questions, namely the coming of Christ to the earth, should be thought of as a special kind of covenant, a covenant *par excellence*, a New Covenant, or (what comes to the same thing), The New Testament. It is new in the sense that God had never so completely taken men into his confidence as he did in coming into the world in Christ. If that is the New Testa-ment, then all that went before, in which God was involving himself with human affairs but in which he persisted in other ways of communicating with men, is the Old Covenant, the Old Testament. And as a matter of fact certain far-seeing minds were able to see that a New Covenant was likely to come sooner or later, that God had not yet spoken his last word, that that would come which would make sense of all that was happening in their own time. Among these was Jeremiah, who wrote of the New Covenant in his thirty-first chapter.

But—why ' covenant ' at all ? Why were not their descendants content to believe that God had simply issued an explanation to Noah, a programme to Abraham, a command to Jacob ? Why is not history to be thought of as a series of statements made by God which men can take or leave ? To give a crude but brief answer—that is what any deity but the living God of Israel might be expected to do. But the men who wrote the Scriptures were quite clear that that was not God's way of going to work. A true picture of life could not be as mechanical or arbitrary as that. They insisted that God's communication with men has always been in the form of agreement, or consultation, rather than of instruction. The incredible truth, yet the only truth that will fit the facts of history from the Exodus to the Korean War, is that he who made the world and life itself, instead of sending down orders as a director would send orders to a clerk, treated men, and is always prepared to treat them, as equal with himself. Man is not equal with God ; but in his dealings with man, God behaves as though he were. God showed confidence in men, and treated them with respect, every step of the way. That is, he treated a drunkard like Noah, a swindler like Jacob, a harlot like Rahab and an adventurer like David all with the same grave respect.

That is what we are saying when we claim that God makes covenants with men ; in a sense (a narrow sense) we are saying what is impossible. God's thoughts are not as men's thoughts. But what else will explain the freedom with which men have been allowed to go into the presence of God in thought and prayer and exploration? Human experience, in the Bible and out of it, demands that we think of God as ready to make agreements with men which men will certainly break, and to show mercy to men who will certainly despise him for doing so.

What kind of incompetence and gullibility are here being ascribed to the Lord of hosts ? Is this not to say just what the barbarians and the godless are overheard saying in the psalms, ' God hath forgotten ; he hideth his face ; he will never see it ' (Psalm 10[11]), ' Tush, say they, God will not perceive it : is there knowledge in the most High ? ' (Psalm 73). Is this not to recall the impudence of Satan in *Job*, the craven stupidity and cowardice of the idolators in *Isaiah*, the cynical security of the businessmen in *Amos* and *Micah* ? But then the very same point is most searchingly put, almost in an aside, in one of the parables of **Jesus**.

The dishonest farmers had turned out the messengers of the owner, so he sent his son, ' saying, They will reverence my son ' (*St Mark* xii. 6). The Gospel's answer to the charge that a covenanting God, a courteous God is a preposterous conception is to yield to the whole weight of men's presumptuousness. What Jesus did amounts precisely to this, that he accepted every kind of insult which humanity could offer to the courtesy of God ; in the most literal and precise and almost pedantic fashion, Jesus kept his side of the covenant. The Resurrection is the last chapter in that part of the story. Love, covenanting love, gained the victory in the end and exposed the triviality of all the devices that the world had brought against it, including the supercilious argument that God was incompetent and uninterested. ' Is there knowledge in the most High ? ' sneered the breakers of the covenant. Yes, indeed, there is knowledge, and there is power, and there is mercy.

Thinking on such things, you will want to associate the word ' mercy ' very closely with the word ' covenant '. Such thoughts about God as we have dared here to entertain would indeed be impiety unless there were some underlying axiom from which we could derive both God's courtesy and God's power. That axiom is there ; it is (once again) love. Say that all God's dealings with men are a loving covenant, and the rest falls into place. God is prepared to rein in his power to the extent of making its operation (as it seems to us) dependent on man's prayers and man's co-operation. God is prepared to delay the coming of his absolute and final reign until men say they want it, until all men say they want it and nothing else. The very delay, the tortuous course of history, its groaning and travailing, its ruins and wastes, the long years through which the nations lurch and stumble, are all part of God's mercy, for he will not deal with men otherwise than by covenant. He will not issue orders or instructions. He will not call down fire from heaven in his wrath—he leaves that to statesmen. He will not, even in Christ, issue short answers to all men's intellectual perplexities and moral questions. He will continue to treat men with respect, to make covenant with them. Nothing so maddens a resentful and hysterical person as to be taken seriously by a friend ; there is, in such a case, nothing to be done but to abandon the grievance and calm down and go back to the point at which reason can prevail. Nothing is so difficult for a man to accept, once he has been lured away by the world towards resenting and rebelling against God's love, than to realize that he is still being taken seriously by God.

But there it is. Just because it is so difficult and un-palatable and unreasonable a notion, so little conformable to the axioms of common life, the Bible insists on it as picturesquely as the consummate art of its innocent scribes can compass. God treated Jacob with seriousness, with deference. Jacob was able to say ' If thou wilt, why then I will. . . .' But that was not the last Jacob heard of this matter. Nor is it the real truth even about what passed at Bethel. The initiative was, and always is, with God. ' If you will, then I will,' said God. God gives the word ; at every stage history and life depend on what answer his child is prepared to give.

10

H. F. Lyte (1793–1847). *Psalm* 103

Praise, my soul, the King of heaven ;
   To his feet thy tribute bring ;
Ransomed, healed, restored, forgiven,
   Who like thee his praise should sing ?
      Praise him, praise him,
   Praise the everlasting King.

Praise him for his grace and favour
   To our fathers in distress ;
Praise him still the same for ever,
   Slow to chide, and swift to bless :
      Praise him, praise him,
   Glorious in his faithfulness.

Father-like he tends and spares us ;
   Well our feeble frame he knows ;
In his hands he gently bears us,
   Rescues us from all our foes :
      Praise him, praise him,
   Widely as his mercy flows.

Frail as summer's flower we flourish,
   Blows the wind and it is gone ;
But while mortals rise and perish
   God endures unchanging on.
      Praise him, praise him,
   Praise the high eternal one.

Angels, help us to adore him,
   Ye behold him face to face ;
Sun and moon, bow down before him ;
   Dwellers all in time and space,
      Praise him, praise him,
   Praise with us the God of grace.

H.H.L. 5, 13, 84, 146, 271–89

History

'PRAISE, my soul' is at present the most popular, in the sense of being the hardest-worked, of English hymns. It finds a place in the repertoire of every kind of Christian gathering, from royal weddings to street corners. This seems to be as much as to say that 'Praise, my soul' comes nearer than any other hymn to saying what all religious Englishmen want, just now, to say. This is not altogether surprising. Years such as those through which he have passed since, say, 1930—so dramatically charged with trials and blessings, cause men to demand not the intimate and the exquisite but rather the objective, outward-looking hymns that speak of God and of his mighty works.

This hymn, like most of the others we have already handled, is a version of a psalm. It is difficult to speak of any psalm without using superlatives. The 148th is obviously the most brilliant, the 23rd equally obviously the tenderest ; the 34th the most fortifying, the 100th the most popular ; the 90th the most solemn, the 104th the most colourful. What is the special quality of the 103rd ? Surely it is that this is the most evangelical of the psalms ; in it we see furthest into the New Testament, in it God looks most like Christ.

'Praise, my soul' is everything we want a hymn to be. It speaks in simple language that conceals a quite unusual degree of skill and concentration. It speaks clearly, but leaves room for the imagination. It has several arresting lines, yet the whole is homely enough for the edifying of the simplest and the comforting of the most distracted.

It has in a high degree the quality of being 'all things to all men', and that is because it was written by a real poet. Its author is also the author of 'Abide with me' (28), and to have written those two is sufficient claim to the true and authentic honour of poetry.

52

For example : it is not usual for a five-verse hymn to provide a paraphrase for more than, say, half a dozen verses of a psalm. (We have had a four-verse hymn paraphrasing a four-verse psalm, and a six-verse hymn written on the basis of a thirty-five-verse psalm : here we have something new again, a hymn of five verses gathering in the substance of the whole of a twenty-two-verse psalm.)   As a matter of fact, the five verses of ' Praise, my soul ' (one is often omitted in the hymn-books) take up no fewer than seventeen of the twenty-two verses of the psalm.   This is the kind of thing that happens :

> Ransomed, healed, restored, forgiven

is a summary of this in the psalm :

Who forgiveth all thy iniquities : who healeth all thy diseases : Who redeemeth thy life from destruction : who crowneth thee with loving kindness and tender mercies.

Again,

> Praise him for his grace and favour
> To our fathers in distress

corresponds to this :

The Lord executeth righteousness and judgment for all that are oppressed.
He made known his ways unto Moses, his acts unto the children of Israel.

So you can go on, comparing word with word, all through the hymn.

But although psalm and hymn are so rich in detail, they have one great and unique word to say.   It is that history, and human life, which is an epitome of history, are the theatre of God's forgiveness.   ' Our fathers in distress '— that is history : ' Ransomed, healed . . .' that is human life.   Things being what they are, and men being what they are, God's love to the world is seen always as forgiveness.

When a man reads some wise and good book on history, such as Trevelyan's *English Social History*, can he be content to say that history is simply a series of events, this happening

H.F.—E

after that, and a third thing following, with nothing to bind them together but their immediate causes ? He can indeed ; many eminent people have taken that view. One of our great historians of the last generation, the late H. A. L. Fisher, wrote in the Preface to his *History of Europe* what have now become famous words : ' Men wiser and more learned than I have discerned in history a plot, a rhythm, a predetermined pattern. These harmonies are concealed from me. I can see only one emergency following upon another as wave follows upon wave.' Those words of an honest scholar warn us against sentimental and doctrinaire interpretations of history that do not pay proper attention to the plain facts, and the warning, in the year 1936, was timely. But as a matter of experience, human nature is not content with that. The human mind tends to seek a pattern in things, and to find it. And Christians say that the ' plot and rhythm ' in history which the Bible exposes is the authentic plot and rhythm.

Dr Fisher said in that same Preface that it is the duty of the historian always to ' recognize in the development of human destinies the play of the contingent and the unforeseen '. The Bible's pattern of history suggests that history is neither predetermined nor shapeless. Every new event is contingent and unforeseen, and at the same time it is directly caused by what went before it. The Biblical interpretation allows for all that, and then adds this, that God, who made history in the beginning, meets every new contingency with a new manifestation of his power and love. Take any isolated event whatever : from one angle it seems contingent or accidental, from another, it is obviously caused by what went before. The Bible says that that event has not caught God in an inattentive moment, and that the love and power of God adjust themselves to it.

There is this further, that since every new contingency has in it something of the impatience and unbiddableness of man, there is in every new manifestation of God's love something of forgiveness. For can any man read the accumulating story of the Old Testament, so human, so full of the things that all men still do as the obvious and reasonable things, without wondering why the omnipotent and glorious God did not here or there throw all history back into the melting-pot? Can any intelligent and informed person avoid wondering why God has not before now crushed together the forming vessel on the potter's wheel, and prepared to make a new beginning? If history has an author, and if that author is anything better than a Nero, why then the only other notion that fits the facts is that the author is a loving creator who treats the stupidity and squalor of what he has made with limitless wisdom and patience.

Human life is of the same sort. What honest man is there who can lay his hand on his heart and say that he never did anything for which God might not justly have struck him dead? Or that he never did anything for which God ought to have punished him but did not? When such a man thinks of the love and grace of God that made aubrietia and Everest and falling-in-love, and compares that with the standard of his daily thoughts and acts, how can he escape the conviction that he would never have allowed any child of his, or any partner in his business, to get clear away with such flagrant denials of his declared purposes and rejections of his offered love. Quite literally it does not bear thinking about, unless the mind can anchor itself to this, that God forgives, and that the shape of life is determined by God's forgiveness. Life is not predetermined by God's grandfatherly benevolence; it is at each point new-fashioned by his infinitely resourceful mercy.

That is what this hymn is singing about—mercy and love, the same yesterday, to-day and for ever.

11

William Cowper (1731–1800)

Hark, my soul ! it is the Lord ;
'Tis thy saviour, hear his word ;
Jesus speaks, and speaks to thee,
' Say, poor sinner, lov'st thou me ?

' I delivered thee when bound,
And, when wounded, healed thy wound ;
Sought thee wandering, set thee right,
Turned thy darkness into light.

' Can a woman's tender care
Cease towards the child she bare ?
Yes, she may forgetful be,
Yet will I remember thee.

' Mine is an unchanging love,
Higher than the heights above ;
Deeper than the depths beneath,
Free and faithful, strong as death.

' Thou shalt see my glory soon,
When the work of grace is done ;
Partner of my throne shalt be ;
Say, poor sinner, lov'st thou me ? '

Lord, it is my chief complaint
That my love is weak and faint ;
Yet I love thee, and adore ;
Oh for grace to love thee more !

H.H.L. 5, 76

Love

IHAD thought the love of God to be beyond descriptions and definitions of the philosopher until I read Dr Nels Ferré's assertion that it is like a self-directing bullet.[1] It would be difficult to find a harsher analogy than that even from the rich store of ugliness that the modern world provides ; yet the very harshness of it is itself a pointer to the stretching and thrusting that the human mind must undergo if it is to comprehend even what is understandable in the divine Love. We must thank Dr Ferré for this, that his picture starts a train of thought that drives clear between two wrong assertions which between them, as many have thought, have covered the truth about God's love—that it is mechanical or that it is capricious. How can it be neither of these? Dr Ferré drives through the horns of the dilemma by stating, with perfect and up-to-date faithfulness to the truth, that the mechanical is nowadays not necessarily the predetermined.

But the Old Testament does the same thing for us, and does it no less minatorily but perhaps with more grace. There is a phrase which many Englishmen now find to be inseparably associated with the voice of the organist of King's College, Cambridge, for as much as it is his duty to read it as part of the third Lesson in the carol service which is broadcast each year from that place. The phrase is, 'The zeal of the Lord of hosts will perform this.' And I know of no hymn which so luminously interprets the bright and deep tone of that word ' zeal ' as does William Cowper's ' Hark, my soul '.

William Cowper wrote ' Hark, my soul ' to expound these mysteries to a village congregation at Olney, Bucks. He has done it with supreme simplicity but without any

[1] Nels Ferré, *The Christian Understanding of God*, English edition (S.C.M., 1952), p. 33.

58

trace of sentimentality. The hymn is very far from being about the imaginary benevolence of a dubiously historical Jesus. The text that Cowper wrote over the hymn was ' Lovest thou me ', from *St John* xxi. 16, the terrible question that was put three times to Peter. The words within quotation marks in the hymn are ascribed to ' thy Saviour ' ; but none the less the subject of the hymn is the love of God. For there is no such thing as a love which Jesus has and which God has not ; there is no truth in the notion of a love of God, a different love of Jesus, and a third kind of love of the Holy Ghost. It is all one love. God, Father, Son and Holy Ghost, three persons and one God, is made and compacted of love.

The special quality about this hymn is the daringly personal way in which it faces the singer with this love. It actually ascribes words to God (or to Christ) in direct speech. It is very difficult, technically, to do this in a hymn and not fail in taste. There is another hymn, well known to many, which does it, and, as I believe, does it without sufficient regard to the enormity of trying to do it at all. ' Behold me, standing at the door ', praiseworthy in intention, written on a terrible text in *Revelation* iii, succeeds only in bringing to the mind Holman Hunt's famous but rather disagreeable picture, and in making our Lord sound resentful and hard-done-by. The thought of this present hymn is remarkably close to the thought of that other, but it is saved from banality by its innocent simplicity, and by the breadth which is given to it by its third verse. ' Mine is an unchanging love . . . '—that verse, than which even Cowper never did anything better in hymns, sets the scale of the whole. Often a pianist, considering what is the correct speed at which a movement shall be played, will turn to some great rhetorical bar of music two-thirds the way through the piece, and will use that as his measure. None of it must be played so fast that that bar, when it comes, is robbed of the least part of its value. In the same way we may say that the whole of ' Hark, my soul ' takes its tempo, its scale, from that great central verse ; that that verse is the one which gives relevance to everything else in the hymn, and whose presence absolutely removes the possibility of triviality.

It is all put in the form of a dialogue, most of which is spoken by God. We are personally confronted with the facts—and are they not facts? Has not life provided enough examples of deliverance, and healing, and illumination, for any man to agree to that? It is the old story —God has been merciful in the past but the immediate future, we are sure, will be too much for Him. ' No,' says the divine Speaker in the hymn, ' I will not be forgetful or absent-minded or caught off my guard ; my love is unchanging.'

Unchanging, yes, but also infinitely compassionate. Here is God talking to a man personally : here, in this hymn, is unchanging, eternal love, higher than the mountains and deeper than the abysses, placed personally at that man's disposal. There is the paradox and the glory of it. It could not be true of a mortal man. Mortal love comes in gusts ; and our perceptions are wholly geared to the fact that it does come in gusts and not in a steady stream. We love life for its rhythms, its heights and depths, we love it for the way in which love and beauty and pleasure come unsought and surprisingly. By comparison we almost suspect an ' unchanging ' love, a love that could never be indignant, a fixed smile, a blinkered and ignorant benevolence, a blind loyalty. ' Unchanging love ' is not part of human life at all. The pitch and toss of life's journey brings out in men the kind of courage and toughness which led the late Bernard Shaw to say (and how nearly true it is) that the idea of heaven, with its uninterrupted bliss, was to him unutterably boring. But the truth is that love, unchanging love, is precisely the essence of God ; and felicity, uninterrupted felicity, is the texture of the life of God.

We need another word ; and the rich language of the Old Testament has it in that word ' zeal '. ' Zeal ' in *Isaiah* is a compound of vengeance and faithfulness. ' Zeal ' is the same, at bottom, as ' jealousy ' in the fourth Commandment. It means (partly) what a man feels when his honour has been outraged or his gesture of love treated with contempt ; it implies an unalterable intention of acting for the rehabilitation of that honour. ' I am a jealous God ' means that God is neither uninterested nor incompetent, that God is involved in the world, and must be expected to react to what is done in defiance of his command. And no doubt ' zeal ' or jealousy of this kind could be ascribed to any powerful deity, or for that matter to any powerful man. It is, after all, a human word used as an epithet for God. There is much more to add, but at least we have here the truth that God is passionate and also unchanging, that what in men would be mutually exclusive qualities are reconciled in God—God, who is all and always the same, and who is all and always love.

For what were the facts ? What did Isaiah say the zeal of the Lord of hosts would perform ? It will bring it about (says he in his ninth chapter) that the people who walk in darkness shall see light ; that a son will be born ; that their joy (the joy of the Displaced persons in European camps and outcastes in India and nameless prisoners in labour camps) shall be like the joy of harvest. Already, those eight centuries before Christ, somebody saw that the vengeance and flaming power of God was directed to the ends of love, to the carrying out not of destructive but of merciful designs. In Christ that was finally and beyond all doubt proved.

What we now know, having witnessed the Passion and Resurrection of Christ, is that the ' zeal ' of God is really the love of God. In that love are all the brightest and the darkest colours in the spectrum. When we compare it with our second-rate response, we are likely to think it presents the appearance of wrath—its heat is too high for human weakness. But it is love, love with the colour of anger in it, love with the colour of endurance and patience and staying-power in it, love as glowing as the lover in the *Song of Solomon*, as patient as that set forth in the parable of the Prodigal Son,—

Free and faithful, strong as death.

Free and *faithful*, not, like human love, feeble and fickle. Five minutes' meditation on those two words, ' Free and faithful ', as a daily exercise, is as likely as anything to be the right prescription for a man of the world in the present day.

12

Henry Williams Baker (1821–77). *Psalm* 23

The King of love my Shepherd is,
  Whose goodness faileth never ;
I nothing lack if I am his
  And he is mine for ever.

Where streams of living water flow
  My ransomed soul he leadeth,
And where the verdant pastures grow
  With food celestial feedeth.

Perverse and foolish oft I strayed,
  But yet in love he sought me,
And on his shoulder gently laid,
  And home, rejoicing, brought me.

In death's dark vale I fear no ill
  With thee, dear Lord, beside me ;
Thy rod and staff my comfort still,
  Thy cross before to guide me.

Thou spread'st a table in my sight ;
  Thy unction grace bestoweth ;
And oh, what transport of delight
  From thy pure chalice floweth !

And so through all the length of days
  Thy goodness faileth never ;
Good Shepherd, may I sing thy praise
  Within thy house for ever.

                    H.H.L. 16, 171, 195

Hospitality

WHEN Isaac Watts published the collection which contains 'Jesus shall reign' and 'Our God, our help in ages past', he called it *The Psalms of David imitated in the Language of the New Testament*. For two centuries and more, Watts has been praised for his masterly skill in carrying out the intention of that title (and, under No. 44 below, we add our own mite to these praises). It is at first sight a rather curious thing, then, that Sir Henry Baker, the author of 'The King of love' has almost been frowned on for treating the 23rd Psalm in very much the same way. 'One cannot help wishing', wrote Dr Percy Dearmer (in *Songs of Praise Discussed*), 'that he had paraphrased some other psalm'; and another commentator has more recently written that this is 'certainly not the best version of Psalm 23.'

Now these judgments have nothing whatever to do with the still unchallenged supremacy of this version in the affections of English people. 'The King of love' remains a tender, simple and beautiful hymn, allied with at least two singularly beautiful tunes ; and those whose 'canon' of hymns is narrower than our fifty, those who know half a dozen only, are likely to number this among their treasures.

The fact is, no doubt, that whereas almost all the psalms are improved by being translated with the accent of the New Testament, it remains just impossible to improve, in any fashion, the 23rd. The only reason for versifying it at all is that the amiable slapdash technique of English congregational singing does not take kindly to the business of singing prose psalms. No, you cannot, by the most sacred methods, improve on the 23rd.

Yet, even while you say that, it has to be admitted that you can never get to the bottom of the richness of truth that is in this psalm. It might well be thought that the psalm is so clear, simple and Christian in its own right that there was no need to comment on it further. But

Dr Micklem's broadcast addresses (now available in published form) [1] showed that in November 1953 there was something new and fresh and relevant to be said about it ; indeed, that precious little book makes it unnecessary to do more here in that line than to urge anybody who reads this to read, and re-read, Dr Micklem on Psalm 23. The fact is, of course, that the hymn-writers, like the preachers, have found endless inspiration here, and that Sir Henry Baker has to stand up and take his place alongside men of the genius of George Herbert and Joseph Addison. There is this, too—that this psalm brings out the best in any poet, be he great or small in his range of technique. It might be possible to say (I have not gone far into this, and perhaps it is too wide a generalization) that no man who has essayed the versification of Psalm 23 has written anything better in the rest of his work.

Whatever may be the issue of such speculations, we have here the cream of Sir Henry Baker's work, and a hymn which everybody loves. Perhaps the truth is that he has here ' imitated ' a psalm of David not only in the language of the New Testament, but also in the language of the Church of England of the mid-nineteenth century. But he is not to be blamed, he is not to be despised for that. Indeed, he is very much to be thanked, for he puts to us, in the special treatment he gives to this psalm, a point which nobody else among its many translators has put, and it is a point of searching importance.

Isaac Watts, we said, ' imitated ' in the language of the New Testament. Note first what he does with this psalm. He versifies it with great faithfulness (I am thinking of the second of his three versions, that which begins, ' My Shepherd will supply my need ', No. 50 in *Congregational Praise*). He makes no attempt, in the five verses in which he paraphrases the six of the psalm, to add or to interpret anything. But he adds, when all is done, a sixth, thus :

> There would I find a settled rest,
> 　While others go and come ;
> No more a stranger or a guest,
> 　But like a child at home.

[1] Nathaniel Micklem, *Two Psalms* (Independent Press, 1954).

That, in this particular case, is ' the language of the New Testament ' ; the finality of it, the peace of it, comes from that which Christ has done. The singer now knows himself to be not merely a lamb tended by a shepherd but a child loved and saved by a Father ; and his Father's house, he now knows (for example, from *St John* xiv) is open to him here and now. No abstract theology here, no rude invasion of the pastoral felicity of Psalm 23 by technicalities about redemption and atonement. Nothing here on the massive scale of ' When I survey '. But none the less—this last verse is what the New Testament adds to Psalm 23 : it is, indeed, not so much an addition as simply an ' Amen ', so smooth is the transition from the thought of David (if it be he) to the thought of the Christian believer.

Now Baker uses the New Testament too, but in his hymn the real emphasis is ecclesiastical in the end. Let us see how he goes to work. The first verse is very much what George Herbert had written two centuries before. ' While he is mine, and I am his ' was George Herbert's inspired reference to the *Song of Songs*. But Baker softens ' The God of love ' in Herbert to ' The King of love '. (What Herbert wrote can be found in any modern hymn-book : it begins ' The God of love my shepherd is '.)

The second verse follows the psalm very closely ; in the third, Baker introduces the New Testament, in a reference to the parable of the lost sheep in *St Matthew* xviii. In the last verse the other great New Testament ' Shepherd ' passage, in *St John* x, is recalled in the phrase, ' Good Shepherd '.

In the fourth verse, the addition to the psalm is in the words ' thy cross before to guide me '. Here we begin to verge into the traditional and ecclesiastical from the simply Scriptural. There is nothing in the Bible about the guidance of the Cross, or even the Way of the Cross, but (and here is the point) anybody who has been to church, anybody who has made any contact with the Church's traditional teaching and manner of speech, will know what this means, and be helped by it. Then in the fifth verse we have an uncompromising reference to the Sacrament of the Holy Communion in the word ' chalice '. ' Unction ', again, links the psalm's ' thou anointest my head with oil ' (a primitive and gracious gesture of hospitality) with the Christian teaching about the ' unction ' of the Holy Spirit (on which see 35). Once again, it is the man who understands the Church's customs and teaching to whom these lines will speak with greatest force. In the last verse ' within thy house ' is clearly ' within the church ', and we all accept it in that sense.

Now all this is the kind of complexity which many people have felt to be foreign to the nature of Psalm 23. But let us consider two things. Let us admit, first, that Psalm 23 is not merely a beautiful piece of writing, but is a record of spiritual experience which came to a man in the course of a busy, hazardous and, for his time, perfectly normal life. Life is not simple for anybody. It was certainly not simple for the author of this psalm. The genius of it is precisely in that its author had allowed the harsh frictions of worry, duty, responsibility and sin to produce in him this clear and simple spark of inspiration. Out of all the muddle of life he was able to see this with perfect clarity—' The Lord is my Shepherd : I shall not want '. That which has to do its good work by making an impact on the complexity of modern man's life comes from just the same kind of complexity. Is it not then proper for a modern writer to interpret it in those terms which he feels will make the soundest connection with modern life ?

But, secondly, this author showed very great faith when he assumed that this contact would be made through the church ; that the church would be, for the singer, the best interpreter of the New Testament. He showed great and admirable faith in that. And I hope it will not appear perverse if I record here my judgment that the true message of this hymn (not of the psalm) is a great judgment on the Church of modern times.

The psalm is a psalm of hospitality. The Lord is represented not only as a shepherd but also as a host, as one who offers shelter and food to a traveller. That meant a great deal in the still nomadic life out of which the psalm

sprung. Isaac Watts adds, we saw, that we may now know
that God's hospitality is not merely a tent of refuge for
a night's lodging, but a home for all time. Baker is making
the astounding assertion that the *church* is not a temporary
refuge but a home. Indeed, he is not so much asserting
that as assuming it. It is the unction, the chalice, the
house of praise that are the abode of felicity and safety.
It is there, in those categories and in that place, that you
will most fully enjoy the Shepherd's care and the Lord's
hospitality. Perhaps (it may be said) that was a natural
and even conventional thing to say if you were a distinguished
high-Church anglican, influenced by the new eucharistic
teaching of the Oxford Movement, to say in the year 1868.
Considerations of that kind, we venture to set aside in
favour of this : that that is precisely what our Lord meant
his church to be—a place of hospitality. He meant it to
be a place where the stranger would feel welcome, and
where, once he had accepted the welcome, he would find
warmth and friendship and the grace and power he was
hungry for. ' This is my Body ', he said, ' which is broken
for you.' ' For you '—that is the divine hospitality, the
costly welcome of God. In a special manner this duty
of hospitality is committed to the Church, to the priests
and ministers of the Church, to the members and officers
of the Church. This hymn is urging churchmen at all
times to make true of the Church what the poet had written
in the 23rd Psalm, that it may faithfully dispense to all
people the symbols and the techniques of overflowing love,
of redemptive reclamation, of comfort in darkness, of mental
and spiritual sustenance—and of physical sustenance too
for those who turn to it for that—and for all the materials
of praise. ' Woe to those shepherds ', said Ezekiel, ' who
feed themselves and not the flock.' ' Feed my sheep,' said
the Lord to Peter. ' Feed my lambs.'

13

Bishop Reginald Heber (1783–1826)

Holy, holy, holy ! Lord God almighty !
Early in the morning our song shall rise to thee ;
Holy, holy, holy ! merciful and mighty !
God in three Persons, blessèd Trinity !

Holy, holy, holy ! all the saints adore thee,
Casting down their golden crowns around the glassy
sea ;
Cherubim and Seraphim falling down before thee,
Which wert, and art, and evermore shalt be.

Holy, holy, holy ! though the darkness hide thee,
Though the eye of sinful man thy glory may not see,
Only thou art holy, there is none beside thee
Perfect in power, in love, and purity.

Holy, holy, holy ! Lord God almighty !
All thy works shall praise thy name, in earth, and sky,
and sea ;
Holy, holy, holy ! merciful and mighty !
God in three Persons, blessèd Trinity !

H.H.L. 131, 195

Holy, Holy, Holy

ALFRED LORD TENNYSON is on record as saying that this was one of his favourite hymns. It is indeed ·a Tennysonian hymn, in that it has a certain almost artificial stillness and symmetry of a kind which is to be found eminently in Tennyson. It is Tennysonian, too, in the almost deceptive way in which it handles a vast subject in language whose texture is so delicate that there is real danger of its being thought trivial. Chesterton said of Tennyson that ' he loved beauty in its completeness, as we find it in art, not in its more glorious incompleteness as we find it in nature '.[1] The thought might well be transferred to this very hymn, in as much as the matter with which it deals is a matter of doctrine rather than a matter of experience, and the hymn presents ' theology in its completeness, as you find it in doctrine rather than in its more glorious incompleteness, as we find it in Scripture '.

Here in sixteen lines the Doctrine of the Trinity is made a matter of common praise. This is, on any showing, a mysterious and exalted matter. And if we are to discuss the meaning of this hymn, we shall be unable to avoid some reference to technical Christian theology. For the hymn causes the singer to utter twice a phrase which is pure technical theology, ' God in three persons, blessed Trinity '. We shall be going beyond our terms of reference if we attempt to expound the Christian Doctrine of the Trinity—for this is not at all what the hymn is designed to do. The purpose of the hymn is to provide occasion for Christians to praise God, the thrice Holy, Father, Son and Holy Ghost, and, in the process, to admit themselves glad that there *is* a doctrine of the Trinity. That thought, and no more, is the subject of what follows here.

[1] G. K. Chesterton, *A Handful of Authors* (Sheed & Ward, 1953), p. 96.

The total appeal of the hymn to our affections arises from three obvious sources—first, the repetition of the word ' Holy ', second, the emphatic position of the word ' Trinity ', and third, the extensive use it makes of the vocabulary of the Book of *Revelation*. This vocabulary is principally derived from the following passage, in *Revelation* iv :

And before the throne there was a sea of glass like unto crystal . . . And they rest not day nor night saying, Holy, Holy, Holy, Lord God Almighty, which was, and is, and is to come . . . and the Elders cast their crowns before the throne. (*vv.* 6, 8, 10.)

The vocabulary is, as it were, part of the scenery ; hymn writers have always found that when they want rather to adumbrate than to explain, the symbolic language of this wholly and heraldically symbolic book is that which serves their purpose best. So far as that goes, we may leave it there ; but the implications of those two great words, Holy and Trinity, we must examine further.

HOLY, HOLY, HOLY

The beginning of the hymn, and indeed the greater part of it, is in the Old Testament. In that word ' Holy ' is epitomized the most august of Old Testament lines of thought and experience. For men of that day, the ' holy ' was primarily the untouchable. Holiness had a religious sense before it had a moral sense, and a superstitious sense before it had a religious. A holy thing was a thing you might not touch ; a holy mountain was a mountain you might not climb ; a holy place was a place you might not enter. From this central notion of holiness you can see spreading out, on one side all the richness of the Christian sense of ' reverence ', and on the other, all the confusion and terror of taboo. And there at the centre, in ' holiness ' you have a category which embraces the dynamic and eternal paradox of love and fear. In the realm of taboo, you keep away from something because you hate and fear it ; in that delicate reticence and courtesy which is part of the texture of the religious life at its most mature, you keep away from something because you love it and feel unworthy to come too near it. At the centre and the root of it all is the idea of ' holiness '.

More particularly, when it was said that God was holy (as Isaiah said it in that sixth chapter where first we have the word written three times in the familiar formula), what was meant was that God might not be seen. No man, they were sure, could see God and live. In that great story in *Exodus* xxxiii, Moses, begging to see the face of the God with whom he had walked all his life, was told that he might hear God's name, that he might see God's ' glory ' (the mysterious illumination which was thought to be a physical accompaniment or sign of God's presence), but that to look on the face of God would be too much for him. Normally the men of the Old Testament were content with this ; they accepted it. So highly developed was their sense of God's ' holiness ' that they did not allow themselves to pronounce God's name. They preferred to refer vocally to God through some periphrasis (in words, roughly corresponding to our ' the Lord ' or ' the Most High '), and to write God's name ambiguously, without vowels, so that it might never be directly pronounced. Thus they reflected in their religious practice what they felt was the gracious evasiveness of God himself. For they came to feel that God withheld his face from them not so much in protection of his own dignity as because the sight of perfection would shrivel up their enfeebled souls. So they said, ' clouds and darkness are round about him ' :

> Holy, holy, holy ! though the darkness hide thee,
> Though the eye of sinful man thy glory may not see.

(Quite so : our author is a little inaccurate ; men *were* allowed to see the glory : and there is no great force in the ' though '. But it matters little just here.) If a man ever claimed to have seen God's face, he knew he was claiming something impossible ; at the very least he was demanding the almost indignant attention of his fellows because he had received so special a grace. So Jacob, after wrestling through the night, called the place ' Peniel ' (which means ' the face of God ') ; and Isaiah

said, ' I saw the Lord,' and the elders in *Exodus* said they
' saw the God of Israel ' (chapter xxiv). These contradictions in Scripture are beyond our power to resolve—so are
the contradictions of life. But the principle is clear.

In the idea of holiness there was always fear, but there
was also a sense of mercy—the thing unapproachable was
both fearful and also in a sense utterly desirable. It is just
here that contact is established between these primitive
gropings and the most sophisticated of Christian doctrines.

BLESSED TRINITY

Perhaps the best point from which to approach a vindi-
cation of the doctrine of the Trinity is the sense of total
missionary obligation in the early Church. The early
Church believed that all things must be claimed for Christ,
claimed not merely by assumption but explicitly, claimed
(what is more) not through enslavement but by willing
consent. This meant among other things that the Church
must not merely out-preach the other faiths by its spectacular
witness and by prominent signs of God's favour to it, but
it must out-think the other faiths. The Christian way
must not merely be gentler, more clear-headed, braver
and more realistic than other ways ; it must be clearly
seen and admitted to be so. In the laborious processes
by which the body of Christian doctrine was built up you
can see the working out of this part of the Church's mission,
the claiming of the free mind of man as well as of his
affections. The story of all this is not primarily a text
for theological students, a technicality to be avoided by
lay-folk who deal in common sense and realities ; it is
a harrowing record of the groaning and travailing of mind
against mind, of tension between honour and honour,
between truth and truth, between loyalty and loyalty, and
in the end of the triumph of common sense and reality.
The doctrine of the Trinity, and the document that classically
embodies it (the ' Nicene ' creed) is the *tour de force* of
intellectual achievement. But—here is the vital truth
without which the whole picture will be thrown out of
drawing—it is also the *tour de force* of intellectual renunciation.

The Old Testament idea of ' the holy ' contains (we said) a majestic moral and emotional paradox. God is mighty, and he is near; God is all-powerful, and he is influenced by the prayers of Abraham; God is too aweful to be represented in drawing or sculpture, but he may be set forth (and is set forth from end to end of the Old Testament) in word-pictures. This titanic counter-point is the force that sets in motion all the music of Old Testament religion, and so persuasive is the language of prophet and poet that we accept it. ' Thus saith the high and lofty one that inhabiteth eternity, whose name is Holy : I dwell in the high and lofty place, but also with him that is of a contrite and humble spirit, to revive the spirit of the humble, and to revive the heart of the contrite ones.' It is all there, and as the Bible puts it it is all easy and evident.

But, said those mountaineers of the mind, the Fathers of the early Church, dare we try to put that philosophically ? Dare we try to state all that in language which will convey the truth to somebody who is not yet morally or emotionally committed to it ? Can we put it in such a way that the *mind* of man can freely accept it ? The missionary work of the Church has always been subject to the very rules which God himself keeps—nobody must be enslaved or bullied or blackmailed or hoodwinked into the Faith. Can, then, the essential truth about God's being be so set out that, without the help of the familiar and compelling rhythms of Biblical thought, a man of clear and cold mind can accept them intellectually ?

The problem is, of course, more urgent now ; for Jesus Christ has come. The paradox of God's holiness was stressful enough before. But now we are saying that Jesus Christ was born at Bethlehem, that his mother was Mary and his father Joseph, and that he is the Son of God. And there has been Pentecost, when men suddenly knew that God was in a sense, working in the world, living in the world, without in any way contradicting everything we had said before about God's utter holiness. All these things, which seem to stand in contradiction, they gathered up in the formula which says that God is three and God is one.

And for the space of three centuries men argued over that. Most Christians *believed* it. For most Christians it was a statement to which they would commit themselves. Hardly any Christian thought his way through it from beginning to end ; but the Bible plus human experience seemed to demand that men believe in God the Father, God the Son and God the Holy Ghost. But there were always men who asked questions. During those centuries there was no question at all that was not asked about this—asked and answered. What are the relations between the Father and the Son ? Can the Father do what the Son cannot do ? In what sense is Jesus human and divine at the same time ? Which of the Persons is Father, and which is Redeemer ? The controversy boiled over into physical persecution now and then ; but it was a controversy over the most important thing in the world : and where it produced the ugly moral paradox of persecution, this was only one unhappy upshot of the fiery paradox at the centre of the truth, which was more than the limited patience and fortitude of the human mind could contain.

And in the end they said what they had always said, 'God is three and God is one.' The structure had been built and tested—every joint and link and girder had been most rigorously tested, and it held. This, after all that the wise and prudent had been able to do, was what men wanted to believe. A creed is, indeed, precisely what men want to believe (it is not by definition what men *must* believe).

But then—when the structure is built, who wants to live in it ? Were not men and religion made before doctrines and creeds ? Indeed they were. All the intellectual discussions that went on then and continues now on doctrines of the Faith are tests of the soundness of the house, the seaworthiness of the ship. But the really important concern is the people who live in the house and who sail in the ship.

In other words, does this make any contact with human nature and human life, or has the whole plan got out of hand ? Who at this time of day *wants* a doctrine of the Trinity ?

The answer may be put shortly by saying that nobody would sing the hymn, ' Holy, holy, holy ', who had no use for the doctrine of the Trinity. Another way of answering the question is to point to the connection we have already established between it and human experience and need as the Old Testament records it. But here are three more considerations.

(1) The codification and clarification of doctrine is entirely necessary to human life. When one talks of creeds and doctrines, there lies in the background a truth that is moral and emotional as well as intellectual. The truth is that it is the duty of every man to thrust out with his mind to its utmost limit. He must find for himself, by experiment, just where that limit is. To abandon his intellectual sovereignty too early will be credulity ; to abandon it too late will be arrogance. He has to find the frontier, and when he has found it, to behave on this side of it with intellectual prudence and responsibility, and on the other side with intellectual submission. It is the Christian's duty to grow up in the Faith, and this is how, as regards his mind, he does it. The mark of the mature Christian is his combination of real skill and clarity of mind with great humility before the holiness of God. The royalty of Jesus embraced his dominion over creatures and his ascendancy over men, and also his obedience before God. There were many things which Jesus did not ask to know ; and there are many things in respect of which the Christian must not seek or claim knowledge. But there were many other things in respect of which Jesus was shrewd and skilful ; there are many things which demand the same response from the Christian. In this doctrine of the Trinity we have both intellectual achievement and intellectual renunciation. The man who dares to hold it has the moral duty of steering between slickness and foolishness ; the Christian way demands that in his mental activities as in all the others he shall be neither gullible nor glib. ' Holy, holy, holy ', that primitive invocation now gathered up into

our hymn on the Trinity, does us a great service in laying all the emphasis on the wonder and majesty of it, and none whatever on the intellectual athleticism of it.

(2) A secret of this doctrine, which it makes clear in its own way, is that God is always to be thought of as *personal*. ' God in three persons ' is a technical expression, and advanced theologians will tell us what ' person ' means. But it may be enough for the ordinary Christian most of the time to be reminded that God is not less, but more ' personal ' than man. No man is without something we call ' personality ', which makes him himself, and distinguishes him from other men. It is tempting and simple to think of God as less than personal ; give God the ' impersonality ' of an idol, and God will be harmless and give you a freedom you have no right to ; give God the ' impersonality ' of a business-magnate or a commander-in-chief, and you will be able to enjoy all the comforts and care-freedom of slavery. But it is not so. God is personal, personal in more dimensions than those which contain human personality. God is loving and zealous and active, yet without change and without caprice (see 11). ' God in three persons '—the old formula directs us to this indispensable truth, that God can be talked to and prayed to and treated as a friend by all men.

(3) But moreover, God's many-sided and infinite ' personality ' is more than can be even understood or worshipped by a single human mind. God *needs* a community of men to whom he may communicate his designs and with whom he may hold council. The varied apprehensions of the Old Testament—God as Father, Judge, Lawgiver, Husband, Lover, Friend, Captain—witness to that. The Church of the New Testament is vindicated on the same ground. Newman wrote (in *The Grammar of Assent*), ' Our image of God is never one, but broken into numberless partial aspects. . . . We know one truth about him, and another truth, but we cannot image both of them together. . . . Attempt to combine them into one, and you gain nothing but mystery.' This multiplicity, this active super-personality of God needs the response of a community of men bound together by

something that corresponds to the force that binds together the diverse Persons in the Godhead itself. That man may understand or experience something of the power and passion of God, man has been made free of the power and passion of love, love between man and woman, love between friends, love supernaturally set forth in the covenanted Church.

All this is mystery. The fruitful attitude towards it is not the analytical and explanatory, but the reverent and expectant. The author of 'Holy, holy, holy! Lord God Almighty!', which is so magnificently incoherent, so ejaculatory in its diction, reflects that necessity in his lines. The accent is on wonder and reverence. The very shakiness and disjointedness in the hymn are a kind of humility. What we think is of less importance than what God is. It is enough, for most of us, that the author clothes the whole in the mysterious shot-silk colours of the book of *Revelation*, and that the musician has set the whole to a tune that strikes the homely and traditional note. Reverence and joy, on this scale, are a sufficient sacrifice of praise.

14

G. Thring (1823–1903)

Fierce raged the tempest o'er the deep,
Watch did thine anxious servants keep,
But thou wast wrapped in guileless sleep,
  Calm and still.

'Save, Lord, we perish!' was their cry,
'O save us in our agony!'
Thy word above the storm rose high,
  'Peace, be still.'

The wild winds hushed : the angry deep
Sank, like a little child, to sleep ;
The sullen billows ceased to leap,
  At thy will.

So, when our life is clouded o'er,
And storm-winds drift us from the shore,
Say, lest we sink to rise no more,
  'Peace, be still.'
    H.H.L. 145, 256

15

William Whiting (1825–78)

Eternal Father, strong to save,
Whose arm doth bind the restless wave,
Who bidd'st the mighty ocean deep
Its own appointed limits keep ;
    Oh, hear us when we cry to thee
    For those in peril on the sea.

O Saviour, whose almighty word
The winds and waves submissive heard,
Who walkedst on the foaming deep,
And calm amid its rage didst sleep :
    Oh, hear us when we cry to thee
    For those in peril on the sea.

O sacred Spirit, who didst brood
Upon the chaos dark and rude,
Who bad'st its angry tumult cease,
And gavest light and life and peace :
    Oh, hear us when we cry to thee
    For those in peril on the sea.

O Trinity of love and power,
Our brethren shield in danger's hour ;
From rock and tempest, fire and foe,
Protect them wheresoe'er they go ;
    And ever let there rise to thee
    Glad hymns of praise from land and sea.

H.H.L. 6, 188, 195

Lord of Creation

THERE are several reasons why it is natural to treat these two popular and picturesque hymns as a pair. Their subjects are, of course, closely allied ; ' Eternal Father, strong to save ' applies to present needs the principle which is recounted in storyform in ' Fierce raged the tempest '. The two were written within a year of one another, and both have been helped towards popularity by the musical genius of Dr Dykes, who employs the same musical device to represent the storm in both.

' Fierce raged the tempest ' is almost entirely pictorial. It is a paraphrase of the Gospel story of the silencing of the storm, as it is set out in *St Mark* iv. 34 ff. (and parallels) ; its climax is a version of the words ' And he arose, and rebuked the winds and the sea ; and there was a great calm.' The application is made in terms of faith, the storm and the sea being taken as symbols of those forces which drive men away from belief into the open sea of doubt and fear. Nothing could be simpler.

' Eternal Father ' is written on the ' Trinitarian ' pattern, giving a verse to each Person of the Godhead, and a final verse of summary, addressed to the threefold God. In the first verse the Scriptural authority is Psalm 104. 9, ' Thou hast set a bound that they shall not pass over ; that they turn not again to cover the earth.' In the second the reference is to the miracle on the Lake of Galilee (the subject of the other hymn), and in the third it is to *Genesis* i. 3, which tells of the Spirit of God brooding over the face of chaos. The whole is directed to a simple prayer for travellers.

The central theme of both, then, is God's power over the elements. In the one it is allegorized, and in the other it is simply invoked for the protection of our friends. And at the heart of it all is a very searching question, which

81

may appear in many forms and may, if it be not answered, throw doubt on the value of both hymns. There are many who must have asked at some time, ' Does God really tell the hurricane and the typhoon to` be silent ? ' or ' Would God tell the storm to stop if I asked him to ? ' ' Fierce raged the tempest ' turns on an understanding of what Jesus really did on the occasion of which it tells ; ' Eternal Father ' turns on man's ability to invoke this power in his own day and for his own needs.

1. We may first consider the authority and value of ' Fierce raged the tempest ' and of the story on which it is based. And to this end we may say, in a very general way, that while it is of great importance for man's intellectual integrity that he shall consider what *explanations* there may be of the miracles of Christ, it is of even more importance that he shall *understand* the miracles ; and understanding is not the same thing as explaining.

Exactly what happened, historically, on the lake that day will remain a mystery. We cannot tell at this time of day how much of the story is history and how much is symbolism. But there is a clear question which we may ask, and to which we can expect a clear answer—What is the story doing in the Bible, and in what way is it supposed to help us ?

It must be clear to anybody who has given any thought to the matter that to regard the miracles of Jesus as conjuring tricks or demonstrations of formidable power, and no more, raises many more questions than it answers. Are such things credible ? Are they of any particular use to anybody but their immediate witnesses ? What character in Christ do they indicate ? The whole thing bristles with difficulties. It must be true that it was never the object of a miracle merely to remove some difficulty, or even to remove some suffering. No miracle can have been designed merely negatively, as the righting of a wrong. ' Miracles ' are technically described in the New Testament as ' signs ' ; there is more in them than meets the materialistic eye. What is more, there is that in them which no amount of embellishment or distortion in the report can finally obscure, and on which the difference in historical sense and scientific apprehension between this age and that has no effect.

For the ' miracles ' were primarily designed to show men who Christ was, and what he was. Augustine puts it that miracles were designed to ' lead men to God '. In a sense all miracles were designed in order to open the eyes of men —not merely of those who were present but of all who should hear about them. It is no accident that St John lays so much emphasis on the healing of a *blind* man ; the blind man is an historical figure, certainly : but he is also symbolic. For two things happened to him—one, that he received his sight, and the other, that he saw Jesus as the Christ, or that he saw and believed. (On this further, see 22.) The paralysed man at the pool of Bethesda in *St John* v was (*a*) given the use of his legs, and (*b*) told, quite abruptly and unsentimentally, to ' go and sin no more '—which means that he was given a new strength that would arm him against the temptation to grievance just as the new physical strength had delivered him from lameness. It is all quite clearly set down in verses 7 and 15 of that chapter. His ignorant satisfaction at being spared a personal inconvenience gave place (we may suppose) to an informed faith in Christ.

This can be generalized and applied to all miracles whatever, that they are primarily for the setting forth of the truth and the helping of men to see it. The personal well-being which followed their working in particular cases—healing, safety, even restoration to earthly life (and in the case of Lazarus how sure can we be that he was *happier* brought back to life than he would have been had he been left alone ?) are an incidental grace. You cannot, in life, separate felicity from the discovery of truth ; nor can you separate that crisis and struggle which is symbolized in the convulsions of the demoniacs, and in the tense silent moment during which the blind man (*St Mark* x. 51) considers his reply to the question, ' What wilt thou that I shall do unto thee ? '

Now in this particular case, we have in the foreground of the picture the remarkable incident of the storm settling at a word from Jesus. But we have in the background (or better, at the heart of it) the miracle by which the men in the boat knew themselves to be safe—because they had found out something new and vital about Jesus. Their fear and doubt were cast out, a large weight of ignorance was in that moment thrown overboard. The way was now clear for the next stage—the demonstration by Jesus that they themselves (in the person of Peter) could with confidence subdue their fears and actually assert their dominion over them (by the sign of ' walking on the water ').

Now the value of this approach to the miraculous in the Gospels is this, that if a man demonstrates that as a matter of plain fact the silencing of the storm was a coincidence, the heart of the thing remains untouched. If a man shows that the healing of the blind man was a simple chemical process, or that the casting out of dark spirits was a perfectly normal process in psychology, that makes no difference to the real story. The real story is about faith *versus* fear or knowledge *versus* ignorance or sanity *versus* darkness, or strength *versus* paralysis. The answer to them all is clear, informed, down-to-earth faith in Christ.

2. But now let us add this. In the account of the storm on the lake, all three evangelists agree that the disciples' first question, after the thing had been done, was ' What manner of man is this, that the winds and the waves obey him ? ' They were persuaded (and so am I) that the storm had calmed down because Jesus had told it to. How did Jesus do it ? The only answer can be that part of the redemptive ministry of Jesus was a complete and loving dominion over nature. The ancient story of Eden (which we shall hear more of, especially under No. 46) tells, symbolically and with uncanny shrewdness, that as soon as man decided to be impatient with the discipline of God, nature became impatient with him. He had been meant, precisely, to exercise loving dominion (*Genesis* i. 28) ; his disobedience, his desertion of the technique of love, infected nature. It continues to do so. Anybody knows that the clue to the enigma of animal ferocity and vegetable obstinacy is in the region of courtesy, understanding and humility.

Anybody can recognize the curious serenity that marks out every good veterinary surgeon, the innocent simplicity of which any lion-tamer must have a share, the patience and submission to routine that characterize the good gardener. And the quality that distinguishes the character of Jesus is, obviously, this faculty of being at peace with God, being obedient to God's routine, being at peace with men and things, reverently and wonderingly but never capriciously or impatiently. That is the manner of man who is never shaken by the winds, who is never shocked by calamity, who is never defeated by the demons.

That is the power which in ' Eternal Father, strong to save ' is invoked for the help of travellers (look again at the Biblical allusions we set out at the beginning). In the light of what we have here set down, we can now say that we are praying, on behalf of the travellers, that God's merciful and miracle-working power will protect them. The real content of the prayer ought to be that God will work for them the miracle that lies at the heart of the miracle Jesus worked on the lake—that he will cast out their fear and give them felicity. We may not pray that God should spare them all setbacks or difficulties ; to put it at its lowest that means praying that God will withhold from them all adventures and all heroism. Jesus did not come into the world to paralyse men into slavery, to rob life of all tension, to make all life like a bad hymn tune, without counterpoint, without shape, flat, stale and servile. He came to give men faith to cope victoriously and without grievance or fear with the challenges and austerities of the truth ; that through the same technique of faith they might be able to turn every such challenge into an opportunity for happiness and victory.

Suppose the worst happens ; suppose the ship in which our friend is sailing is fired on, or wrecked on the rocks ; suppose there is room in the boats for three-quarters of those on board because one or two of the boats are out of action. It is possible that our prayer for our friend to be saved might be a selfish prayer ; that a literal answer to it might mean his safety at some other passenger's expense. It is

H.F.—G

never selfish to pray that, however it goes, our friend may
be happy, without anxiety, without fear.   The granting of
that prayer might mean that he proved himself a hero, a
martyr to courtesy by giving up his chance of escape to
a neighbour.   The granting of that prayer might be his
death—a happy and heroic death, but death.   It might
leave us with the laborious, embarrassing, and perhaps
harrowing duty of comforting his relatives and bringing
them also to the peace of God : it might indeed be our
duty, because after all his heroism might easily be our own
fault—we prayed for it, did we not ?   That kind of prayer
is realistic.   And whether or not the prayer is realistic, the
answer will be : Casual, selfish miracles are not to be
demanded of God.   In plain fact, God *cannot* work them.
Jesus did not and could not have set his hand to anything
so trifling.   But *The* miracle, the precious gift of peace,
courage and felicity, will always be worked for the asking.

16

Bishop Thomas Ken (1637–1711)

Glory to thee, my God, this night
For all the blessings of the light ;
Keep me, O keep me, King of kings,
Beneath thy own almighty wings.

Forgive me, Lord, for thy dear Son,
The ill that I this day have done,
That with the world, myself, and thee,
I, ere I sleep, at peace may be.

Teach me to live, that I may dread
The grave as little as my bed ;
Teach me to die, that so I may
Rise glorious at the awful day.

O may my soul on thee repose,
And with sweet sleep mine eyelids close,
Sleep that may me more vigorous make
To serve my God when I awake.

When in the night I sleepless lie,
My soul with heavenly thoughts supply ;
Let no ill dreams disturb my rest,
No powers of darkness me molest.

Praise God, from whom all blessings flow,
Praise him, all creatures here below,
Praise him above, ye heavenly host,
Praise Father, Son, and Holy Ghost.

H.H.L. 132

Sleep

BISHOP KEN'S 'Glory to thee, my God this night;' is the simplest, the oldest, and the most popular of the traditional English evening hymns. Many others have been modelled on it; some of these are inferior imitations. But this, written for the scholars of Winchester College (and carrying the rubric, 'Be sure to sing the Morning and Evening Hymn in your chamber devoutly') is as solid and as sensible, and at the same time as lyrical, as the seventeenth century could make it.

Evening hymns are to be found among the very earliest Christian hymns. The oldest hymn we ever sing, 'O gladsome light' (or 'Hail, gladdening light') is an evening hymn from perhaps the second century. Many of the quaint and venerable pieces called 'office hymns' are evening hymns from not much later. And there is no doubt that there is something eminently creaturely about evening hymns. More than morning hymns, they gather up into Christian devotion much that is primeval in human experience and aspiration.

Man did not have to reach a very advanced stage of self-consciousness before he knew that the night-time is the time of mystery and fear. The evening incantation, the invocation of some Great Spirit to ward off the demons of the night, correspond in any primitive religion to the more mundane precautions which must be taken against the wild beast and the marauder. Bolts and bars, burglar-alarms, and popular science have done a good deal to make modern man feel confident in the night-time; and he is now at leisure to admire and love all that is beautiful in the evening. That happier condition is rather surprisingly seldom celebrated in hymns, but the magic of Robert Bridges' 'The duteous day now closeth' is in that it so happily and richly fills that need. But man can only appreciate the subtle pleasures of darkness when he is at leisure and at peace.

Men who are worried and busy and anxious by day are liable to be fretful at night.   Most Christian evening hymns therefore sound the note of protection and peace.

But of course the evening is the time of leisure and rest, a time when men are tired.   They may be pleasantly sleepy or grievously overstrained, for there are many degrees of tiredness.   To all the thought that ' he giveth his beloved sleep ' comes with a sense of gratitude.   And men who sleep soundly know nothing of the tortures of insomnia.   Sleep is a gift for which to be very grateful to God.

Yet sleep is a mysterious thing.   Look at any sleeping man, be he a dustman or a director or a young conscript in a railway carriage ;   how helpless he is, how defenceless ! Sleep is a great leveller.   It makes you think of death. Men have often softened the word ' death ' by substituting ' sleep '.   As you enter sleep you enter a kind of death, and as you wake up you enter a kind of resurrection.   You cannot go to sleep without making an act of faith ;   you cannot wake without a moment of elemental thanksgiving.

All this is in this grand old hymn, as it was in the lines which Sir Thomas Browne wrote earlier, ' The night is come, like to the day,' and which form to some extent the basis of this.   It says all the obvious and creaturely things.

It begins with an act of thanksgiving for the day past, and a prayer for protection through the night.   It goes on with a prayer for forgiveness for all that was amiss in the day, and the plea that the singer may be at peace with ' the world, myself and Thee '.   Then comes the greatest verse—' Teach me to live . . .   Teach me to die.'   Life leads to death as day to night, and death leads to resurrection as night leads to day.   The prayer is that life, death and what follows may all be encountered without fear and without dishonour ;   the man who is at peace with himself, the world and God will be able thus to live and die.

From this the hymn proceeds to a characteristically matter-of-fact petition for a sound sleep ;   a quiet mind brings good sleep, and good sleep brings renewed strength. But should sleep be denied, should we be too tired to sleep or kept away through pain or worry, then indeed we shall need help, and need it badly. For things look their worst at two in the morning. The powers of darkness will at that hour have their way with body and mind and soul, except God be present with light and help.

So the singer prays for ' heavenly thoughts '. That does not mean anything romantic or remote. It does not mean that the singer aspires to write religious verse in the small hours. For the ordinary Christian heavenly thoughts mean thoughts about real things, as contrasted with thoughts about imaginary things. The weary mind ' overrunning ' in sleeplessness is the prey of imagination, and imagination is played on by all manner of gross physical and psychological humours. That is just what makes things look bad at two in the morning. Well may a man pray that at that hour his thoughts may be as disciplined and courageous and sane as they are at two in the afternoon. Heaven on earth is truth and love, and heavenly thoughts are sane, straight thoughts ; they are the activity of the pure in heart who see God. A sound and God-regulated mind will be safe in the small hours whether the body be sound or sick, asleep or awake.

Nothing can be more for the fortifying of everyday life and common faith than this kind of simple and direct prayer, nor better for the advancement of the Christian in faith and love than the simple praise which closes the hymn. ' Praise God, from whom all blessings flow '—that is the beginning and end of life ; the humble creature's prayer is in the end absorbed in universal praise.

17

Bishop Thomas Ken (1637–1711)

Awake, my soul, and with the sun
Thy daily stage of duty run ;
Shake off dull sloth, and joyful rise
To pay thy morning sacrifice.

Redeem thy mis-spent time that's past;
Live this day as if 'twere thy last ;
Improve thy talent with due care ;
For the great day thyself prepare.

Let all thy converse be sincere,
Thy conscience as the noon-day clear ;
Think how all-seeing God thy ways
And all thy secret thoughts surveys.

By influence of the light divine
Let thy own light in good works shine ;
Reflect all heaven's propitious ways
In ardent love and cheerful praise.

Wake, and lift up thyself, my heart,
And with the angels bear thy part,
Who all night long unwearied sing
High praise to the eternal King.

Glory to thee, who safe hast kept
And hast refreshed me whilst I slept ;
Grant, Lord, when I from death shall wake
I may of endless light partake.

Heaven is, dear Lord, where'er thou art ;
Oh never then from me depart ;
For to my soul 'tis hell to be
But for one moment void of thee.

Lord, I my vows to thee renew ;
Scatter my sins as morning dew ;
Guard my first springs of thought and will,
And with thyself my spirit fill.

Direct, control, suggest, this day
All I design, or do, or say ;
That all my powers, with all their might,
In thy sole glory may unite.

Praise God, from whom all blessings flow,
Praise him, all creatures here below,
Praise him above, ye heavenly host,
Praise Father, Son, and Holy Ghost.

H.H.L. 132

Waking

THIS and ' Glory to thee, my God, this night ' are, of course, twin brothers. They were written by the same hand for the same community, and no doubt for the same tune (probably in the first instance the 100th Psalm). But they are by no means identical twins. In themselves and their relation with one another they may be described with some accuracy as non-identical twins, for in character and in import they are not merely very different—they are complementary. Where the evening hymn has solemn grandeur, this morning hymn has springing grace ; where the evening hymn prays for protection, the morning hymn prays for strength—and so on. That is all obvious enough, but here is another thing.

It is a matter of historical fact that while of the twelve verses in the original of the evening hymn few editors have ever printed more than six and none (in the last hundred years) more than seven, in the fourteen of the morning hymn many editors print eleven and few less than eight. That is to say, more of the morning hymn has stood up to the erosion of time than of the evening hymn.

The mythology of English hymnody treats morning hymns very differently from evening hymns. There is a real danger (whose origin will be obvious from the preceding article) in evening hymns of sounding too forcibly the note of resignation, the general strain of, ' Well, none of us is getting any younger.' It is the morning hymns that more generally sound the note of praise and hope. For the writers of evening hymns (as we saw) are drawn towards the imagery of death, while the writers of morning hymns find it difficult to resist the imagery of resurrection. That is a generalization to which there are honourable exceptions among evening hymns and mournful ones among morning hymns ; but it is the tendency, and we can observe its effects in this morning hymn of Bishop Ken.

It shares with the evening hymn, of course, a supremely innocent mode of speech, and a firm contact with human instinct and experience. That is an important factor in its greatness. Here in the first verse we begin with the obvious image—the sunrise. The sun awakes to run his course, and men will do well to emulate him. The energy and power of the sun, immortally depicted in the 19th Psalm, provide a good starting-point for a morning hymn. The natural imagery continues. Ken has not the astronomical imagination which makes him able to make much use in the evening hymn of natural images ; but we have here the sun, the noonday, the light of heaven, and the morning dew.

All is done with that common sense and efficiency which are among the characteristics of the true Puritan. Puritanism you can also see in the deeper note sounded in the second verse. ' Live each day as if thy last '—' The precious time '. Christianity is not a religion of the future but a religion of the present. Men do well to live not by ends or origins but by daily manna. To live in the past is one error ; to strain towards the future is another. Between them they engender despair and worry, they stifle true hope and courage. As day succeeds to day the thought that that means one day less of life becomes more and more insistent. I woke up not long ago to the thought that, on a reasonable estimate, I was now half-way to the day of my death. Yet I remember a distinguished and magnificent old gentleman, whom, when near his ninetieth birthday, I saw transported into pleasure and gaiety when he first discovered a certain Beethoven movement. It is possible to worry about the little life that is left—that is wasting time. It is possible to pay no attention to the passing of time, as though any good deed and any fresh vision can wait until to-morrow—that also is wasting time. But to live as long as may be allotted, thirty years or a hundred, and to let no day pass without some new knowledge of God's goodness and some opportunity taken of doing good—that is living. That is redeeming the time.

' Let all thy converse be sincere '—honest dealing, a good conscience, and everything done as in the sight of God. ' Let your light, reflecting the light of God, shine in good works.'

> Reflect all heaven's propitious ways
> In ardent love and cheerful praise.

There is the homely, upright, efficient Puritan in Ken ; all
is direct and relevant, praise in the common things of life.

So ends what we usually mark off as the first part of the
hymn.   That part is a soliloquy in the second person singular
—unusual, this, and very difficult to do as well as Ken does
it.   Then he turns to God with high thanksgiving.

' Glory to Thee ', he begins, Glory to God for answering
last night's prayers.   The mercies of sleep have given me
confidence about that other matter—death—which was
raised in the evening prayer.   Once having begun to
think about God, the author cares not to turn away immediately.   Heaven is God's presence, hell is separation from
him.   May this day then be, in that simple sense, heavenly.
Let the vows be renewed, the courage newly put on, sins
forgiven, thoughts and speech guarded afresh, acts and
ambitions controlled, and all things done for God's glory.

We shall at a later stage discuss a much profounder
morning hymn, ' Christ, whose glory fills the skies ' (24).
That hymn makes the theme of resurrection more explicit
than does this one.   And after all a hymn written for
schoolboys (as both Ken's were) is better kept to the simple
things.   But any morning hymn, in giving thanks for the
resurrection of waking from sleep, implies a prayer for protection from the things which would prevent or make
nonsense of that resurrection.   The question at the beginning of every day is this—will the things that the day brings
advance or set back my faith in God and knowledge of
him ?   The beginning of the modern day is a particularly
trying event in most lives.   The morning paper screams at
you from the front-door mat ; the cultivated and imper-
turbable news-reader announces the dooms of nations.
The children have to be got out of bed and packed off to
school, the 8.15 to Town is remorseless ; and with it all,
that dark and ill-humoured interval, which usually includes
breakfast (and which may or may not be dulcified by the

B.B.C.'s offer to lift up your heart), between physical waking
and the awaking of that mental faculty which sets things in
due and fit proportion. There is enough there to make
the whole day and the whole family morose and miserable ;
there is enough there to last until the broadcasting comedian
or the cinema make their evening effort to disperse the
gloom. The man who can best cope with this daily emergency, this singularly varied and malevolent monotony of
irritation, is the man who has said his prayers, and has said
in them the kind of thing that is written in ' Awake, my
soul ' ; if he has done that, and ended with the doxology,
he is more likely to move into life responsibly and good-
humouredly than to allow life, in its blundering way, to
move into him.

18

John Keble (1792–1866)

New every morning is the love
Our wakening and uprising prove ;
Through sleep and darkness safely brought,
Restored to life, and power, and thought.

New mercies, each returning day,
Hover around us while we pray ;
New perils past, new sins forgiven,
New thoughts of God, new hopes of heaven.

If, on our daily course, our mind
Be set to hallow all we find,
New treasures still, of countless price,
God will provide for sacrifice.

The trivial round, the common task,.
Will furnish all we ought to ask,
Room to deny ourselves, a road
To bring us daily nearer God.

Only, O Lord, in thy dear love
Fit us for perfect rest above ;
And help us this and every day
To live more nearly as we pray.

H.H.L. 110, 144

Work

NOT long ago a good story about Iona was going the rounds. Iona is a community of work and worship, whose headquarters is in Glasgow, where most of its work is done ; three months of the year the community spends on the Island of Iona, and you may go and spend a week or a fortnight there by way of holiday—if you intimate your intentions early enough. But for the duration of your stay you will be offered the privilege of lending a hand with the work that goes on there. It may be in helping to rebuild the Abbey of Iona ; it may be in digging the garden, it may be in washing up. One day (it appears) the leader of the community and a guest were working together on some necessary but repulsive detail of domestic routine, and the guest said to the leader, ' Now, why have you asked me to do this job ? ' The leader replied, ' To prevent your doing what I used to do—talking about the dignity of labour.'

Nothing is easier than for those who have interesting lives to exhort those who have dull work to do. I have heard a trustworthy authority declare that a good deal of the complaint about the dullness of other people's lives is made by people who ought to be helping but would rather take refuge in romance than actively help ; and that such complaints do not so frequently come from the victims of dullness themselves. That is probably true. Ministers of religion, anyhow, are the people who lead the most interesting and adventurous lives of all, and in the matter of trivial talk about the dignity of labour and vocation we are among the worst offenders. We mean no harm, but we here and there do a great deal.

This is the context of ' New every morning '. Here is a hymn that deals with just this point without facility and without patronage. It does it much better than our sermons do it. The keynote is sounded in that very first word, ' new '.

That would be, probably, the reason why we tend to sing this hymn beginning at this verse, ' New every morning '. But that is not where the author began it, and we very slightly distort the meaning of the hymn if we are not careful to divine the thought that lies in his opening quatrain.

> Oh timely happy, timely wise,
> Hearts that with rising morn arise !
> Eyes that the beam celestial view
> Which evermore makes all things new.

We must regretfully admit that that is a shade romantic for the robust temper of the modern congregation. But those final words are vital, ' which evermore makes all things new '. For as we commonly sing it, we begin with a verbal reminiscence of the *Lamentations of Jeremiah*, ' His compassions fail not : they are new every morning ' (iii. 26). But it is only a reminiscence, for there is nothing else in *Lamentations* that will find a place in this hymn. The real thought comes from the text in *Revelation* xxi. 5, ' And he that sat upon the throne said, Behold, I make all things new '. There may also be a hint of *Zechariah* iv. 10, ' Who hath despised the day of small things ? '

The hymn begins by stating a fact on authority, ' New every morning is the love ' of God, which preserves us through the hazards of the night and brings us back to life again. There is always something to be thankful for that distinguishes one day from another, and on that evidence God will provide some means of sacrifice, whether through discipline or through praise, in the day that lies ahead. The very limitations of the daily round provide a means, if nothing more, of making, through self-denial, a cheerful sacrifice. This we pray, and may we be given grace to live up to the prayer.

The backbone of all this is Biblical and Christian ; indeed it is only by understanding this deeper issue that we can rescue the hymn, and the Church's thought, from that triviality against which Dr MacLeod at Iona was warning his guest.

As we glance through the Old Testament, one of the

penetrating paradoxes which emerge from it is this : that
while it was forbidden to men to worship any material
thing, there was nothing which men were not prepared to
regard as standing for, or as symbolizing, the Holy.
Palestine must still be littered with stones set up to commemorate solemn covenants and religious crises, like
the stone Jacob set up at Bethel, or the stone Ebenezer
which Samuel erected to commemorate the Dunkirk of the
Philistine war (*I Samuel* vii. 12). Certain things, themselves
merely material, were yet never to be touched by human
hands because of their ' sacredness '.

Without taking this further here, we may appreciate
that it shows the willingness of the Hebrew mind to leave
room for a kind of derived holiness in things. It was always
to be sharply distinguished from that holiness which is God's
alone. You might worship only God ; but for the sacred
things you were entitled to feel something akin to respect.

Again, it is clear from the whole climate of the Biblical
view of life that words without actions never appealed to
the Hebrew mind, nor to the mind of Christ ; that actions,
like things, could be symbolic, that they were thought of as
possessing the power to lead the mind beyond themselves to
something in the spiritual background. It was common for
a prophet of the Old Testament to perform physical acts in
the course of his allocutions ; he would break a vessel in
pieces to drive home his message that God would bring
disaster on an erring city ; John the Baptist used water at
least in part because of the readiness with which it would
be accepted as reinforcing his teaching of repentance,
cleansing of the soul, and a new moral start in life. And he
who was greater than all the prophets and the crown of all
prophecy took bread, and broke it, and said, ' This *is* my
body.'

Things, then, are as important as words, and actions as
ideas ; neither can exist without the other to any good
purpose. It is all associated with the principle made known
finally in *St John*, where it is written that the Word was
made flesh : that the material and the spiritual were in
Christ wholly and harmoniously allied. This means that

the mind of God is willing to suit act to word, to clothe his Word in flesh, and thus to give men the authentic principle upon which they can found their doctrines of work and of material things. Tracing the same principle in the other direction, we find that the whole sacramental system of the Church depends on it, that worship, for almost all Christians, issues not only in word, but in word as preparation for act. To this day Protestants and Catholics cannot agree on the pregnant detail of how much *holiness* we are allowed to ascribe to that physical object which is used in the Holy Communion as the vehicle of the sacrament.

These are great issues. Here we are concerned with issues on the particular and domestic level. Christians have come to believe (and this is one of the beliefs that lagged behind the great credal beliefs of the early Church : a modern, Western article of faith) that the old principle can be generalized in New Testament terms for the good of common life. Where men of the Old Covenant would set this and that aside for some special holy purpose, men are to-day tending more and more to work out the consequences of believing that *anything* can possess this derived holiness, because every material thing (and *a fortiori* every person) has not only an aspect visible to us but also another aspect permanently turned towards God. This, without doubt, is the truth hidden in this familiar hymn.

Consider one or two very familiar things. Is it not obvious, for example, that when you are dealing with the land, you are dealing not merely with a *thing* ; that to get the best from it a man must observe rules of restraint and respect which are demanded by some kind of holiness in the land, by its character as made by God and lent to men ? If a man repudiates these rules and ignores the hidden holiness, the land will be his enemy. Again, it is possible to murder a motor-car by stupid, insensitive driving ; it is logical for the Christian to believe that, being a worshipper and a child of the God of Christ, he is obliged to treat with understanding and respect a machine that works according to laws that may have been discovered by Otto Daimler but were made by God.

H.F.—H

As concerns daily work, the Christian tends to speak similarly in sacramental terms. Some kinds of work must be characterized as irretrievably dull and sub-human. Where life has imposed such kinds of work on men, life has sinned, and we have to deal with the situation as a sinful situation demands. Perhaps a rough-and-ready guide which distinguishes redeemable work from sub-human work is this : Would it or would it not make sense to say, ' Ah, there's nobody like Jack Jones for that job ! ' After all, you can always ' tell ' a Willis organ, a Grinling Gibbons carving, a Nash street (when there were any). In a community where work is being done as God meant it to be done, you could, one supposes, talk that way about each one of the workers and each of the jobs ; men's hands and brains would be reserved for those things which, being able to carry the personal impress of the skilled workman, could obviously carry also the conception of sanctified vocation. Work of which such things could not be said would be handed over to machines. If it is nonsense (for all I know, not being a technician, it may not be nonsense) to say, ' There's nobody who empties dustbins like Jack Jones,' then let human ingenuity evolve mechanical means for emptying dustbins and give Jack Jones something better to do. There is no need to be romantic here, or to be too facile in judging other people's ways of life. In a recent broadcast we were told of a very fashionable restaurant-proprietor who treats his washer-up like an artist and pays him ten pounds a week—with the result that a ' clean food ' survey pronounced his establishment one of the four of hundreds surveyed which are really as hygienic and well run as human nature can make them.

But the principle is clear. And meanwhile the jobs are to be done. It is no help to be told that Jesus was a carpenter (or a builder). Carpentry and building are aristocratic callings compared to what most men do for their living to-day. It is no help to generalize about the dignity of labour or to assume *a priori* that this or that piece of work is necessary but beyond redemption. But here is something that does help :

If on our daily course our mind
Be set to hallow all we find,
New treasures still, of countless price
God will provide for sacrifice.

If the mind be set to hallow it, if it be believed that what is impossible with men is possible with God, then miracles will surely happen, and water will be turned to wine. Man's irreverence and impatience will do much to deepen the curse of labour yet ; but the power and love of God are greater. It is, to put it summarily, astonishing what a God-centred mind can find *interesting*.

Brother Lawrence, who spent the last twenty-five years of his life as a servant in the kitchen of a monastery in Paris and died in 1691 at the age of eighty, is the classic type of the man who can redeem dull work. His wisdom is crystallized in the little devotional tract known as *The Practice of the Presence of God*, and the following is a characteristic passage :

The most excellent method I have found of going to God is that of doing our common business . . . purely for the love of God. . . . The time of business does not differ with me from the time of prayer, and in the noise and clatter of my kitchen, while several persons are at the same time calling for different things, I possess God in as great tranquillity as if I were upon my knees at the Blessed Sacrament.

That is a good way in which to cast one's thoughts on the dignity of labour.

19

Cecil Frances Alexander (1818–95)

Once in royal David's city
   Stood a lowly cattle shed,
Where a mother laid her baby
   In a manger for his bed.
   Mary was that mother mild,
   Jesus Christ her little child.

He came down to earth from heaven,
   Who is God and Lord of all ;
And his shelter was a stable,
   And his cradle was a stall :
   With the poor, and mean, and lowly
   Lived on earth our Saviour holy.

And through all his wondrous childhood
   He would honour and obey,
Love and watch the lowly mother
   In whose gentle arms he lay.
   Christian children all must be
   Mild, obedient, good as he.

For he is our childhood's pattern,
   Day by day like us he grew ;
He was little, weak and helpless,
   Tears and smiles like us he knew ;
   And he feeleth for our sadness,
   And he shareth in our gladness.

And our eyes at last shall see him,
   Through his own redeeming love,
For that child so dear and gentle
   Is our Lord in heaven above ;
   And he leads his children on
   To the place where he is gone.

Not in that poor lowly stable,
   With the oxen standing by,
We shall see him ; but in heaven,
   Set at God's right hand on high ;
   When like stars his children crowned
   All in white shall wait around.

H.H.L. 214

Childhood

ONE of our well-known hymn-books places this
hymn in the section for children, and dourly
adds a rubric, ' suitable also for adults '. There
is much to be said for taking the other line, and
placing it in the section for general use at Christmas, and
adding a footnote ' suitable, if judiciously chosen, for children '. It is one of the most famous of children's hymns,
true : it was written to expound to children the Apostles'
Creed at the point where it is written, ' Who was born of
the Virgin Mary '. This it does faithfully. It goes to one
of the loveliest of tunes, and every child loves it. But for
all that, it is a hymn that carries a hidden message which
only the grown-ups can appreciate, and which all the grown-
ups need very much.

For we can say that the inner message of the hymn is
wholly suitable and necessary for adults ; and we are bound
to say, in our day, that there is one line which most certainly
does not chime with our thought about the proper virtues
of childhood. ' Mild, obedient, good ', with the best will
in the world, we can hardly do much with to-day.

But the singing tradition of the Church has invested the
hymn with a quality, and made it the vehicle of a message,
which may not have been present in the author's first intention. The style of the words, the felicity of the music,
and the association of the whole with Christmas make the
hymn the symbol of Gospel childlikeness. It gives its best
value when it is closely associated with our Lord's words
about children in *St Matthew* xviii.

Jesus said, on the various occasions which are gathered
together in that chapter, that to enter the kingdom of
heaven a man must ' be converted ' and become as a little
child ;. that to have a proper sense of values it is essential
to have a right respect for the value and grace of childhood
(verse 4) ; that to corrupt that grace of childhood, or to be

the initiator of the grievous process by which a child may grow up wrongly and perversely, is the worst crime in the world (verse 6), and that contempt for the special qualities of childhood is the best way of indicating contempt for the essential qualities of the Kingdom (verse 10).

All this is often sadly misinterpreted. There is a gracious condition called infancy, and there is a sour disease called infantilism, and it is a pity to confuse the one with the other. It is impossible to conceive our Lord's encouraging men and women to cultivate childishness (imitation of children by grown-ups) or infantilism (fear of growing up at all). But of course if a man can deceive himself into thinking that this is really the content of the Lord's teaching at this point, he can excuse himself for a whole lifetime of sloth, and can give himself a weapon to use against those, whom he will call highbrows and æsthetes, who take life with more courage and faithfulness.

Consider for example the attitude of a man to books and literature. There are many good reasons for a man's reading children's books. He may read them for his children's amusement ; he may review them or publish them ; he may read them in the course of teaching children to read. But he is only half a man if his whole literary world consists of children's books. We should look with pity and concern on a middle-aged man who read nothing in the 8.15 to Charing Cross every morning but *Peter Rabbit* or a comic paper—for that would be childishness. It is a matter for real anxiety that what is as a matter of fact read in the 8.15 is literature deliberately geared to the fear of growing up— the infantilism—that is peculiarly characteristic of this universally literate age. The spiritual sloth and cowardice that issue from yielding to the fear of growing up are one of the special curses of modern civilization ; dictators and oppressors thrive on it. It is very far indeed from the Kingdom of heaven, and the contents of any railway station bookstall provide ample evidence of it. In the context of books, the man who knows how to live is surely the man who can read responsibly and with attention the classics of his own and other ages, but with the same kind of courage and surprise and freedom which his child shows on first discovering for himself the experience of reading *Peter Rabbit*. What is said in Scripture amounts to this, that being converted is rather like a recapturing of the graces of childhood. In another place Scripture takes an image from the other end of life and says it is rather like a resurrection. It is, in any case, a radical change from bondage to freedom (see 22). This is what is notable and admirable in the child whom Jesus placed in the midst of the disciples as their example—that he is innocent of those things into which men enter as they advance in years. The very act of pointing to the child was occasioned, the Evangelists tell us, by the dispute among the disciples about ' which was to be greatest '. The child has not yet learnt to sulk. He is still free of the world, adventurous, afraid of no new thing. His elders will see to it that he is well stocked up with the fears and selfish axioms and codes of rights that are the proper appurtenances of civilized life. If they get their way he will become skilled in the ' adult ' arts of suspicion, self-regard, caution and worry.

Jesus never forbids a man to grow up. He was only desperately indignant and sorry every time he saw a youngster growing up into *that*. The child was born into a context of sin and self-regard. And inevitably there will be some who ' offend ', in making that context more real, and the Kingdom of heaven less real to that child. ' Woe to him through whom offences come.'

This is, however, not merely a disconnected moral precept. It is a truth made of the same fabric that the Incarnation itself is made of. ' Let this mind be in you ', said the Apostle, ' that was also in Christ Jesus ' ; and when he wrote those famous words (*Philippians* ii) he was writing to a Church whose chief defect was a tendency to sulk and stand on its dignity, both corporately towards himself and individually one towards another. Let us read on in a modern translation :

Let Christ himself be your example as to what your attitude should be. For he, who had always been God by nature, did not cling to his prerogatives as God's equal, but stripped himself of all privilege by consenting to be a slave by nature and being born as mortal man. And having become man, he humbled himself by living a life of utter obedience, even to the extent of dying, and the death he died was the death of a common criminal. That is why God has now lifted him so high, and has given him the name beyond all names.[1] . . .

Jesus ' stripped himself of all privilege '. In his loving purpose all his rights were set aside. Much good will be done by those who are able to live as men who have set aside their right to sulk, their right not to be taken advantage of, their right to score over their neighbours. The passing passion of the child is a small thing, almost a happy thing, compared with that principle of security and right which is at the root of the habitual unwillingness of the grown-up to forgive and to have in him the mind of Christ Jesus.

' For he is our childhood's pattern ' : ' *suitable for adults* ' indeed !

[1] From *Letters to Young Churches*, translated by J. B. Phillips (Bles, 1947).

20

Isaac Watts (1674–1748)

When I survey the wondrous Cross,
  On which the prince of glory died,
My richest gain I count but loss,
  And pour contempt on all my pride.

Forbid it, Lord, that I should boast
  Save in the death of Christ my God ;
All the vain things that charm me most,
  I sacrifice them to his blood.

See from his head, his hands, his feet,
  Sorrow and love flow mingled down ;
Did e'er such love and sorrow meet,
  Or thorns compose so rich a crown ?

His dying crimson like a robe,
  Spreads o'er his body on the tree ;
Then am I dead to all the globe,
  And all the globe is dead to me.

Were the whole realm of nature mine,
  That were a present far too small ;
Love so amazing, so divine,
  Demands my soul, my life, my all.

The author's first version of verse 1, line 2, was ' Where the young prince of glory died '.

H.H.L 5, 29, 66

Prince of Glory

THE curse of journalism is, it is often said, the adjective. For since the adjective is the most powerful instrument for subjective expression in the writer's repertory, it is a weapon that can easily turn against himself. If he is careless he can smudge the whole picture with adjectives ; if he is unscrupulous he can turn truth into tendencious half-truth and make it impossible for his reader to separate fact from interpretation. Nouns state facts, adjectives provide ornament, emphasis, comment. ' The house ' may be any house in the world ; ' The Great House ' brings up a picture not merely of a large house but of a large eighteenth-century house in a park.

In ' When I survey ' there are five adjectives (six if you read the original second line). This does not include adjectival words used as predicates. The purely descriptive adjectives are these : ' wondrous ', ' richest ', ' vain ', ' rich ', and ' amazing '. Yet it must surely be agreed that this is the most penetrating of all hymns, the most demanding, the most imaginative. It is these things precisely because its style is so simple. It is drawn throughout in strong, clear, simple lines and colours.

This restraint corresponds with the same qualities in the Gospel narratives of the Passion. ' And they crucified him.' ' He gave up the ghost '—simple, elementary sentences like those are the units of the story on which the whole of world history hinges. A similar interpretation through textures will be found in Charles Wood's *St Mark Passion*, in which, at the ushering in of the last scene, all the pomp and richness and barbaric splendour appropriate to the crowd, the Prætorium and the court of Herod are set aside, and the story goes on to the end in simple, unaccompanied, archaic, and austere music sung with solemn quietness.

This is a technical and relatively superficial matter. Indeed, it would be wrong to press the analogy far in this latter case : for whereas the composer without question knew what he was doing, the author of the hymn is like the Evangelists in that he produced this stylistic effect quite without self-consciousness, being concerned only with writing down what had to be written, as clearly and simply as he might. The author, indeed, wrote his hymn as a comment on a text of Scripture ; and you might very conveniently describe the difference between this and ' There is a green hill ' (which follows) by saying simply that this is written to illuminate scripture while that is written to illuminate the Catechism.

The verse of Scripture which is here paraphrased is this :

God forbid that I should glory, save in the cross of our Lord, Jesus Christ, by whom the world is crucified to me, and I to the world. (*Galatians* vi. 14.)

And just as the texture of the hymn, considered as a Passiontide hymn, corresponds closely with the texture of the Passion narratives of the Gospels, so the context of the hymn corresponds with the context of the particular verse on which it is based. For the hymn was conceived by Isaac Watts as a hymn for the Lord's Supper, and the Epistle to the Galatians comes straight from the busy mind of the Apostle Paul to the confused and perplexed life of a group of primitive churches. The Holy Communion, the sacrament of common life, is always in a sense a table ' furnished in the wilderness ' (Psalm lxxviii. 21), a table ' spread before me in the presence of mine enemies ', a defiance of the secular and transitory through the very use for holy purposes of common and perishable things ; and both the hymn and the great verse in *Galatians* are, as it were, points of stillness and adoration snatched out of the bustle and trouble of daily life.

Galatians is Paul's most indignant and forthright letter (except perhaps that very strong letter to Corinth preserved in part at the end of *II Corinthians*). It is his reaction to the very situation in the churches which was most likely to

make him deeply anxious and angry. We will attend to
that situation, and our reason for doing so shall be this :
that the Cross is the throne from which the Prince of Glory
reigns, not over holy thoughts, but over common life ; and
that ' When I survey the wondrous Cross ' is not a holy and
romantic thought but a song of the abasement and offering
and sanctification of common life. It is as much about
common life as ' New every morning '. There is nothing
of Holman Hunt about this. We will, then, glance at
common life as it erupts in the Galatian troubles.

A group of churches, it seems, had been led into error by
people who were more anxious to make their voices heard
than to wait patiently on the truth of the Gospel. The false
note in their teaching was that they presented Christianity
as a new version of an old faith, a new variation of a faith
whose most obvious appurtenances were a set of *regulations*.
The general and public danger of this was that it became
possible for the candidate for conversion or baptism to say,
' I see : if I obey the regulations and sign where you tell
me to sign, then I can take it I have arrived ? ' He could
go on—nothing was to prevent him—to regard himself as
socially and perhaps morally superior to those who did not
commit themselves to these regulations. That was bad
enough. What made it ten thousand times worse for Paul
to bear, what drew from him human and near-frantic wrath,
was that it was that very error which had been formerly
his life and his livelihood and his passport to academic distinction. At great cost to himself he had set it aside, he had
resigned from his position as the youngest and most violent of
its persecutors, he had risked his life over and over again to
preach to these people a faith whose only regulation was the
law of love, and whose only requirement was the courage of
the crucified ; all this—and here were superficial and vain
people, half-baked, inflated religious Philistines undoing all
his work, making Christianity easy and making it cheap.

On this Paul lets himself go. ' O you dear idiots of
Galatia, who saw Jesus crucified so plainly, who has been
casting a spell over you ? ' So reads one passage in J. B.
Phillips's tranlsation. Paul shows himself indignant and

grieved : but one thing he never does. Not for one moment
does he say, ' That is a fine way of repaying me for all I have
done for you.' Not for a moment does he boast of his own
achievements in the spreading of the Gospel.

On the contrary, as the letter nears its end he snatches
the pen from his secretary's hand, reads over the draft, and
adds an immortal postscript. ' Look at these huge letters
I am making in writing these words to you with my own
hand ! ' (vi. 10), he begins, and the substance of the postscript is really gathered up in the very verse we have here
under review. It is as much as to say, ' Never mind about
all these arguments, true though they are. Here is the
heart of the matter. I am proud of nothing but this, that
Christ has died for me.'

' God forbid that I should glory. . . .' ' I have no
authority to say anything but the authority that comes from
that.' Isaac Watts fastens on that and writes three verses
on it. Where is pride, where is grievance, where is pomp,
in the face of what Christ did ? Nothing there but sorrow
and love, love and sorrow. It is not merely grief, not
merely heroism, but sorrow going forth in brave love ; love
adding triumph to sorrow.

But Paul has another word yet, and so has the hymn
(though there are hymn-books that leave out this verse).
' . . . the Cross of Jesus Christ, by which the world is
crucified to me, and I to the world '. ' Crucified ' means
everything here. It means not merely dead, but disgraced
and discredited. Those who crucified a man did it publicly,
on the main road. When in cruder days Englishmen hanged
traitors at Tyburn (which is now Marble Arch), the point
of it was that they were hanging them at the junction of
the main road to Holyhead and the main road to Fishguard
—in the most populous place they could think of. This
was not merely to end the life of the criminal but to show
the world that what he stood for was discredited in English
public opinion, that his treachery could do no more harm
because it had been cut off at the root. They hanged Jesus
on a cross with the express intention of discrediting his
claims as well as making away with his Person. The

Apostle cannot here mean less than that in his eyes now all the claims of ' the world ', all its values and standards and axioms, are similarly pilloried and discredited, and that he, in the eyes of the world (what must the old gang at the University of Tarsus have thought of it all ?) is discredited and proud of it.   Now he knows where to find the truth, now he knows where to find strength.   His mind and his will and his affections are now made free of the truth and love of God ; he now knows what is really wisdom and what is really goodness.

All this is interpreted in that mysterious and beautiful verse about the precious blood of Christ, the poured-out life carrying with it to every mind the poured-out love, the utter faithfulness of the King of kings.   ' Then am I dead to all the globe '—for if a man will attend to this thing that had been done, he must either write Jesus off as an impostor, or he must take the consequences of accepting him as King of life.   So much of human valuation is associated with the rejection of the Cross ; perhaps the application of this to contemporary life, whose distinguishing character is literacy and abundance of information and great ease of communication, is to denounce those mental habits, and in particular the mental cowardice and meanness, which are at the foundation of most of the barriers that cut off modern man from the sight of the Cross.   All these false values ' I count but loss ', says the Apostle.

What are the consequences of this ?   That immortal last verse tells what the consequences are.   In whatever region the great change has been made, whatever form the sacrifice has to take, the consequence is a new and abounding generosity.   All must be given.   Giving, not receiving : duty, not right : obedience, not mastery—these are the response.   The reckless pouring out of divine love demands a reckless abandonment of earthly defences against it. ' Lift up your heads, O ye gates, and be ye lift up, ye everlasting doors, and the King of glory shall come in.'

' When I survey ' is a hymn of common life.   The Gospel demands a response, on this scale, in common life.   The very last thing the Cross demands is an increase of specialized and fugitive holiness. The very first thing it demands is the throwing down of the barriers. ' The sacrifices of God are a broken spirit ; a broken and a contrite heart, O Lord, thou wilt not despise.' A broken and a contrite heart, a heart that has willingly borne the weight, and been broken and renewed under the weight, of the love of God ; a heart ground down and set free by the joyful burden of gratitude to God. The broken heart is not the mournful heart ; for what is broken is the shackles that prevented its being free. The contrite heart is not expressed in the grim and cheerless outlook, for it is the heart's prison-walls that have been ground to powder (and ' contrite ' means precisely ' ground to powder '). He who has allowed the love of God to break over him will not, probably, appear to all his neighbours all at once to be a specially pious man. What his neighbours will be unable to miss will be the freedom of his heart from all impediments to love, and the freedom of his mind from all impediments to generous speech. He will be just like a man who has laid down a heavy burden, or a man who has just recovered from a wasting disease, or a man who has just seen the world for the first time after a lifetime of blindness. He is free, because he has yielded to the demand for *his* life, *his* soul, *his* all. The possession has gone, the right to them has gone, and, considered as a man with a life to live, he knows he is far better without the burden of possession. Life is altogether richer and saner now that he has exchanged that for the burden of praise, for the weight of glory.

21

Cecil Frances Alexander (1823–95)

There is a green hill far away,
    Without a city wall,
Where the dear Lord was crucified,
    Who died to save us all.

We may not know, we cannot tell
    What pains he had to bear,
But we believe it was for us
    He hung and suffered there.

He died that we might be forgiven,
    He died to make us good,
That we might go at last to heaven,
    Saved by his precious blood.

There was no other good enough
    To pay the price of sin ;
He only could unlock the gate
    Of heaven and let us in.

O dearly, dearly has he loved,
    And we must love him too,
And trust in his redeeming blood,
    And try his works to do.
              H.H.L. 214

Atonement

THIS hymn is by the same author as 'Once in royal David's city'. Those and many other hymns by the same author, one or two of which besides these two are well known, were written for a high and holy purpose, to answer the questions of children concerning the great doctrines of the Faith. They are based on the Catechism, which contains the Apostles' Creed ; and they presuppose a child, preparing for catechism, looking up from his prayer-book and saying, 'Yes, but *why*?' The hymns are, therefore, essays in simple theology. This is the finest of them all, and it begins from the question, '*Why* did Jesus die?'

We begin with history. Oddly enough, not all that appears in that first verse is in the strictest sense history. The modern literal and well-travelled mind will make some reservation about the green hill ; for to Englishmen green hills are places of solitude and peace, whereas this thing happened on a main road near the front garden gate of a substantial citizen called Joseph of Arimathea. That hardly matters. It is no more than a piece of scene-painting to catch the imagination. It is more important to have a picture of the thing that really happened there, when you are dealing with a child, even if the picture be geographically inaccurate, than to wait until the child can cope with abstract ideas. What matters, and what the child will not doubt after singing this verse, is that the thing did really happen.

Reverently the hymn proceeds in the second verse to say what, on the one hand, we may not try to explore, and what, on the other hand, we firmly believe. The dereliction and sorrow of the Cross are facts, but they are impenetrable. They are the sacred concern of Jesus of Nazareth and of nobody else ; we are wise to avoid too much imaginative dwelling on the personal suffering involved in this thing, except as an occasional private exercise in mental prayer. It is better to cultivate clear thinking and a brave and decisive response than public hysteria or the kind of thing exhibited on that day by the daughters of Jerusalem. ' We believe it was for us '—that is the heart of it. ' For us.' ' Now,' says the intelligent seeker, ' what do you mean, " for us " ? '

> He died that we might be forgiven,
> He died to make us good.

That is very baldly stated. The second clause makes the sophisticated raise their eyebrows. ' To make us good ? How can anything *make* us good ? ' But this, properly understood, is good Biblical teaching.

Taking an overall estimate of the condition of mankind as it is displayed in the Old Testament or in the daily newspaper (it really hardly matters which you prefer to take as evidence), the shortest way of describing it with any accuracy is to say that it is out of touch with truth and at odds with goodness. Or you can say that it is separated from God. Something is very wrong with the world. It looks, on this evidence, as if God and man just do not understand one another. Man (on the whole) either ignores God or speaks ill of him, making him out to be neither comprehensible in his words nor kindly in his manners. God seems to take much the same view of mankind. That is a reasonable generalization about the world from the outside, as soon as God has been brought into the conversation at all.

If God has been supposed to be not only good but also active, what will be his intention when he knows that men are thinking in that way about himself? His first intention, you would say, would be to restore the relation which existed before things began to go wrong. The restoration of that relation can only be done from God's part, because it is God who precisely has not gone wrong, and man who has gone wrong. And God is the creator of the whole system in which the error has taken place. The great need is for the restoration of friendliness and *understanding* between men and God. This is, precisely, forgiveness. Forgiveness at the human level is the restoration of a relation which has been upset by some deed of violence against it. Such, by analogy, is the forgiveness of God. This is what God did in the events with which the hymn is concerned.

But the very act of forgiveness means that the person to be forgiven is to be treated as though he wants to be forgiven, as though he wants the relation restored—even though it may turn out that he does not want it, and rejects the offer of forgiveness. When a man turns to another in an act of forgiveness, and is resolved that, come what may, everything he can do shall be done, it may well be that he will have to try first one way, then another, of forcing his way through the barrier of fear and resentment in the other man. Clearer and more emphatic notices of readiness to forgive will have to be presented. Most of us, in human relations, do not get far along this road ; but it might in the end come to this, that the other man will not be persuaded of our readiness to forgive until we have actually died for him, by (for example) giving our life to save him in some emergency, or (like the great heroine of the concentration camp) taking his place in the queue for the gas-chamber. It is more than probable that it will come to this, at least, that the man who would forgive will have to give clear evidence that he is ready to abandon some important right in the case, ready not to stand on his dignity or take advantage, ready, in that limited way, to die for his rights. Above all, he must show some active *respect* towards the other, at the moment when the other deserves, knows he deserves, and fears, contempt.

That is the manner in which men have interpreted the strategy of God in dealing with the world's trouble and rebellion. Our Lord himself summed it up in the parable of the wicked farmers, to which we have already made reference (9). ' He sent first one . . . then another . . . then he sent his Son.' God gave all the evidence required through law and conscience and prophet and singer ; but mankind would not accept that as evidence. So at last he came, and died.

' He died ', then, ' that we might be forgiven.' There

is more in this than a merely passive sense. He died that
we might not only be, but be clearly seen to be, forgiven and
forgivable. What greater respect could Almighty God pay
to men than to place himself thus physically in their power ?
' He died ', it goes on, ' to make us good '—not to make us
feel good or to change human nature by waving a wand,
but to make us see that we are being *treated* as good. The
technical word which theologians toss about in their discussions at this point is the word ' impute ' : God ' imputed '
goodness to men, though men had no shadow of claim to
be so treated. The hymn insists that God ' made out '
men to be good precisely at that moment in all history when
mankind least deserved it. And once that has been grasped,
it becomes tolerable to say simply, ' He died to make us
good ' because the surest way of getting the best out of
anybody is to treat him with respect. The man of whom
most is expected will, as a matter of fact, produce the best
response. Once a man has bowed his head to the truth that
God respects him, he becomes from that moment, simply,
a better man.

  ' That we might go at last to heaven '—that means, of
course, that the object of it all is that a man may go back
into the presence of God, into friendship with him, into
the condition he need never have left. ' Saved ' means
' rescued ', or brought back from exile, or restored to friendship after estrangement, rescued from the spiral of despair
and grievance which only this public demonstration of God's
love could break.

  And from here we proceed to that remarkable and controversial fourth verse.   ' There was no other good enough.'
Frankly, it is possible to interpret that as a mistake in terms.
The author, to achieve that simplicity which is appropriate
to the youthful mind, has rightly paid the youthful mind
the compliment of not expecting it to suspect heresy. But
more sophisticated singers ought to deal with this point.
It robs the Gospel of its power, it makes the act of God
artificial just where we want it to be spontaneous, if we
say that God chose Jesus to be our Saviour because Jesus
was an eminently good man. Some have thought that at

his baptism Jesus, son of Joseph, was ordained by God to become the Saviour. But that is out of key, because it makes God order somebody *else* to take the heavy part of the work, whereas the Christian conviction is that God did it himself. We must not take this phrase that way.

We do better to start from the expression in the second line, ' To pay the price '. This means changing the whole metaphor on which the previous verse was based. If it is a matter of forgiveness, there is no payment involved. For-giveness is free or it is false. But then perhaps someone was saying, while reading what is written above, that it is not really very satisfactory to set out the acts of God as though they were human acts. The two objections answer each other. That is precisely the point. You cannot tell the truth about this or about any of God's acts by the use of only one picture. You need many pictures, and the truth is that all those ' doctrines of the atonement ' that form the subject matter of examinations in theology are nothing but the various pictures which have so far been drawn. We are now turning to another picture.

Suppose we take the original generalization, that ' some-thing has gone wrong with the world ', but instead of making it the ground of being sorry for ourselves and saying ' What will become of us ? ' make it the ground of moral concern and say ' This puts us under a great debt to God. How can the debt be paid and honour restored ? ' Then we shall be in the condition to which this verse is speaking. We are now right down alongside the man who has done the wrong, and in a way this is healthier than associating ourselves with the people who complain of the suffering brought on themselves by the consequences of the wrong. It is not our place to forgive (if that is where we now stand) ; it is our place to undergo the discipline of receiving forgive-ness—but that is not yet. What a man in this position feels most strongly is that it is his business, somehow, to *pay*.

Suppose a man has swindled or robbed another. He can do a good deal by simply paying back the money. Yet even in this simple case there are two difficulties. He may not have the money—swindlers are not usually brought to book until they have spent the money. But beyond that, even if he can repay in full, the injured man will probably have his whole view of human nature soured by what happened. He may be made less able to trust, forgive, and respect men because of what happened. That is the real mischief. And if the trouble in question is not a civil offence but a crime, where there is no medium of repayment, then that is all the criminal is left with. Suppose then that a man has grievously injured another man but that the case is one from which we can exclude legal processes. The sinner has only one thing he can do, and he will be a brave man if he can do it. He must go to the man he has injured, and give *himself*, in order that, ' dying to ' his own pride and rights, he may by that means sweeten the bitterness of the injured man. This ' giving himself ' means, of course, nothing so crude as committing suicide on the spot or offering to work for no wages. It means making a spiritual offering of a kind which will bring no advantage of self-righteousness to the giver. That will be the test ; that will be the measure by which a spiritual adviser will diagnose the situation and prescribe the restitution.

Not unnaturally, men have felt that way about the relation between mankind and God ; there has been a sense of *guilt* towards God, a sense of the love rejected and the forgiveness set aside, and men have felt they must, here and now, *do* something. They must pay off something of their moral debt. ' What shall I render ? ' says the psalmist, and ' Wherewith shall I come before the Lord,' said the prophet Micah. Man felt he must make sacrifices (as it is written) of unblemished and valuable animals. The animal for sacrifice had to be the best specimen in the flock, a ' whole burnt offering '. The very cruelty and wastefulness and barbarity of these ancient rites reflects the moral tension which resulted from a perfectly healthy and realistic religious sense of debt to God.

When the Crucifixion was done, and the Resurrection accomplished, men began to see what had happened that day. Not a soul knew what was happening while it was in process. Men began to say, ' but this was a *sacrifice* ! It was *the* sacrifice, not a lamb or a bullock, but a perfect and sinless man. Behold the Lamb of God ! ' The sinlessness of Jesus became an essential part of what he had done, and the sacrifice became at last an effective sacrifice, which made all the bulls and goats of the old days look like play-acting. That is just what they had been—sacred and pious play-acting. ' There was no other good enough '—he was the only spotless man, who could go forth and offer himself as a payment of the debt of man to God. This, we repeat, is only one of many pictures which interpret to us what was done there ; but its shrewdest point is this, that it includes the conviction that we sent him to his death. The other way of thinking (forgiveness) includes the conviction that God went, of his own free will, to death.

Both convictions are true. Matthew, Mark, and Luke make Jesus say ' The Son of Man must suffer many things ' ; John makes him say, ' No man taketh my life from me, but I lay it down of myself.' It is no use arguing which of these is right, because they seem to exclude each other. Both are true, and the mind and imagination of the Christian must be broad enough to encompass both.

So we are brought back to the same point to which the previous verse led—to ' heaven '. The effect of it is to show mankind the way to friendship with God. Jesus let men drive him to death (or he went to death) to procure for us this friendship. Active and passive are mysteriously mixed up in the great Act, even as past and present and future are intertwined in the Being of God. It is all beyond human language and grammar, but that is what we should have expected the Acts of God to be.

' And we must love him . . . and trust him . . . and try to do his works.' ' If ye love me, keep my commandments.' A simple, almost tame finish. It may appear so. But let a man set his hand to that task, and he will find the whole story of the Cross and of the Resurrection coming to life in his own life. ' Doing his works ' will involve such a man in costly love, will use every ounce of his strength of body and brain as well as will. We believe it was ' for us ' ; we believe he said, ' Follow me '.

22

C. Wesley (1707–88)

O for a thousand tongues to sing
  My dear Redeemer's praise,
The glories of my God and King,
  The triumphs of his grace !

Jesus—the name that charms our fears,
  That bids our sorrows cease ;
'Tis music in the sinner's ears,
  'Tis life, and health, and peace.

He breaks the power of cancelled sin,
  He sets the prisoner. free ;
His blood can make the foulest clean ;
  His blood availed for me.

He speaks ;—and, listening to his voice,
  New life the dead receive,
The mournful broken hearts rejoice,
  The humble poor believe.

Hear him, ye deaf ; his praise, ye dumb,
  Your loosened tongues employ ;
Ye blind, behold your Saviour come ;
  And leap, ye lame, for joy !

My gracious Master and my God,
  Assist me to proclaim
And spread through all the earth abroad
  The honours of thy name.

H.H.L. 67–72.

Conversion

IF there is one word which divides the world, it is the word 'Conversion'. Bring it into a conversation, and you will immediately arouse emotions which will divide unbelievers against believers and believers against each other. It arouses all the defence-machinery in the minds of the sensitive, and all the aggressive energies in the zealous. It is, to use a vivid but (as so often) precise Americanism, the 'hottest' word in the Christian vocabulary.

'Conversion' is, of course, associated especially with the name of Wesley. But it is no monopoly of any family or denomination or way of Christian thought. It is, to begin with, a Scriptural word and a Scriptural notion. To be sure, the word is not very often employed in the English Scriptures. It and its cognates appear about a dozen times in the Bible. Its two most famous contexts are in the 51st Psalm—'and sinners shall be converted unto thee', and in *St Matthew* xviii. 3, 'Except ye be converted, and become as little children, ye shall not enter into the kingdom of heaven.'

But the idea is part of the essential teaching of the Bible. After all (provided you do not use this offensive word) there is something almost platitudinous in saying that, things being as they are, there is great need for a radical change in people's outlook ; that in order that things may be as God meant them to be there needs to be a change in the centre of gravity, or the focus of attention, from self to God. The idea of conversion is inseparable from any evangelistic activity, whether or not it be Christian or even religious.

It is the effects of religious conversion to Christ in particular people that cause the trouble ; and the subject of this hymn is just that—the effects of conversion. Originally it ran to eighteen verses, and when you read the original you see no reason why any but purely physical and pru-

dential causes ever brought it to an end.   It is an astonishing
outpouring (even for Charles Wesley) of high spirits and
joy.   But then even among Wesley's hymns it has a special
place, since it was written to celebrate the first anniversary
(May 21, 1739) of what he always called his ' conversion '.
It is our business here, then, not to attempt to examine the
mysteries of the process of conversion, but to put a point
which arises out of the text of this hymn, and which has to
do with conversion recollected in tranquillity.

Observe, first, that almost every line in the hymn bespeaks
a great change from darkness to brightness.   ' Jesus, the
name that charms our fears : that bids our sorrows cease '—
anxieties are dispersed, sorrows and grievances evaporate.
' His blood can make the foulest clean '—the dirt and
blurring and tarnish of the ineffective and aimless life give
way to the fresh brightness and cleanness of a life with a
purpose.   Further, the author insists that the results of
conversion are spectacular and demonstrative.   The dumb
men not only speak : they praise.   The lame man not only
walks, he leaps and capers about in public.   The blind not
only see ; they see Jesus.   The mournful are not merely
relieved of their sorrow, but are taught the technique of
joy.   (Upon all which, see 14/15.)

In fact, the whole texture of the converted life can, on
the evidence of this hymn, be summed up in a single word—
freedom.   That is one of Wesley's favourite ideas—he rarely
omits it from a hymn on any subject.   Freedom from
blindness, from bondage, from deafness, from sorrow, from
death.   ' Restore unto me the joy of thy salvation,' says
that 51st Psalm again, ' and uphold me with thy free spirit.
Then will I teach thy way to the ignorant ; and sinners
shall be converted unto thee.   *Deliver* me. . . .'   This is
the freedom, the fearlessness, the innocence that our Lord
was pointing out in the child whom he held up as an example
to his disciples.

Freedom is the keynote—but freedom, we must say,
issuing from sanctified habit and directed by purpose.
William James, lecturing and writing on conversion fifty
years ago, said that conversion means ' that religious ideas,

previously peripheral to man's consciousness, now take a central place, and that religious aims form the *habitual centre of his energy*'. 'Religious aims' mean, not a narrow or oppressive piety, not religious pomp and 'lifemanship', but a religious habit of mind, a Christlike way of talking and thinking and acting. That is the mark of the converted man.

Who does not know the difference between two kinds of musician? Here are two men who can both play with skill and dexterity and even virtuosity; but the one plays with authority while the other plays by rote. The one plays with understanding, the other with skill only. The technical subtleties of this do not matter here; but this common experience, an experience of criticism which is available to the non-expert listener, can be put with some accuracy thus, that the understanding musician is he who takes his instructions from the composer with all the dignity of a free man, while the other takes his instructions as a pupil or as a slave. The one is 'free of' the music, and therefore free of this particular music, while the other is, by comparison, in a kind of bondage.

Alongside this, to provide an example authentic if embarrassing from another sphere of mental activity, I ask leave to place my own experience with geometry. Geometry I found unintelligible at my preparatory school until a certain day which I can remember as though it were yesterday. Up to that time I would take the word of the book or the schoolmaster for anything, but I was incapable of using my mind freely on the subject, of seeing the logical connection between this proposition and that, and of moving by the free discipline of logic into further deductions. On this particular morning the schoolmaster drew on the blackboard the diagram appropriate to the proposition that the angle in a semicircle is always a right angle. Up to that moment this was to me nothing more than 'Theorem forty-one', just one more boring, unrelated, unpersuasive proposition. But then I threw up my hand with indecorous eagerness and said, 'Please, sir, I see why that is!' The master turned round and listened to my explanation, and

then said, ' Well ! So you have started at last ! ' So
astounded was he that, as I recall, he gave me about five
times the appropriate number of marks. But the point is
that I had ' started at last ', I had moved of my own free
will from one proposition to another in the field of
geometry. From that day I felt, not more knowledgeable
than I was before, not greatly advanced in my store of
learning, but (what was infinitely more to the point), *free
of* the subject.

Anybody can produce an experience parallel to that.
Indeed, the analogy with religious conversion is so close
and exact that I am myself persuaded that God means such
things to be a type or training for that time when a man
accepts from God the freedom of life : for that, in a word,
is what conversion is.

The details are so important that I would rehearse them
again. The experience is one of freedom, not of omniscience.
It is impossible to lay too much stress on that. The whole
notion of conversion is distorted and soured by the failure
to grasp that. Conversion is not omniscience. Conversion
is not a title to lay down the law to the schoolmaster or to
say you know more than the textbook. Conversion is much
more like making the schoolmaster your friend and the book
your pleasure.

Now we will take a third and classic picture. Consider
the story of Bartimaeus, who was healed of his blindness
(*St Mark* x. 46 ff. and parallels). Observe, in all versions
of that story, the vital fact that Bartimaeus not only received
his sight, but proceeded immediately to follow Jesus *in the
way*. That is to say, he joined the group who were following
Jesus on that impressive and solemn journey to Jerusalem.
(The very next story in *St Mark* is that of Palm Sunday.)
He is delivered from darkness, and he is impelled, thus
made free, to use his freedom to follow Jesus.

The converted man, the man who is made ' free of life '
is in that condition precisely. He was like this blind man,
who had had to be guided along the road by some friend,
who was full of natural fears because of the dangers around
the road which he knew nothing of. The road was a

dangerous and irksome discipline. But now he not only sees the road and the Master, but he wants to go along it. He is free of the countryside, free to walk on the road and admire the scenery. He is free, but he does not think of himself as free to do what he likes. To be free of mathematics is not to be free to do what you like. It is to be free to walk without schoolmasters and textbooks along the road, to want nothing more than to see what lies round the next corner. The gift which God offers to every man is just this freedom. The difference between unregenerate freedom and converted freedom is the difference between the freedom to stumble and break your neck and the freedom to walk with confidence along the road and enjoy it.

It is this truth which gives to the hymns of the Wesleys such high spirits, and to the Christian life such zest.

> My chains fell off, my heart was free,
> I rose, went forth, and followed thee !

That is the note they so often strike, and the note which the Christian life should strike. And the Christian pilgrim may be sure of this further, that once this freedom has been given, it can never be taken away. I am now no mathematician at all. I should have to turn back to the textbooks to follow through again the arguments before I could recount them to anybody else. But I shall never be again as desperate and blind as I was before the revelation of geometrical principles came to me that day. The musician of authority and freedom may get rusty, he may have to go back several stages and practice again as he had done in his youth before he can give a decent account of a Mozart sonata ; but he will never be as though his freedom of music had never been given to him. It is always said that once you have learnt to swim or to ride a bicycle you can never forget, even though you lapse for a lifetime from the practice of such skills. Nor can the gift of freedom of life be taken away. A man may sin grievously, he may become spiritually rusty, he may become despaired of by his friends ; but this remains, that he has been given freedom to follow, and at any point he can take it up again, even if he has to go back to the Jerusalem Road at a point several miles behind that to which at one time he had attained.

Neither of the Wesleys, I think, would want to contradict this, though they would wish to add much depth to it. They were both highly religious men before their conversions (John was converted three days after Charles, in 1738). Taken all round they were good professional religious men, distinguished in piety. But they were, compared with what they became, religious ' by rote '. There was so little to show for all their piety. After the freedom of life had been given them, all the stored-up power began to flow through them into the world, with what results we know very well.

And this itself is authenticated by the experience of the disciples of our Lord. In a moment, as they tell us, they suddenly became free of the life that the Lord had ordained for them. After that strange thing happened at Pentecost (the queer and uncanny thing was that it happened to all of them at once ; it was a communal conversion—that was the only odd thing about it, but it was a very remarkable thing), they found themselves no longer waiting for instructions from the historic Jesus, but able to walk freely on their own in the countryside of the Faith, and to gather others to walk beside them. They had ' started at last '. They were free of life. And they knew then that though the earthly Jesus had left them, the power and presence of Jesus were still with them. They knew that the Holy Spirit was at work.

What then has this to say to the ' ordinary Christian ' who is put off by the idea of ' sudden conversion ' ? First, it is probable that there are many more Christians who can point to some day or hour of ' conversion ' in this sense than would admit it or have realized it. This will be chiefly because few people practise the exercise of self-examination to any extent. Few spend much time looking back over their lives and discerning a pattern in them. To do this for the purposes of self-pity or self-justification is poisonous ; to do it in order to discern the plan of God is necessary and healthy. No Christian who knows himself to be in any

H.F.—K

sense ' free of ' the Faith can say there was no time when he remembers being delivered from bondage ; it is only that that kind of statement, and the activity that leads to the discovery of its ground, is unfashionable and unusual to-day.

But, secondly, the error of thinking that conversion means the end of the road is always possible. It is no use looking for some occasion in the past when you suddenly found you knew all about life. If a man claims any such experience, he is to be suspected. The failure of many to find any point of conversion to thank God for is probably due to their looking for the wrong thing. What most of us must be content with is to discern in our lives many moments which mark turnings in the road resulting in new and wider views of the country. We shall probably call our ' conversion ' the first of these. But we may well feel that the picture is one of freedom always increasing rather than of the whole of freedom being given all at once.

But the journey along the road is another story altogether. What we are here concerned with is the process of receiving the freedom of life. The journey along the road is called in the technical theology of the Bible, ' sanctification '. This giving of freedom is called ' justification '. And if once we can agree that it is a real experience, and a common experience, we shall be able to agree on this also (which will make us realize how faithful and factual these lines of Charles Wesley's are), that it is nothing but a gift of God, and that nothing is more precious or more deserving of our cheerful gratitude.

23

C. Wesley (1707–88)

Love Divine, all loves excelling,
  Joy of heaven, to earth come down,
Fix in us thy humble dwelling,
  All thy faithful mercies crown.
Jesu, thou art all compassion,
  Pure unbounded love thou art ;
Visit us with thy salvation,
  Enter every trembling heart.

Come, almighty to deliver,
  Let us all thy life receive ;
Suddenly return, and never,
  Never more thy temples leave.
Thee we would be always blessing,
  Serve thee as thy hosts above,
Pray, and praise thee, without ceasing,
  Glory in thy perfect love.

Finish then thy new creation,
  Pure and spotless let us be ;
Let us see thy great salvation,
  Perfectly restored in thee,
Changed from glory into glory,
  Till in heaven we take our place,
Till we cast our crowns before thee,
  Lost in wonder, love, and praise !

H.H.L. 67–72, 276

Sanctification

THERE is nobody like Charles Wesley for packing a volume of pregnant thought into a short hymn. In a sense, when we come to ' Love divine, all loves excelling ', we come to the climax of the whole series formed by the familiar hymns collected into this book. It would be possible (but we shall not here attempt) to show that all the other hymns are as it were tributaries of this one ; that thoughts expressed by a word or two here are elaborated elsewhere ; that all the other hymns of praise and penitence and triumph make contact at some point with what is written here.

The primary subject of this hymn is the sanctification of daily life. Indeed, although no hymn is more exalted in its aspirations, its very literary form has a secular origin, for in its metre and in the language of its opening lines it imitates that famous poem of Dryden's, memorably set to music by Purcell, beginning :

> Fairest isle, all Isles excelling
> Seat of Pleasures and of Loves ;
> Venus here will choose her dwelling
> And forsake her Cyprian Groves.

But the secular associations are soon forgotten. It immediately becomes obvious that we are dealing here with that ' sanctification ' which we described at the end of No. 22 as being the process which keeps a man walking along the road. The sense of this will emerge if we look closely at the hymn verse by verse.

It begins with a prayer that Christ will come. He is addressed as the Divine Love, and the Joy of heaven, and he is invited to make his habitation in the heart of the Christian. Here at once is the tension between time and eternity, between life and Life, between the joy of conversion and the grim practicality of the daily round. In

history, Christ has come.   In the end of history it is promised
that Christ will come.   Yet we all pray daily, and must
pray, that Christ may come personally to ourselves.   What
does this mean ?

This is to some extent explained in the second half of
the first verse, where we sing ' Visit us with thy salvation '.
That word ' visit ' is here the keyword.   The line is itself
a reminiscence of this, in the 106th Psalm (verse 4) :

> Remember me, O Lord, with the favour that thou bearest unto
> thy people ; O visit me with thy salvation ; that I may see the
> good of thy chosen, that I may rejoice in the gladness of thy
> nations, that I may glory with thine inheritance.

' Visit ' means, in the Bible and in older English, a good
deal more than it means in modern speech.   ' To visit '
is nowadays to pay a call, to stay only a short time, to be
a passing and even casual guest.   If I have spent an hour
once in my life at Corfe Castle, I am entitled to say that
I have visited Corfe Castle.   If the Prime Minister spent
five minutes in my house, you may be sure that I should
ask him to sign the visitors' book, and should boast thereafter that I had been visited by the Prime Minister.   But
the old word ' visit ' was originally a very strong word.
' The Bishop our Visitor ' does not mean the Bishop who
sometimes drops in to tea, but the Bishop who is at any
time entitled to come and inspect us, admonish us, correct
us and even punish us.   Bishop Grosseteste of Lincoln in
the thirteenth century was regarded by his canons and
clergy as a pestilent tyrant because he revived, in the
literal sense, the ancient episcopal duty of visitation, and
made life a good deal less comfortable and self-indulgent
for these unfortunate clerics than it had previously been.
The matter can be illustrated even by the etymology of
the word.   In the Latin language it is possible to strengthen
a verb by coining a new verb out of the original according
to certain etymological rules which we need not go into
here.   The Latin word ' sto ' means ' I stand ' ;   its
frequentative, ' sisto ' means ' I stand firm and defy you
to move me.'   Similarly, the Latin word ' Video ' means

' I see ' ;   its frequentative, ' viso ' means, ' I stare.'   But
you have to repeat the process before you get the word
' visito ', which means ' I am coming to see you and you
won't forget it.'   And so the Biblical translators use the
word ' visit ' to translate a very strong Hebrew word, in
such phrases as ' Visit me with thy salvation,' and its
converse, ' Visit me not in thy wrath.'

What we then are asking here is that Christ will come,
again and again, and drive his ' salvation ' deep into our
minds and wills.   Salvation is the freedom, the rescuing,
that is the content of conversion.   We need that to be
renewed daily, we need to pray against getting rusty, or
being tempted to leave the road along which he is leading us.

The second verse reinforces this by reminding us of the
great Messianic text, ' The Lord, whom ye seek, shall
suddenly come to his temple ' (*Malachi* iii. 4).   We are
asking that Christ shall come without warning, without
further request, and work his will, ' visiting ' as seems best
to him.   We want to be ' always blessing ', ' praying and
praising without ceasing ', our life fashioned and fortified
by ' perfect love '.

In this way the hymn searches the problems of daily
life.   Conversion, the giving of freedom, is a blessed thing,
but what disappointments, what disillusion, what slithering
back into all the old errors and ignorances, what fading
of the first love, lie before the free mind and soul !   There
was a time when he knew it all in principle, when the
relevance and rightness of God's design were luminous to
him, when the problems were all stripped of their power
and terror, when he felt that one by one he could, in
Christ's power, tackle all the dragons and serpents that
infest the path of life ; but here is night again.   Here is
domestic trouble that makes him resentful ; here is illness
that makes him impatient ; here is anxiety that makes
him thoughtless ; here is economic worry that tempts him
to shady dealing ; here is a cold in the head that makes
him bad tempered ; here is breakfast-time at which he is
never at his best ; here is bereavement that makes him
want to curse God and die.   Or it may be not adversity

but prosperity that softens his spiritual muscles and makes him careless of keeping guard, that tempts him to be proud and self-sufficient and secure. That is the time to sing ' Love divine, all loves excelling '. Human affections and faith are transitory, but the faithfulness of God is eternal. ' The Lord, whom ye seek, shall suddenly come to his temple, even the messenger of the covenant, whom ye delight in.' (A glance back to No. 9 will do no harm here.)

' But ', the old prophet went on, ' who may abide the day of his coming ? ' Dare we take the consequences of this ' visitation ' for which we ask ? Can we stand the sight of the holiness of God ?

This question is taken care of in the enigmatic expression, ' changed from glory into glory ' in the last verse. The reference here is to a great passage in St Paul about conversion (in a context which need not trouble us here). The heart of what he is saying (*II Corinthians* iii. 18) is that when a man receives the Gospel, when he is made free of the faith, he is now able to look on Christ without the fear that religious Jews had always had (see 13) that one might not look on God and live. There need now be no shading or veiling of the eyes. For God will see that his glory and brilliance will not be too much for a man. For one thing, he will temper it to that man's need, for another, he will make that man stronger to bear it. Indeed, once a man surrenders himself to that light and truth, he begins to absorb it and even to reflect it. There will be something of the abounding strength and brightness of God in that man's character—he will go on from ' glory to glory ', from the less to the greater degrees of ability to reflect the brightness of Christ's character. That precisely is sanctification. That is what happens as he goes along the road— the vision becomes brighter and brighter and he becomes stronger and stronger to bear the increase of brightness, and (as part of the same process) becomes a cleaner and truer mirror for reflecting the brightness. The humility that obviously is involved in this, the cleaning off of the smears of pride and self-love from the reflecting surface, are just the same as ' casting our crowns before ' God.

A moment's thought will see how faithfully this expounds the ordinary course of life. Consider a man whose life is really ' lost in wonder, love and praise '. Of course it will be a happy life ; but equally inevitably it will be a life that spreads happiness. He will be not only a good man but a man whom it is good to know, refreshing to talk to, strengthening to follow.

This is sanctification, the changing from glory into glory, the increasing of the power to absorb for oneself and reflect for the world the glory and brightness of the character of Christ. There is no progress but this ; there is no making of history but through this process. ' He that began a good work in you ', said St Paul in another place (*Philippians* i. 6) ' will perform it.' He who gave the felicitous gift of freedom will also give, day by day, food for the journey and protection against its dangers.

24

C. Wesley (1707–88)

Christ, whose glory fills the skies,
 Christ, the true, the only light,
Sun of righteousness, arise,
 Triumph o'er the shades of night ;
Day-spring from on high, be near ;
Day-star, in my heart appear.

Dark and cheerless is the morn
 Unaccompanied by thee ;
Joyless is the day's return,
 Till thy mercy's beams I see ;
Till they inward light impart,
Glad my eyes, and warm my heart.

Visit then this soul of mine,
 Pierce the gloom of sin and grief ;
Fill me, radiancy divine,
 Scatter all my unbelief ;
More and more thyself display,
Shining to the perfect day.

H.H.L. 67–72

The Sun of Righteousness

'THE sun,' said Father Brown, 'is the cruellest of all the gods.' G. K. Chesterton's Father Brown stories [1] are one of the great unrecognized spiritual tracts in English ; not one of those stories but enshrines not merely subtle detection but a vital Christian truth. They are as surely ' required reading ' for intelligent Christians as *The Screwtape Letters* or *The Man Born to be King*. The story entitled *The Eye of Apollo* is concerned with the harsh and murderous side of heathenism, in particular with sun-worship. History confirms that sun-worship has its ugly side.

But it is not surprising either that men once worshipped the sun, or that sun-worship is a dangerous cult. For primitive men the sun, the source of heat and light, indispensable to life, was the obvious thing to worship. But the sun-god could never be more than a god of naked and capricious power—the power which (as we saw on an earlier page) Dr Karl Barth identifies with naked evil.

We have had occasion elsewhere to notice Christianity's uncanny faculty for putting back on the right track religious instincts which had gone astray. Its boldest conquest of the kind, without doubt, was that of the sun-myth. The ' sun of Righteousness ' is now built securely into the picture-language of the Faith, and the impotent power of Apollo is tamed. ' Hail, thou heaven-born prince of peace,' we sing at Christmas, ' Hail, thou Sun of Righteousness.' And in this greatest of morning hymns here again is the phrase, ' Sun of Righteousness, arise '.

This expression comes from Scripture—from the last page of the Old Testament, where it is written (*Malachi* iv. 2), ' but unto you that fear my name shall the Sun of Righteousness arise with healing in his wings '. But even Scripture

[1] See G. K. Chesterton's story, ' The Eye of Apollo ', in *The Innocence of Father Brown*.

seems to regard this as a bold way of speaking of the Messiah. There is no other place where the word ' sun ' is used, from end to end of the Bible, otherwise than literally. There is only one other place where another word is used for ' sun ', and used to represent the Christ, and that is the famous verse in the *Benedictus (St Luke* i. 78–9), ' Through the tender mercy of our God, whereby the *Dayspring* from on high hath visited us ; to give light to them that sit in darkness and the shadow of death, and to guide our feet into the way of peace.'   Even Scripture dared only in these two places to speak of God as ' the sun ' ; there is something sombrely triumphant in that assertion, on the last page of the New Testament, that the eternal city had ' no need of the sun '.   But ' Sun of Righteousness ' caught the imagination of Charles Wesley, and here we find it, along with that other picturesque and old-fashioned word, ' Dayspring '.

Now this gives ' Christ, whose glory ' a universality which places it apart from all other morning hymns.   Compare it with Bishop Ken's, which we noticed above, or with Keble's.   The Bishop gives us solid, down-to-earth, honest puritan counsel ; the country parson gives gentle advice about the sanctification of daily routine.   But Wesley talks all the time about the glory of Christ.   ' Christ, whose glory fills the skies '—the late Bernard Manning called the phrase ' Dantesque ', and that is not undue praise.   It is as bold a conception as you will find anywhere in all the hymn-books.   ' God, whose glory fills the skies ' would have been understandable, and commonplace.   Here the idea of Christ, the Sun of Righteousness, filling the very natural order with his glory is little short of an epic idea. But the generous arms of Christian doctrine gladly receive it and contain it ; for Christ is indeed the ' Sun of Righteousness ',—not now the ' sol invictus ' of heathen religion, the ' unconquerable sun ' whom Constantine worshipped before he was a Christian (and secretly for some time after) ; but Christ unconquerable, powerful in righteousness, in justice, in goodness and truth, powerful not irresponsibly and wildly and capriciously, but powerful in a sense limited by love.

And so he becomes the Sun (as John the Scot put it a thousand years ago) in whose rays all good things flourish and all mean things wither and die. He is the sun who ' triumphs o'er the shades of night ', and who can be called on to ' scatter all my unbelief '.

The hymn remains on that level all through its modest length. So universal and cosmic is it that it hardly suffers even the limitation of being especially appropriate to morning. ' Awake, my soul ' can hardly be sensibly sung after 8 a.m. A hymn beginning ' Summer suns are glowing ', still popular in some parts, has often been the occasion of a parson feverishly thumbing through his hymn-book for an alternative on some torrential July Sunday. But ' Christ whose glory ' depends neither on time nor on season. You could sing it at an evening service with perfect propriety, for it is dealing with the eternities all the way.

For whereas Ken's excellent lines tell us to do our duty, and Keble's tell us that God can make the dullest work profitable to his glory, what Wesley is here saying amounts to no less than a prayer that, through the present day, my life may be conformable to the mystery of the Gospel. The ' Sun of Righteousness ' is an advent phrase—Malachi and the Benedictus. It is Christ, in the humility of his incarnation, arising like the sun to dissipate the gross darkness of the world. To pray, ' Sun of righteousness, arise, . . . Daystar, in my heart appear ' is to pray that the miracle of the incarnation may be re-enacted in my own person ; that will and affections may be the very habitation of Christ even as Bethlehem's stable was his habitation. We sing, ' Visit then this soul of mine ', and we mean just what we meant when we sang ' Visit us with thy salvation ' in ' Love divine '. We mean (as is explained at that place), not merely ' come ', but ' come and convert and conquer '.

And the whole context is joy ; the dominant colour is golden. Never was written a more thoroughly and richly happy hymn than this. This is indeed a good way to begin the day, praying for the radiancy of the mercy of Christ.

25

Augustus Montague Toplady (1740-78; *altd.*)

Rock of Ages, cleft for me,
Let me hide myself in thee ;
Let the water and the blood,
From thy riven side which flowed,
Be of sin the double cure—
Cleanse me from its guilt and power.

Not the labours of my hands
Can fulfil thy law's demands.
Could my zeal no respite know,
Could my tears for ever flow,
All for sin could not atone ;
Thou must save, and thou alone.

Nothing in my hand I bring ;
Simply to thy Cross I cling ;
Naked, come to thee for dress ;
Helpless, look to thee for grace :
Foul, I to the fountain fly ;
Wash me, Saviour, or I die.

While I draw this fleeting breath,
When mine eyes shall close in death,
When I soar through tracts unknown,
See thee on thy judgment-throne,
Rock of Ages, cleft for me,
Let me hide myself in thee.

H.H.L. 105–9

I—The Rock

WHEN a hymn achieves that order of merit which makes it impossible that it be omitted from any hymn-book, broad, high or evangelical, you will find in that hymn a combination of three properties—familiar teaching, vivid language, and a commanding opening phrase. By these means it engages and retains the attention and inscribes itself on the memory of the singer. In ' Rock of Ages ' all these qualities are present, but especially the last has established its popularity. ' Rock of Ages '—it is those three words that give rhetorical and persuasive power to a hymn which without them would still have been great. Suppose it had begun with the line, ' Jesus, who didst die for me ' ; it would still have been good and admirable. But what writes the hymn not only on the memory but on the affections of the singing Christian is that great·line, ' Rock of Ages, cleft for me '.

It is worth while pausing to examine both the effect and also the true meaning of that phrase. Its effect is to face the singer at once with the reliable and friendly power of Christ. Now the hymn is about the power of Christ, but its universal application is to sin. It is the only popular and universal hymn about sin. But whereas many lesser hymns on that theme begin at once with confession or petition, this one begins with praise. You address Christ, who is as firm and friendly as a great rock ; it is only when you have thought of him for a moment like that that you can address him on that other subject without shyness or reserve.

But whence comes this immortal expression, ' Rock of Ages ' ?[1] A man will look in vain for it in the text of the

---

[1] On the influence of Biblical language on English letters, and especially on the limits of that influence, see C. S. Lewis, *The Literary Impact of the Authorised Version* (Athlone Press, 1951).

King James Bible ; but that will be not because he went
to the wrong source but because it was not given to him
to penetrate to the heart of it.   For though many hymn-
writers take their vocabulary from the King James Bible,
it is given to few to take it from the venerable Hebrew
text itself.   That is what Toplady did here.

The Hebrews were great poets but would have been
bad journalists ; for they love verbs and are uncommonly
shy of adjectives.   That is what makes their language as
hard as nails and as colourful as fire ; and that hardness
and colour have penetrated to some extent through the
King James translation.   Indeed, the distinguishing rhythm
of the King James Bible comes not so much from the fact
that it was written in the early seventeenth century, as
from the fact that it is a literal translation of Hebrew into
seventeenth-century English.   The particular application of
this fact is this, that what we should translate as ' the holy
hill ' would be in Hebrew (and sometimes remains in
translation) ' the hill of holiness ' ; ' the glorious God ' is
in Hebrew ' the God of glory '.   So behind a certain verse
in *Isaiah* (xxvi. 5) which we translate, ' Trust ye in the
Lord for ever ; for in the Lord Jehovah is everlasting
strength ' lies the Hebrew for this : ' Trust ye in the Lord
for ever ; for the Lord Jehovah is the Rock of ages.'   Our
abstract ' strength ' is in the original the very solid ' Rock ',
and our ' everlasting ' is the prophet's ' of ages '.

It was men who knew their Bible as intimately as this
who gave us our greatest hymns ; and this particular
phrase found its way into several hymns about the time
when ' Rock of Ages ' was being written.   It is in John
Newton's ' Glorious things of thee are spoken ', and it is
in that superb twenty-second Paraphrase,

> Supreme in wisdom as in power
> The Rock of Ages stands.

The Old Testament is, in other places than this passage,
fond of the image of the Rock.   Isaiah, especially the Isaiah
of the first thirty-nine chapters, is full of it.   ' A man shall
be as an hiding place from the wind, and a covert from

the tempest ; as rivers of water in a dry place, as the shadow of a great rock in a weary land ' (xxxii. 2) ; ' What hast thou here, and whom hast thou here, that thou hast hewed thee out a sepulchre here, as he that heweth him out a sepulchre on high, and that graveth himself an habitation for himself in a rock ? ' (xxii. 16).   For a people whose country contained so much desert, and whose whole history had so much in it of wandering in a dry and storm-swept region, the overshadowing rock was a refuge, and a cave in the rock was a place of warmth and security. No doubt we have to dismiss the story that ' Rock of Ages ' was written by a man sheltering from a storm in Somerset, but it has everything to do with the God of whom these tough and resourceful folk thought as a rock of refuge.   Nor is it without solemn overtones to men of modern times who, like the people of Chiselhurst and Stockport, used the natural caves of the rocks for air-raid shelters in the winter of 1940.

The first two lines, then, establish the thought of Christ as a rock in whose cleft a man can seek shelter from the storms of life.   But there is more than this, to which the hymn turns at once.   The cleft in the Rock is not merely an empty hole.   It is the source of a stream.   And here the author takes us back to the ancient story of the people of Israel which is recorded in the Exodus.   So pivotal is this story to all Christian thought, and especially to the language of Christian hymns, that we must here attend to it.   For in the thought of a stream issuing from the Rock, the author brings to mind one of the central experiences of the Exodus, the water struck by Moses from the rock. ' And they thirsted not when he led them through the deserts : he caused the waters to flow out of the rock for them ; he clave the rock also, and the waters gushed out ' (*Isaiah* xlviii. 21).

II—*The Rock and the Journey*

Nobody can read far in the Bible without noticing the importance which was attached to the story of the Exodus from Egypt by the writers and prophets of later times. Whenever a prophet wished to vindicate the righteousness and mercy of God, he knew no more solid piece of evidence for it, no more resounding confirmation in the popular mind, than this, that God is the Lord ' who brought up his people out of Egypt '.

Archæologists will not contradict the story. They will tell you that some twelve hundred years before the birth of Christ there was a great movement of population in the Middle East from Egypt in the direction of Palestine. They will not assert it to be impossible that first and last the mass emigration took forty years—the Biblical measure. They will not contradict the statement in the Bible that this was a movement towards Palestine of the descendants of people who centuries before had migrated in the reverse direction, and that therefore these people were in a sense not so much going out (as Abraham had done) as going home. The Pharaohs and the Israelite slaves are there in their place in the historical picture.

But of course nobody kept a diary of the journey. There was no *Times* correspondent or news-reel operator to present the facts to later generations. The whole story of the journey was transmitted from one man to another in speech. And speech always means interpretation. As we say, the story did not lose in the telling. It was impossible for a man to tell his son of what had happened during that migration without here and there saying, ' and now it's all over, of course we know what it all *meant* '. Nobody could tell the adventures and temptations of the journey without saying, or at least implying, ' of course, we didn't know at the time, but now we can see where it was all leading '. So when it came to be written down centuries later by various people, and the whole story to be edited

H.F.—L

in the end seven or eight hundred years after it had happened (as though the Oxford Press were to publish an authorised account, chiefly from Elizabethan sources, of the Norman Conquest), the emphasis is heavily on the purpose of the whole thing at the expense of bare statements of fact.

Now modern history is not written that way, for obvious reasons. Equally obviously this could not be written down any other way. But, prejudice apart, what is the important thing to tell in recounting a series of events ? The statistics, or their purpose ? Nowadays history tends to be popularly written in the form, ' English people spent x million pounds on football pools and y million pounds on drink in the year 1953.' Admirably accurate, these figures ; but what is of greater importance, to have the figures by heart or to understand what it is that makes people do these things ?

It is, at any rate, the shape of the story rather than statistics about population and mileages that interests the chronicler. And he is persuaded of this, that that journey out of Egypt was the best opportunity the Israelites, as a nation, had ever been given of learning about the great issues of life. These days were days in which the best of them penetrated to the secrets of the universe, and the worst of them showed their true quality. For one thing, at every step the people seemed to be faced with some impossible situation. Pharaoh will never let them go. Pharaoh, having let them go, will change his mind, chase them, and trap them on the shore of the Red Sea. They will die of thirst. They will die of hunger. The wild desert tribes will make short work of them. At every point there were plenty of people who were prepared to say, ' This is it. God may have coped with the other emergencies, but this will be one too many for him. We never ought to have come at all. We had better go back.' In its homely fashion, under the figure of the story, the Bible sets down there a great secret of life. The great question, which nobody at the time could positively answer, was ' Is there any purpose in this journey ? ' The best of them, pre-eminently Moses, acted on the assumption that there was a purpose, and a good purpose. After it was over the purpose was clear. But while it was in process the immediate question was always, ' What is the next step ? '

These spiritual and universal colours in the story held fast when the material and ' historical ' colours had largely faded ; indeed, the fading of the historical colours made the spiritual ones stand out the more brightly. What more natural than that the whole story should be taken up into the mythology of the faith of the Jews, and later of the Christian faith ? We must always be able to present the Christian faith as a story as well as in the dimension of abstract ideas ; for life itself is a story. Everybody needs a sane and coherent story, and one way of telling the story has always been to take the Exodus framework and build the supernatural story into it. Egypt, then, the place which had been in far-off time so attractive to the material needs of Israel but was now the place from which they prayed to be delivered—Egypt is, quite simply, hell. (In Old Testament times it was not merely thought politically unwise, but actually impious, to have dealings with Egypt—see *Isaiah* xxxi. 1.) Palestine is the end of the journey, the Promised Land, and therefore (for Christians) either heaven (after death) or eternal life (after surrender to Christ). Between the two lie the three great physical barriers—the Red Sea, the desert, and the river Jordan. The desert is temporal life, and the Red Sea and the Jordan more or less interchangeably represent those crises which stand between this life and the life to come (death) or between unregenerate and converted life (spiritual death or surrender). The fear of the Red Sea and of the Jordan recorded in Exodus (that was historic enough : they never forgot that) represents the tension of these crises—fear of death, unwillingness to surrender ; and the part played by Moses in, through his act of faith, leading the people across the Red Sea (here history is probably confused and the moral meaning alone stands out as clear as Mount Sinai itself) corresponds to the part played by Jesus, in rising from the dead, in the architecture of the Christian's faith. The image of the Red Sea is to be met with in Easter hymns and in Psalm 114, which is traditionally one of the Easter psalms (see further, No. 47).

All this can be traced through the Old Testament, and then through the New. It is all a very natural process, a little strange, perhaps, to our own document-ridden age with its statistics and reports and insistences on proofs and evidences, but none the less for that natural and sensible. The Exodus is the allegory of life as surely as is the *Pilgrim's Progress*. And the smaller details can be fitted into the story—details such as the provision of manna and (what especially concerns us here) the striking of water from the rock.

Now let us pursue a little further those parts of the allegory which have been traditionally referred to Christ. It might well be supposed that the type of Christ in the story is Moses—Moses, the leader and statesman and hero and man of God. As a matter of fact this is not the view taken by the most ancient of Christian authorities on this, the Apostle Paul. Paul very often contrasts Moses with Christ, but he never identifies him with Christ. What did Moses do in the story ? Moses was the leader ; he interpreted to the people the moral code (in the Commandments) which contained the basic regulations for living. He directed the administration of justice. When the need was urgent, he prayed for direct guidance and got it. When the people went clean against the regulations, when he was betrayed by Aaron, his right-hand man (in the matter of the Golden Calf) he prayed that God would forgive the people and turn their punishment towards himself, Moses. Nothing could be more Christlike than the patience and skill of Moses. Never man walked nearer to God than Moses did. But for all that—Moses is a man. Moses is Everyman at his best, man at his best strained and dragged down and turned from his purpose by man at his worst.

Paul says something altogether more daring. ' Our fathers', he says, ' all shared the same spiritual food and drank the same spiritual drink—for they drank from the spiritual Rock that followed them ; and that rock was Christ ' (*I Corinthians* x. 3–4).·

Broken up into its constituent parts, that remarkably compressed phrase seems to mean this : the Israelites had the experience of the water being struck from a rock, which experience they did not expect, and on the ground of not expecting it they had already come near to losing their faith. But it happened. That single incident was the *sort of thing* that was always happening ('the Rock followed them '). And if there was any man there who could see beyond and through the isolated events to the truth underlying them, if there was any man there who, because he had seen the principle of one, positively *expected* the next, and the next, then that man was looking straight in the direction of Christ. That kind of mind is the mind that can accept Christ. It is hardly too much to say that these people had seen Christ. They had at any rate heard the true Word of God and seen the glory of God (*Exodus* xxiv), and had understood the truth of God—which is hardly different from seeing Christ himself.

Moses was the lawgiver, the interpreter, the dispenser of justice, the administrator of sacred things. Moses, if you like, was the priest. Christ was the truth of it all, the context of it. Christ was the ' rock that followed them ', the spirit of love and salvation that lay in that experience of the Rock.

' Rock of Ages, cleft for me ; let me hide myself in thee ' : we have returned now to Christ the rock, and to the mind that can see the Rock, move towards it, hide in it, and take of the healing stream from it.

III—*The Fountain of Forgiveness*

The author of ' Rock of Ages ' is quite clear about the greatest need of man. He says that the root of it is ' sin '. The Rock split for the release of the refreshing stream has now become Christ crucified for the release upon the world of God's forgiveness. That which flowed from the body of Jesus after it had been rudely pierced by the soldier's spear is the type, or the earnest, of that which he will provide, and of the cost at which he will provide it, for the forgiveness of sin. The author further adds the prayer that man may be ' cleansed ' from the ' guilt and power ' of sin.

Now ' sin ' is a blunted and corrupted word. Let us substitute, for the purpose of making contact with daily life, something else. Let us substitute ' my past '. Time is a great enemy for most of us. Time has an ugly habit of locking up the past and suddenly releasing memories of it at unfortunate moments. Time can release our past to plague us, but we cannot go back and undo what was wrongly done in the past. It may be doubted whether there is any greater source of personal frustration in life than this, and if that be so, then we have in ' my past ' a very fair substitute for the older and clearer expression ' my sin '.

The past, as the author sees with luminous clarity, does two things to a man. On the one hand it worries him (that is guilt) ; on the other it has objective consequences which he cannot prevent (that is power). Both lead back to the same point. Take as an example some notable error. Here is a man who advances himself in the world by a shady piece of business. He may deny it to his friends, but that shady act has marked him for life. And it has consequences. He will never know just how many people know the truth. How are they talking about him at the office, at the club ? Does that slight that somebody offered to his wife mean that something has leaked out there ? Will it all catch up with him one day ? Those simple and admirable mythologies of human morals, the detective stories, are full of that kind of situation—the accumulation of sin suddenly toppling over and engulfing the sinner and, as often as not, engendering new sins in others. The murderer is involved in the blackmailer's sin (though not in his original guilt).

What answer is there to a simple situation of that kind ?

One way is to fend for yourself, to see that it does not catch up with you. The price of such vigilance will be inability to relax ; as likely as not, insomnia. But suppose the opportunity comes of really wiping out the evil. Will not the man who avails himself of it feel, precisely, clean and washed as well as unburdened ? ' *Cleanse* me ', says the hymn. ' Cleanse me from its guilt and power.'

But it may not be so simple. Suppose the man who committed the wrong says something like this : ' I now know that it was wrong. I am sorry, I will make restitution. But I am not at all sure that it won't all happen again, because I am afraid that, in temptation, I could not help myself.' As soon as you begin saying ' I couldn't help it ' you are talking, not about a sin, but about *sin*. And the Bible commonly treats sin as if it were a disease. So does this hymn, when it talks of the ' healing stream '.

Suppose then another man in a doctor's consulting-room. He is ill, and he thoroughly trusts the doctor. The doctor will probably have to say at some point, ' Will you allow me to go to work in my own way ? You say that the trouble is in your head. My view is that all that is needed is a simple operation on your feet. Will you trust that ? ' Granted the undoubted skill of the doctor, it will be unwise for the patient to insist on his own diagnosis of his malady (cf. *St John* xiii. 1–8). But he may have to say also this. ' I put it to you, my dear sir, that you do not wholly *want* to be cured. I must tell you that I can do nothing unless you are prepared to renounce all the moral capital you have made out of being an invalid.'

The technique of the Forgiveness of Sins, in the divine sense, is in some ways like that. There is a sense in which the man who would really be clear of his sins, really be given that sense of being washed and clean and free, must wholly trust his Physician, and must also declare himself as it were bankrupt of moral capital. He must say ' nothing in my hand I bring '—for he has nothing in himself that can help the situation.

Now the hymn was not written for a special condition ; it was written for all who want to put away the shyness, the secretiveness, the laborious deceptions, the hysterical self-defence, the mournful caution, the boring and exhausting routine of covering up defects and keeping up a reputation that make up so many civilized lives. It is written for anybody who ever felt that he would give anything (*anything*) to exchange the perverse busyness of life for the friendship of somebody who is powerful and understanding and effective. It is written for all who want life to be more of peaceful conversation and less of strident wrangling. And the word which means all that this man is looking for, is the word ' salvation '. It is a technical word which Christians are shy of. But the author is not shy of it. He says ' Thou canst save, and thou alone.' Christ, the Rock of Ages, is the source of peace and health. ' Could my zeal no respite know '—I have tried that, constant vigilance, careful piety, doing my duty, seeing that no further black marks go up against me ; ' Could my tears for ever flow '—I have tried that too, I have fretted all night and made myself miserable and ruined my health with worry. It is no use. It is *no use* ! ' All for sin cannot atone : Thou canst save, and thou alone.'

There may be a haunting fear that it is too late, that the doctor may say, ' If only I had known about this six months ago ! ' But it is not too late, because he is the Rock of Ages. The mercy of Christ, in which is included the effectiveness of Christ, is timeless. Nothing is too late for it. His mercy extends beyond death and judgment. The unknown beyond death, so terrifying and mysterious and physically repulsive—' even there shall thy right hand lead me '. All sociology, all psychology, all medicine and science come to this at last, that a man needs friendship with God, and in that will find friendship with the world. He needs a rock for shelter, a rock for refreshment, a rock for forgiveness. That Rock is Christ.

26

John Henry Newman (1801–90)

Lead, kindly light, amid the encircling gloom,
Lead thou me on ;
The night is dark, and I am far from home ;
Lead thou me on.
Keep thou my feet ; I do not ask to see
The distant scene : one step enough for me.

I was not ever thus, nor prayed that thou
Shouldst lead me on ;
I loved to choose and see my path ; but now
Lead thou me on.
I loved the garish day, and, spite of fears,
Pride ruled my will : remember not past years.

So long thy power hath blest me, sure it still
Will lead me on
O'er moor and fen, o'er crag and torrent, till
The night is gone,
And with the morn those angel faces smile
Which I have loved long since, and lost awhile.

H.H.L. 85, 111, 160, 256

Light

WE love this hymn for its strong, dark colours. If a hymn-writer knows how to use his colours, and can draw his picture well and true to the heart of life, he is sure of a hearing. How many of our hymns beguile us, in one way or another, with the dark colours. We have already encountered primitive darkness, the night that is the abode of ghosts. The darkness here is open-air darkness, the darkness of ten o'clock on a moonless October night on the North Derbyshire moors. Get off the track, find yourself two hours late on your time-schedule and the youth-hostel still five miles off, know that to go off the track may lead you into the sinister swamps of Kinder Scout, and you will soon be thinking that every rabbit-hole is a precipice and every stream a torrent. Above all, you will know what darkness can be, and you will be prepared to sell your soul to any stranger who can provide you with a light; you will feel that the first glimpse of a lighted farmhouse window is like the breaking of day.

That is not the condition of most people most of the time. Most of us work by day and come home in the evening. We have our electric light, our eyes and our brains, our bus-services and our town-plans. It is, on the whole, not a common experience to lose one's way home. That makes it all the worse when we do lose it. Then suppose a man of unusually acute and civilized mind and strong faith, a man whose name is already headline news, a man to whom many are already looking as men look to a leader, a man whose good opinion is coveted by many and whose good counsel is valued even by those who do not agree with everything he says. Such a man, at thirty-two, was John Henry Newman, the author of this hymn. He was on a Mediterranean voyage with his friends, Hurrell Froude and his father. He fell sick of an illness which was probably less than half physical in its origin, and more than half occasioned by the great mental tension through which he was passing. Some think he was actually on the sea when he wrote the lines, and that the ' kindly light ' is the light of the harbour ; but the images in the poem suggest a man travelling by land, not by sea. However that may be, when such a man is, for reasons his best friends may never know, spiritually and mentally out in the dark, then he will either write a hymn like ' Lead, kindly light ', or want to sing one.

It is the kind of hymn which you may not be needing most of the time but which, when you do need it, you need badly. ' The night is dark, and I am far from home.' The healthy, muscular and intelligent—especially the younger among these—may not often feel so. That is, at least, what we generally believe, though the truth may be that these people admit to such a condition less often than they experience it. But there must be few who have any effective contact with their neighbours, and who have not seen somebody stranded in this way. It does not take more than a moment for the bottom to fall out of the securest and most successful life. Some stroke of fortune may cut clean through a plan which a man thought of so confidently as the plan of his life. Or there may be no evident exterior cause ; it may be just a cloud falling across his mind ; in the most literal and sinister sense, perhaps, a deep depression. The effect may be anything from irritability to the conviction that God has deserted him ; anything from passing perplexity to downright dereliction. That is the man this hymn is designed to help. How might William Cowper have done had he lived fifty years later and been able to sing this hymn ?

' Keep thou my feet : I do not ask to see the distant scene.' That is one secret of pathfinding when the night is dark. When the world dissolves into this kind of confusion, consider at least, says the author, whether there is not something very close at hand that can readily be done. The darkness reduces visibility to five yards, perhaps, but it may be really five yards and not positively nil. If God's guidance on the great problem is not forthcoming at once, he is very likely waiting to say something on a matter that appears by comparison trivial, but which God's attention renders important. It is very possible that by fixing your eye on the farmhouse window in the distance you may end up in a ditch with a twisted ankle. ' But as for me,' said the psalmist, ' my feet were almost gone ; my treadings had well-nigh slipped.' He had lost his way, and what almost brought him down was mounting resentment at the distant scene of other people's prosperity. But then—' So foolish was I and ignorant, even as it were a beast before thee '— for it came to him just in time that ' nevertheless, I am continually with thee ; thou hast holden me with thy right hand ' (Psalm 73).

What this hymn says is much the same. ' I was not ever thus '—indeed, I cannot remember ever feeling like this before. I thought I knew where I was going. I thought I had a firm grip on life. I thought I understood the geography. There was light enough in those days. If I was afraid of anything, I did not give way to my fears. I was in charge—but now, ' Lead thou me on '. For now I begin to see that the light I walked by before was about as much use as the light provided by the illuminations at Southend or Blackpool : adequate, no doubt, for careless, inexact and slovenly living, but no use for an undertaking that requires assiduous concentration. If it be possible I would make a new beginning, ask for real light, wash out the memory of those ' past years ' in which I took such pride, but which now look so shabby. This is an emergency. Lead thou me on.

The last secret is the secret of faith—faith retrospective as well as forward-looking. For God, to whom I pray for light, has been very forbearing so far. I have invited his impatience, and he has never let me down, nor left me quite alone. ' So long thy power hath blest me ' ; ' Surely goodness and mercy shall follow me all the days of my life.'

It is a singular sorrow of human intercourse with God, that men take it for granted that what God has done in the past he can never repeat. But the mercy of God is from everlasting to everlasting on them that fear him. It is **not**

limited to occasions ; it is the very fabric of history.   ' Sure :
it still will lead me on '. . . .

'. . . Till the night is gone, and with the morn those
angel-faces smile.'   Here is a curious expression that has
often puzzled thoughtful people.   Just what its author
meant by it is as obscure and conjectural as the precise
meaning, to their authors at the time, of many phrases we
read in the Bible.   Yet it means something to the singer ;
it is only by taking thought that we succumb to perplexity,
and having succumbed we must work through to the truth.
The truth may well be this, that the traveller, looking for
a light, is promised the daylight.   By the light he prayed
for he might see what he had expected to see.   By the light
he will be given, if he keeps faithfully on, he will see what
will surprise him.   He will see something that he loved long
ago and thought he had lost.   Some say that what he will
see will be the faces of loved ones who are dead.   In some
cases this will be true.   But more than that may well be
meant.   The most grievous toll that the years took was the
tax of faith, of sense of proportion.   The traveller lost his
capacity, in so far as he had had it as a child, to see things as
they really are.   Seeing things with the insight of heaven is
one of the gifts of the Spirit which are given to men of
faith ; it is one of the things that go with childlike innocence
and are distorted by the corruptions of life.   When the
morning breaks on the traveller he will see, and will see
straight.   He will see not only the path but also the scenery.
He will see the plan as God has devised it.   He will see the
past and the present in true proportion.   He will then
know how long it is since he last felt sure of himself and
of God.

27

Sarah Flower Adams (1805–48)

Nearer, my God, to thee,
    Nearer to thee,
E'en though it be a cross
    That raiseth me ;
Still all my song shall be,
Nearer, my God, to thee,
    Nearer to thee.

Though like the wanderer,
    The sun gone down,
Darkness be over me,
    My rest a stone ;
Yet in my dreams, I'd be
Nearer, my God, to thee,
    Nearer to thee.

There let the way appear
    Steps unto heaven ;
All that thou sendest me
    In mercy given :
Angels to beckon me
Nearer, my God, to thee,
    Nearer to thee.

Then, with my waking thoughts
    Bright with thy praise,
Out of my stony griefs
    Bethel I'll raise ;
So by my woes to be
Nearer, my God, to thee,
    Nearer to thee.

Or if on joyful wing
    Cleaving the sky,
Sun, moon, and stars forgot,
    Upwards I fly,
Still all my song shall be,
Nearer, my God, to thee,
    Nearer to thee.

H.H.L. 163, 209

163

Bethel

ON an earlier page we gave some thought to the hymn, 'O God of Bethel', which paraphrases the final verses in the story of Jacob's vow in *Genesis* xxviii. 'Nearer, my God, to thee' is a meditation on the earlier part of the story. The older hymn deals with the consequences of the incident ; this one handles its immediate causes.

Jacob was, by normal standards, a thoroughgoing scoundrel. He lived by his wits ; he had an eye to the main chance. He did not care, if we may believe the stories about him, what means he used to gain his ends. The only thing that complicates the moral issue at all, that gives us any need to pause in writing him off as an incorrigible adventurer, is that his ends were in every case more religious than those of his brother Esau, and that (incredibly enough) his God seems to have liked him for it.

Take the story of the birthright, in the two parts which are recounted in *Genesis* xxv. 29 ff. and xxvii. It is obvious from the earlier story (about the 'mess of pottage') that Esau cared little for the birthright that was his by hereditary right, and that Jacob cared very much indeed for it. But the moral import of the story is precisely that Jacob was serious where Esau was frivolous about sacred things. For birthright was an extremely sacred thing. It was, in that tribal society, the right to be head of the family after the father's death, an hereditary right to leadership, and to responsibility. There is nothing in modern society to correspond to the Hebrew idea of 'birthright'. The nearest analogy is perhaps in the modern attitude to royalty in England. Englishmen have come, in recent generations, to expect, and have received with high thanksgiving, a tradition almost amounting to spiritual fatherhood in the Sovereign. Royalty to us is not merely eminence ; it is also service—we have been taught to believe this by the faithfulness of the Sovereigns themselves. Royalty is a responsibility from which we can imagine a royal personage shrinking. The assumption of that responsibility, of the spiritual burden of royalty, is now a close parallel to the assumption in Hebrew society of birthright. Now Esau is represented as being a very slothful person for whom birthright was too much trouble. It is without surprise that we learn that he made a mess of his marriage (*Genesis* xxvi. 34–5), and the more we look into the long-term effects of his temperamental laziness in sacred things, the less are we disposed to differ from the venomous comment of the author of *Hebrews* that he was (here we translate the queer Greek word quite literally) a ' rank outsider ' (*Hebrews* xii. 16).

These two men are presented to us in this ancient story as examples of two very common types—the easy-going decent fellow who has a fundamentally frivolous view of life, and the unattractively cunning and serious-minded person whose view of life is ultimately responsible and serious. Of the two, it is the latter who comes nearer to God. It was (one might say) an embarrassing choice for the Almighty to have to make ; but then when may we say that God is not embarrassed by the remarkable variety of sinfulness that his children display ? ' We have all sinned, and come short,' says the Apostle, and when it comes to an issue as vital as that which was in question at Bethel, there is very little to choose between any of us.

God, says the story, chose Jacob. Jacob was, in religious matters, single-minded and reliable. God's choice of Jacob had a profound effect on history thereafter : it remained a standing puzzle to thoughtful people. ' Jacob I loved : Esau I hated ' was a phrase which summed up the enigma of history for all who came after. St Paul uses it as a peg on which to hang profound thoughts about God's omnipotence and the mysterious and unfathomable ways in which he works in history (*Romans* ix. 13). But the point here is that God did use Jacob, a flagrant sinner, for a purpose of very great importance.

The situation Jacob left behind him at home was confused enough. That house was inhabited by a foolish old father,

H.F.—M

a shrewish mother, and a brother with a mountainous grievance. The household had always had to bear the consequences of the father preferring one and the mother preferring the other of twin brothers. All in all it was a common kind of domestic background, the kind that has produced many a great sinner and many a saint. Jacob might well wonder whether it would ever be safe to go home and claim the birthright he had legally secured.

The whole story is faithful to life. It is not a simple moral tale of a good man and a bad man. It is a tale of two sinners, a microcosm of history, which is a tale of a million sinners. It is full of that intricacy in which ordinary people are constantly being involved, and in the context of which they are always having to make decisions.

At Bethel when Jacob had his dream about the ladder going up to heaven from earth, all his life at once took shape. He was enabled to see more clearly than he had ever seen or was likely to see again, the pattern of his life. He saw what he had taken on in assuming the birthright. He was exalted and frightened and humbled. All the perplexity, all the tension of his past life had been part of a pattern God was preparing. The ladder was a symbol of the communication between God and man, reinforced by its angelic traffic—communication which was made complete and universal by him who said, in his day, ' Ye shall see angels ascending and descending on the Son of Man ' (*St John* i. 51). Jacob came ' near to God ' in that night. He was, for a brief space, a whole man, a sane man, a man who knew where God meant him to go, a man who could stand up straight and talk with his God. Before he had been a shady character ; afterwards he was to know much humiliation and much suffering. Indeed, he was not going for some years to be very obviously a ' changed man ' even in his personal conduct. He was going to fall in love, and have children, and lose his wife by an untimely death, and prove a rather ineffective father who half-ruined more than one of his sons by over-indulgence. But just here he was a whole man. The issue of life was clear to him. He knew what he was going to be used for. He saw that no matter how darkly he had sinned, it was God's purpose to give him a place in the overarching design of bringing back the nations to God. ' In thee shall all the families of the earth be blessed.'

That is the background of this very familiar hymn. Its second verse recalls Bethel, the third verse tells of the ladder set up on earth, the fourth of the new brave vows that come of such an experience. Interwoven with this are thoughts of the Gospel and of common life. And the end of the matter is that which is expressed at the beginning, ' E'en though it be a cross that raiseth me.' The way to God is, we now know, the way of the Cross. Jacob learnt just that when he wrestled at Peniel (*Genesis* xxxii). And what he learnt is a truth which is universal and inescapable. Paradox answers paradox and mystery answers mystery. It is granted to any man, no matter what his past may be, no matter how deeply he be sunk in iniquity, to come ' Nearer to God ' as soon as he will. God does not impose a means-test. God simply says ' come ' to all who will hear. God could use Jacob, and God can use every man and love every man. The answer to that is this other mystery, that (as Jacob found) the way to God was not, in the end, in pious aspiration but in renunciation ; not in visions but in life's duties ; not in ecstasy but in faith ; not in power but in love.

28

Henry Francis Lyte (1793–1847)

Abide with me ; fast falls the eventide ;
The darkness deepens ; Lord, with me abide ;
When other helpers fail, and comforts flee,
Help of the helpless, oh abide with me.

Swift to its close ebbs out life's little day ;
Earth's joys grow dim, its glories pass away ;
Change and decay in all around I see ;
O thou who changest not, abide with me.

I need thy presence every passing hour ;
What but thy grace can foil the tempter's power ?
Who like thyself my guide and stay can be ?
Through cloud and sunshine, Lord, abide with me.

I fear no foe with thee at hand to bless ;
Ills have no weight, and tears no bitterness ;
Where is death's sting ? where, grave, thy victory ?
I triumph still, if thou abide with me.

Hold then thy cross before my closing eyes ;
Shine through the gloom, and point me to the skies ;
Heaven's morning breaks, and earth's vain shadows flee ;
In life, in death, O Lord, abide with me.

H.H.L. 5–6, 84, 146

Companionship

ABIDE with us ', said the friends on the Emmaus-road, ' for it is towards evening, and the day is far spent.' The memory of the Crucifixion was still fresh in their minds, and within a few minutes they were to learn that their fellow-traveller was the risen Christ. Death was behind them, and life before. Many hymns have been inspired by that most remarkable of ' pastorals ' in *St Luke* xxiv, but none has reached so far into the English Christian mind as ' Abide with me ', and none has so penetratingly searched the mystery of death and life as this hymn, which was written three months before its author's death.

Death and life are presented in this hymn, as they often are in the Bible, under the figure of darkness and light ; and although the hymn begins from the Emmaus-text, the real clue to it is to be found in such texts as this, from the Old Testament :

If I say, surely the darkness shall cover me ; even the night shall be light about me.
Yea, the darkness hideth not from thee, but the night shineth as the day ;
The darkness and the light are both alike to Thee
(Psalm 139. 11–12)

or perhaps this, from the New :

God is light ; and in him is no darkness at all
(*I St John* i. 5).

Every device of language available to a real poet is here used to draw attention to this central theme—light and darkness. The uninterrupted succession of day and night is introduced, or suggested, in the first line as a mere ornament of the structure. Day and night are only an example, and a relatively superficial example, of that tension between light and darkness which makes life and history.

' Abide with me ; fast falls the eventide '—yes, we may begin in the physical manifestation of darkness, in the deepening evening. It is, of course, ' Abide with me ', not ' abide with us '. The change to the singular has already moved us away from the Emmaus-context. It is a solitary man, a lonely man who speaks. For the sociable and the well-off, night-time means cosiness and fellowship ; for the lonely and the poor, except he be very strong minded or very well occupied, it means silence and a touch of primitive fear. Things walk by night that dare not encounter the light of the sun, ' the arrow that flieth by night . . . the pestilence that walketh in darkness '. It is in the evening that the lonely man or woman misses good company, it is in the evening that the recluse is most haunted and the solitary most open to temptation. This homely if sombre truth is the starting-point of the hymn. It says, simply, ' Stay with me ', and many a man or woman in advancing years, saying the lines over in quiet solitude, gives them the overtone of the prayer put in the mouth of Jacob by Charles Wesley :

> My company before is gone,
> And I am left alone with thee.

This simple human need for companionship, together with the unchanging faithfulness of God, occupy the first verse.

The second verse shows what line the rest of the hymn is going to take. Here at once we have a contrast between the transitoriness of creation and the eternity of God. It is a curious thing (perhaps it is the fault of the tune, or of those whose business it is to choose hymns for public worship) that we have come to think of this verse as sounding a mournful, sub-Christian note of pessimism. We have made the hymn much more subjective than its author intended it to be simply by thinking too exclusively of an old man dying or a lonely man seeking companionship. The true message of the verse is in the words ' Thou who changest not '. It is not only the pessimist, not only the desolate, who notice the changeableness of things. It is, on the contrary, the realist who dares to observe them for what they are, and to notice that they point away from themselves to the eternal. But yes—it is surely the accident that the familiar tune has a dying fall on the line ' change and decay ' that misleads us. No scientist, no philosopher would wish to disagree with what is really being said here, that the change-fulness of things bespeaks an unchanging and faithful creator.

The ' passing hour ' in the third verse links the thought with what went before in the second (and indeed in the three verses of the original which are usually omitted here). But the second line introduces the theme of temptation. It is human moods, the tides of emotion and affection, that are here the ' darkness ' and God's constancy that is the ' light '. ' O thou who changest not ' we sang before. Now we are more urgent—' I need thy presence every passing hour ', for the ebb and flow of night and day is nothing compared with the ebb and flow of the soul's fortunes in the spiritual battle.

We wrestle not with men of flesh and blood (said the Apostle), but with every kind of intangible darkness, and ultimately with death. It is natural that the next thought should be the decisive engagement in the battle of life. So many hymns mention heaven in their last verses, and are wrongly despised for so doing (cf. 47). This one goes further. It looks death itself in the face. This is its most triumphant verse, its healthiest and most down-to-earth and most realistic verse : for the man who has never faced the enigma of death has never faced anything. In interpreting these two verses, the third and fourth, we may once again be guided by the Apostle. ' It is sin ', he wrote (*I Corinthians* xv. 55), ' which gives death its power, and it is the Law which gives sin its strength.' That, in inverse order, is the way life's problems present themselves. We know that there is an unfriendly side to life ; we have a conscience that warns us when we are approaching it. We know that there is much to fear. We feel in our bones that life is made very difficult, and that it is impossible to keep all the rules and go to heaven with a clean sheet. All that kind of natural thought is implied in the Apostle's word ' Law '.

Then we know, if we look further into it, that most of this is our own fault, that even our way of looking at it and the propositions in which we clothe our thoughts are our own fault, and there is precious little hope of mending matters— all that is ' Sin '.   If we have not something to hold on to, we shall at this point either run away from the problem or look despair in the face, and say that the universe is running down, that in any case men are bent on destroying themselves, and that all things are vanity—that, in the Apostle's language, is Death—Death in his frightening and uncouth aspect.   The hostile thing, the dark thing in conscience is sin, and the dark centre of sin is death.   But the Apostle says, ' Where is death's sting ? '   Given that which will answer the first of these conditions, given the forgiveness of Christ that roots out the fearfulness and despair of sin, then there is nothing to be frightened of in life ('Law') or in death.   The man who believes that can see sin and death with solemnity, and with sorrow, but not with despair and loathing and resentment.   Neither is greater than the love and faithfulness of God.   The darkness is no darkness with him.

And so, when death comes, with the Cross in view and the victory of the Cross in mind, the singer knows himself secure. He can, on the evidence of Christ risen, contradict the conclusions of the senses ;   each time he closes his eyes at the end of a day he can think without fear of the day when he will close them for the last time ;   for he who had been asked to abide with the friends on the Emmaus-road was Christ risen.   And when he broke bread with them in their own house, the last darkness fell from their eyes.   ' And their eyes were opened, and they knew him.'

29

C. Wesley (1707–88)

Jesu, lover of my soul,
    Let me to thy bosom fly,
While the nearer waters roll,
    While the tempest still is high :
Hide me, O my Saviour, hide,
    Till the storm of life is past ;
Safe into the haven guide,
    O receive my soul at last.

Other refuge have I none ;
    Hangs my helpless soul on thee ;
Leave, ah ! leave me not alone,
    Still support and comfort me.
All my trust on thee is stayed,
    All my help from thee I bring ;
Cover my defenceless head
    With the shadow of thy wing.

Thou, O Christ, art all I want ;
    More than all in thee I find :
Raise the fallen, cheer the faint,
    Heal the sick, and lead the blind.
Just and holy is thy name ;
    I am all unrighteousness ;
False and full of sin I am,
    Thou art full of truth and grace.

Plenteous grace with thee is found,
    Grace to cover all my sin ;
Let the healing streams abound ;
    Make and keep me pure within.
Thou of life the fountain art ;
    Freely let me take of thee ;
Spring thou up within my heart,
    Rise to all eternity.
                        H.H.L. 67–72

Protection

NOTHING proves the comprehensiveness of Christian teaching and faith more cogently than the fact that this hymn and ' Soldiers of Christ ' (33) are from the same hand. Indeed, in the end we may find that, despite their wide superficial divergence from each other, they are really saying very much the same thing.

' Jesu, lover of my soul ' is one of those hymns about which you can always tell a dozen stories. John Telford, in *The New Methodist Hymn Book Illustrated*, has collected several of them. W. S. Kelynack, in his *Companion to the School Hymn book of the Methodist Church*, adds some more. A glance at these or any other such collections shows that all the stories have this in common, that they are stories about men and women in extremity, about people either about to die or in danger of death or in great spiritual darkness. It is a hymn for the crises of life.

The expression ' lover of my soul ' was suggested to Charles Wesley by the last words of a passage in the *Wisdom of Solomon*. It reads thus in the King James Version :

Thou lovest all the things that are, and abhorrest nothing that thou hast made : for never wouldest thou have made anything if thou hadst hated it. And how could any thing have endured, if it had not been thy will ? or been preserved, if not called by thee ? But thou sparest all : for they are thine, O Lord, thou lover of souls.

' Lover ' here means all that we found to be implied in ' creator ' when we were discussing ' O worship the King ' (2). The thought in Wesley's opening is that the man in great need appeals to Christ on the ground of the limitless love, authority, and power which are attested in the order of nature and history. It is fortifying to a man's sense of the love of God if he can reflect that God has preserved and

176

not impatiently destroyed this rebellious creation. But as soon as that has been said, the hymn becomes an intimately personal prayer ; and it is natural to associate it with those occasions when the whole issue of life and death, bodily or spiritual, is a matter between a man and his God.

It is no contradiction of this to say, as history insists that we say, that ' Jesu, lover ' is part of the public praise of the whole English-speaking Protestant Church. So is ' Abide with me ' ; so is ' Lead, kindly light '. There is no explaining the mystery which makes the Church gather together to sing such intimate lines as these, as though the whole singing company were a single singing person. But the authenticity of the experience, its claim to be more than a sentimental myth, is confirmed by the number of genuine conversions which have been the result of the congregational singing of these words. Something in its arresting language, its honesty, and its appealing simplicity, has caused one man after another to rise up and praise God.

The message of the hymn is an honest and a stern one. The first verse is disarmingly simple. You might be singing any mild religious lyric—' Jesu, lover of my soul, let me to thy bosom fly ' . . .—taken by itself it is hardly more than ' escapist ', and a man might properly say that it is not his business to pray to be protected from the storm of life, but rather to pray for strength and courage to walk on the water. That is very true, and Charles Wesley knows it. It is almost as though he begins with this simple and almost cosy image in order to win the attention of the man he wants to save through courage.

This, however, is the truth with which the singer is faced before Wesley has done with him, that there is one enemy against whom mere personal courage and a defiant attitude are shaky and unreliable weapons. There is one enemy who makes the difficulties and the great waves and storms of life look like pigmy enemies to be warded off with one hand. This most intractable of enemies is oneself. The self is the source of all those troubles from which in these lines a man prays to be protected. That third verse (left out by some books) is pivotal to the whole scheme. ' False and full of sin I am : thou art full of truth and grace.' **But** already in the second verse there is a warning that this **is** the heart of the matter—' Leave, ah, leave me not alone.' Do not leave me to cope unaided with myself and my solitariness—that is the line Wesley is taking all the way.

This is good diagnosis. We may test it by common life. Here is a man in the extremity of mental perplexity ; he has a decision to make that he knows will affect the next twenty years of his life, and involve his family as well. He prays for light, and so far as he can see, light has not come. Time begins to grow short and the crisis becomes more urgent. Anxiety, fear, and probably grievance begin to fill up his mind. Will not such a man be (at least) wise to ask that God may help him to set aside everything selfish in his desires ? Is it not possible that on the answering of that prayer, he will find that all the time, long before the self-loving affections began to churn themselves up into a storm of resentment and anxiety, these affections were fogging the issue and generating perplexity ? We may not tread heavily and clumsily in such intimate areas of personal life ; we may only leave it there as a question.

Or again : here is a man in danger of death, a soldier on a special mission, a scientist experimenting on himself for the benefit of medical knowledge, a mountaineer or a test-pilot. What does he most want ? Surely he will never pray that his difficulties be removed. He does not want to be taken off the mission, to throw away the hypodermic, to have the mountain flattened or the aircraft grounded. What he wants is to be purged of all those things that tempt him away from the duty at the heart of whose difficulties and dangers he knows his own felicity to lie. He wants to be delivered from fear and the source of fear, which is selfhood.

The man who knows he has only a little while to live, the man so often mentioned in stories about this hymn—this man does not pray that death may not come, for he knows it is already at hand. He prays that he may face it cheerfully and fearlessly. He knows that this is the kind of prayer God will hear and answer immediately and literally.

That transition in the hymn from prayer for protection to confession of sin is so natural and easy in its expression that many singers miss it. So do those commentators who say that the hymn is too intimate for congregational use. It is one of the bravest things even in Wesley. ' False and full of sin I am '—I am in bondage to my past, my affections, my fears ; they paralyse me so that a trifling breeze blows on me like a hurricane, and a pleasant lake in August looks like a raging sea, and every bicycle is a serpent and every motor-car a fiery dragon bent on killing me, and every railway-timetable is a sinister enigma designed to drive me away from home into the wilderness, and every man's hand is against me. ' Then were they in great fear, where no fear was,' said the psalmist of the men of bad conscience and evil life ; and again, of those who prefer to neglect the way of God, ' I will send a faintness into their hearts in the lands of their enemies ; and the sound of a shaken leaf shall chase them ; and they shall flee, as fleeing from a sword ; and they shall fall when none pursueth ' (*Leviticus* xxvi. 36). This is the real storm of life, the bad conscience, the unruly self-love that is in every man. ' I will send faintness into their hearts in the land of their enemies '—' Thou preparest a table before me in the presence of mine enemies ' ; ' False and full of sin I am : thou art full of truth and grace.' This really is the way of things ; it is no pious legend. There are peaceful and courageous men and there are hectic and troubled men ; every man is now peaceful, now troubled. The ebb and flow is controlled by his own will, by his own mind. Here is the question for the worried man, the dying man, the afflicted man, the question which his best friend hardly dare ask, but on whose answer hangs, for him, the issue of the crisis : ' Where is reality ? Where is the fountain of life ? Is it in yourself, or is it in him ? '

' Plenteous grace with thee is found,' we sing, and there we pronounce the most precious word in the Christian vocabulary. Grace is for the man in the street and the man in trouble. Grace is first and foremost the conqueror of fear. Not strength, not instruction, not wisdom, not even gentleness can do it ; for though these may make a man realize more completely how weak and bad and ignorant he is, though they may bring him to some knowledge of how far he is making his own difficulties and generating his own fear from within, yet none of these can put back the confidence that he has allowed to seep away through a soul like a leaky bucket. Grace can do this ; grace alone. ' He is able : my grace is sufficient for thee.' For grace is the quality by which God says not only ' be healed ' but ' your faith has saved you : sin no more '. Grace is that through which he says not only, ' You are forgiven,' but ' You are my son, and you and I understand each other.'

30

Charlotte Elliott (1789–1871)

Just as I am, without one plea
But that thy Blood was shed for me,
And that thou bidd'st me come to thee,
　　O Lamb of God, I come.

Just as I am, though tossed about
With many a conflict, many a doubt,
Fightings within, and fears without,
　　O Lamb of God, I come.

Just as I am, poor, wretched, blind ;
Sight, riches, healing of the mind,
Yea all I need, in thee to find,
　　O Lamb of God, I come.

Just as I am, thou wilt receive,
Wilt welcome, pardon, cleanse, relieve :
Because thy promise I believe,
　　O Lamb of God, I come.

Just as I am (thy love unknown
Has broken every barrier down),
Now to be thine, yea, thine alone,
　　O Lamb of God, I come.

Just as I am, of that free love
The breadth, length, depth, and height to prove,
Here for a season, then above,
　　O Lamb of God, I come.

H.H.L. 85, 207–8

'Come'

THE most familiar and persuasive of the Gospel imperatives is the word ' Come '. ' Come unto me, all ye that labour and are heavy laden, and I will give you rest.' The hymn ' Just as I am ' is a simple expansion of that single word, the invitation of Christ.

Secular life, in which it is the Christian's duty to engage, seems often to be a conspiracy to prevent his accepting the invitation. It drives him, if he be not on his guard, in the direction of two other answers, both of which are quite wrong answers. On the one hand, the more life adds to a man, the more deeply he becomes involved in it and committed to it, the greater the danger that he may never come to the point of saying ' I come ' ; on the other hand, the more life frustrates and buffets him, the more life takes out of him, the greater the danger that he may come to doubt the love and suspect the invitation as being a hoax. Be he rich man or poor man, suffering or successful, he stands in danger of saying either ' I am good enough as I am ' or ' I am not good enough to come '.

Let us agree on one simple and preliminary caution. Let us agree never to think of the words ' Just as I am ' as anything more than a convenient title for the hymn. Think of them as the whole message, and you will be grievously misled. There was a rich young man who came to Christ just as he was, but who had to resign his hope of being a disciple because he wanted Christ to leave him just as he was. There was a young fellow who came to Jesus and offered himself just as he was, but found that when it came to the point domestic claims must take priority. He too wanted to be left just as he was. Ananias and Sapphira provide an excellent example of this kind of limited liability which is all a man will ever rise to so long as he claims to be good enough for Christ just as he is.

But the wise and brave authoress of this hymn means nothing of this sort. What does her first verse say ? ' Just as I am, claiming no rights, but knowing that you want me —knowing that because of what you have done—I come.' Every verse is on the pattern 'Just as I am, *but . . .*' Every verse contains the conviction that once a man has come he must expect to be changed. Once the invitation has been accepted, a man will no longer be just as he was. When the man came to the wedding-feast, unexpectedly invited by the generosity of the host, not having any social right to be there, and came without his wedding garment, the host (says St Matthew) was quite unusually and unexpectedly furious. There is something specially repulsive in the attitude of the man who, being (as all men are) in no position to claim God's goodness as a right, none the less makes just that claim, saying ' Well, here I am, take me or leave me,' with no word of thanks or of wonder. That man will not be a kindly man, a humorous man, a courteous man. He will perhaps not even be a very efficient man. But this assuredly he will miss, and this will be the worst of it for him : because he wants to be and remain ' just as he is ', because he knows he is good enough for God, he will miss the ' breadth, length, depth, height ' of love.

But, loathsome though it is to say ' I am good enough for Christ,' it is the excess and abuse of humility to say, ' I am not good enough, and so I will not come.' At the time of accepting the invitation, we must accept it just as we are. We cannot accept it any other way. Perhaps it was this thought that was uppermost in the mind of the authoress, who was writing at a time when she was especially oppressed with a sense of her own inadequacy ; she had, it appears, been left at home while all the other members of the household had gone out to help with a church function. The writing of these lines was for her a gesture of defiance against her own invalidism.

But there are many who, for reasons quite different from Charlotte Elliott's, feel that they are not good enough to come to Christ ; some say they are not good enough to come to church. There is something initially attractive in that attitude, for, to be sure, it is better to be backward than to be forward in claiming favours. But behind it there may be a kind of fear or sloth which no man should be content to entertain. This man is the man who must learn to receive, where the other was the man who must learn to give. Receiving, for some temperaments, is far more difficult than giving. (Recall, perhaps, what we said about ' Now thank we all our God ' (6).) But even more important, there is a fact which must not be overlooked— a fact, not a feeling. This is that which we discussed under ' There is a green hill ' (21), that ' He died to make us good.' Precisely : he died to make us good enough for him, to demonstrate that he could think of us as good enough for him. It is not at all that we *are* good enough ' just as we are ' ; on the contrary, we are full of just those impulses that led, in that day, to his crucifixion ; we are full of jealousy and fear of the truth and hatred of the good. The truth is that he is prepared to treat us as good, to deem us good, to speak to us as to responsible and spiritually intelligent people, to give us heroes ' work to do. That we must accept, and to persuade a shy and sensitive and spiritually sedentary person of that truth is one of the most difficult of the evangelist's duties.

But the Gospel leaves us in no doubt. Neither fear nor price, neither fear of what Christ will take away nor fear of what he will give, need prevent a man's accepting the truth. The result, it is promised, will be the proving, the free knowledge and understanding, of the depth and breadth of the love of God. ' Take my yoke upon you, and learn of me ; for I am meek and lowly of heart : and ye shall find rest to your souls. For my yoke is easy, and my burden is light.'

31

John Newton (1725–1807)

How sweet the name of Jesus sounds
  In a believer's ear !
It soothes his sorrows, heals his wounds,
  And drives away his fear.

It makes the wounded spirit whole,
  And calms the troubled breast ;
'Tis manna to the hungry soul,
  And to the weary rest.

Dear name ! the rock on which I build,
  My shield and hiding-place,
My never-failing treasury filled
  With boundless stores of grace.

Jesus ! my shepherd, husband, friend,
  My prophet, priest, and king,
My Lord, my life, my way, my end,
  Accept the praise I bring.

Weak is the effort of my heart,
  And cold my warmest thought ;
But when I see thee as thou art,
  I'll praise thee as I ought.

Till then I would thy love proclaim
  With every fleeting breath ;
And may the music of thy name
  Refresh my soul in death.

H.H.L. 75–8

The Name

WHEN a composer writes a piece of music he is able to choose between two very broad principles on which he will go to work. Either he may state his main theme and make it the basis of a continuous argument which will run logically through the whole of a movement lasting as much as a quarter of an hour, or an opera-Act lasting an hour and a half; this is the more usual method in classical and modern music. But he may decide to state his theme, and then to write ' variations ' on it. These variations consist in a series of short movements, each of which does something new with the basic theme. It may be simply a matter of adding superficial ornaments. Or it may be a matter of drawing out the implications of certain phrases in the theme. Or it may be done by holding the theme up against some other musical idea or convention and watching what new light may thus be thrown on it. Now most hymns are in a form that corresponds to the first of these, the continuous argument of sonata or dance or fugue. But there are some great classics, like ' God moves in a mysterious way ' and ' Fight the good fight ' and ' Just as I am ', which suggest rather the variation-form, a great and familiar theme decorated and varied and expounded, each verse taking the same theme and a new exposition of it. ' How sweet the name ', on the name of Jesus, is the finest and the best known of all these.

J. H. Newman has this excellent passage in his book, *A Grammar of Assent.*

A Deliverer of the human race through the Jewish nation had been promised from time immemorial. The day came when He was to appear, and He was eagerly expected ; moreover, One actually did make His appearance at that date in Palestine, and claimed to be He. He left the earth without apparently doing much for the object of His coming. But when He was gone,

His disciples took upon themselves to go forth to preach to all parts of the earth with the object of preaching *Him*, and collecting converts *in His Name*.

' In the name of Jesus of Nazareth,' they would say, ' rise up and walk.' ' In my name,' he had said, ' ye shall cast out demons.' In those first days it was the name of Jesus that worked the miracles and brought the converts. The *name* of Jesus, you might almost say, could do what the physical presence of Jesus could not do. The *name* could sound through all the world, when it was pronounced by faithful men.

What a singularly complex thing a name is. My names (modern life demands that I have at least two names) are for one thing an epitome of my history. My surname tells you that I come from a certain Somersetshire family on my father's side. My Christian name has a meaning and a history which a textbook will easily furnish. No name is an accident. Christian names are given to children at their baptism (to put it at its lowest) because of some pleasant or noble association they may have for the parents, even if their etymological meaning be hidden from them. The name of Jesus had an earthly meaning. It meant ' Deliverer ' or ' Rescuer ',—indeed, it is the Greek form of the Hebrew ' Joshua ', and Joshua is for all time the type of the leader who by courage and faithfulness brings to completion the purpose that God has for his people. Jesus was in this sense the new Joshua, the deliverer of men from their spiritual enemy by means of spiritual courage and faithfulness.

But again, a name is a precious possession. It is a great crime to steal another man's name. A man's name signed at the foot of a cheque indicates his purpose and his capacity to honour the debt named in the cheque. Forgery is the theft of the goodwill for which the name stands. Those who would promote companies or charitable concerns load their notepaper with ' names '—not fictitious or obscure names, but names which carry prestige, names which associate the qualities of their owners with the business being promoted. Similarly there are many who will borrow the

name of Christ in order to lend prestige to themselves or
some design of their own.   These are they who covet the
prestige but not the responsibility.   They are glad to carry
the name of Christ, so to speak, on their notepaper, but the
personal presence of Jesus may be the last thing they wish
for.   And the crime of forgery is a sinister mixture of an
offence against morals and an offence against truth.   There
is an axiom of speech and thought, without which the whole
world immediately goes mad, which says that a thing is not
another thing, that A is identifiable with A and not with B.
It says that Smith is Smith and not Jones.   A name identifies
a man.   His name is a part of him, inseparable from him.

This has one important consequence.   If a man's name
is really his property, it is easy to see that it is sinful to steal
it.   But can he give it away?   In the ordinary commonplace sense of giving it away so that he has no longer any
title to it himself, he cannot, of course.   But when a man
tells another his name, he has given away something of
himself.   It comes more pointedly from the other angle :
if a man resolutely refuses to disclose his name, he does it
either because he wishes to retain a power over another
which the other cannot have over himself, or because he
wishes to defend himself against some power that he
fears.

This sense of the power of a name is the most primitive
and universal association of the notion of naming.   I was
for a short time a minister in a busy industrial town.   The
Manse was on a main street, and just round the corner was
a large school.   The small children who poured out of this
school at four in the afternoon were inclined to use my front
garden as an extension of their playground.   I could find
no way of curbing their depredations ; one day I was
remonstrating with a few of them and getting very much
the worse of the argument.   My neighbour appeared at his
front door and took in the situation at once.   He produced
a notebook and pencil, looked sternly at one of the children,
and said, ' Now then.   What's your name ? '   Within ten
seconds they had altogether disappeared, indignantly and
tearfully saying that he couldn't do that to them, and

implying that once they had let him know their names they were as good as imprisoned already.

And there is the well-known story of the small child who, lying awake in a large and lonely house, was frightened by the thought that Somebody was coming up the stairs. She was only comforted when her uncle gave her this advice : ' Next time you hear him coming, call out " That you, Percy ? " ' Give the unknown a name, and it is no longer unknown. To know a man's name is to have him to some extent in your power.

From this one naturally passes in thought to some of those primitive experiences of the character of God which are set down in the Old Testament. Jacob, making contact with God at Peniel so close that he felt himself to be physically wrestling with the Most High, his soul torn asunder by the weight and breadth of the truth he was trying to take in, called out, ' Tell me thy name ! ' In the story of the Exodus there is a mysterious passage in which certain chosen men of Israel swore they heard God pronounce his own name ; and they set it down for just this purpose—to place on record an occasion when they had received new insight into the purpose of God, and new knowledge of God's character.

It is significant, too, that in times of that kind, when it was an issue between God and some particular person, and when something of the nature of a conversion (of the sort we considered under 22) is at stake, very frequently a *change of name* is involved. Abram becomes Abraham ; Jacob becomes Israel ; Jerubbaal becomes Gideon ; Saul of Tarsus becomes Paul ; Levi becomes Matthew. If the passages be looked up in the scriptures it will be found that each one of them has at its centre the surrender of a man's soul in exchange for a new freedom of the truth given by God. This is the only kind of situation in which you hear of a man wholly and literally giving his name away. Let us insist on this and press it. Men who were given a new name were given it after a conversation of great weight and intimacy with God (or with Jesus). Press that far enough, and a new and venerable word will begin to suggest itself—

a word which has already been our concern—the word
' covenant '.

Now at last we are at the heart of the matter. God deals
with men in conversation, in covenant (see No. 9). In the
course of such a dealing God may cause a man to give away
himself, to give himself up utterly. And the man will do
that because he knows that God has given himself up for
men. God has made his name known to men in the name
of Jesus. God has placed himself in men's power, in the
life and death of Jesus. That we are allowed to know the
name of Jesus is the direct result of Jesus' having died and
risen again.

That is why the name of Jesus is so powerful as the hymn
says it is. To say ' Jesus ' is to bring to mind all that Jesus
was and did, and to know that it was done to gain the
friendship of man, to demonstrate the confidence that God
still had in his creation. Given this covenant on both sides,
the surrender of God answered by the surrender of man,
things can be done ' in the name of Jesus ' that may indeed
set the world by the ears. For such a covenanted person
has Christ in him, and the power of Christ. He is free of
the Christian way, and has a skill and patience that defy the
world. The name of Jesus is his rock, his shield, his protection, his treasury of wisdom and grace. He sees, as life
brings one emergency upon another, just how rightly men
have given Jesus every name of praise they could think of
—shepherd, husband (or guardian), friend, prophet who
not only speaks but is the truth, priest who not only calls
for the sacrifice but is himself the sacrifice, King who not
only rules but also serves. All the other names of Jesus are
the notes his grace has struck out of life. They represent
all the glowing colours in the spectrum of the world's praise.
But they are all gathered up in that name which is as powerful and as health-giving as the sun itself, the name of JESUS.

32

John Bunyan (1628–88)

Who would true valour see,
Let him come hither ;
One here will constant be,
 Come wind, come weather ;
There's no discouragement
Shall make him once relent
His first avowed intent
 To be a pilgrim.

Whoso beset him round
With dismal stories,
Do but themselves confound ;
 His strength the more is.
No lion can him fright,
He'll with a giant fight,
But he will have a right
 To be a pilgrim.

Hobgoblin nor foul fiend
Can daunt his spirit,
He knows he at the end
 Shall life inherit.
Then fancies fly away ;
He'll not fear what men say ;
He'll labour night and day
 To be a pilgrim.
     H.H.L. 168

Courage—I: The Pilgrim

IT is a singular fact, which has been not without its influence on Christian moral teaching, that courage is on the whole not a Biblical word. Its synonym, fortitude, which finds its place among the seven cardinal virtues of medieval teaching, has no place at all in the text of the King James Version. Apart from the venerable and famous first chapter of Joshua there is hardly a mention in the Bible of courage itself, and none later than the book of Deuteronomy. It is almost as though courage were not a Biblical virtue at all, but there are two considerations which weigh against any such conclusion apart from its obvious unlikelihood. One is to say that courage is a quality so universally inherent in all the specific virtues which the Bible does mention that there is little occasion, except that classic one, for particularly mentioning it. (After all, in Greek the same word stands for ' courage ' and for ' virtue ' ; courage is, in a sense, inseparable from the exercise of any virtue.) The other consideration is the vital place which Joshua, the embodiment of courage in the Bible, plays in the story of salvation. We observed in the article before this one that the name Jesus and Joshua are the same, and the implications of that are far-reaching enough to establish courage as a quality of life which is indispensable to any who aspire to follow the way of the Master.

Courage, we are bound to say, is not so much a virtue in its own right as the preservative of all the other virtues ; conversely, for a good action, courage needs the presence of at least one other virtue. Consider, for example, the qualities which St Paul enumerates as the ' fruits of the Spirit ' in *Galatians* v. 22. He enumerates them *currente calamo*, so to speak, not intending them to form a technical or exhaustive list ; but they are—love, joy, peace, long-suffering, gentleness, goodness, faith, courtesy, self-control. Not one of these but will become sentimental and vapid without a stiffening of courage. Faith, hope, and charity themselves need courage for their effective operation in daily life. ' Charity never faileth '—courage provides its staying power. There is no real love without courage, only obsequiousness or romance or lust or moonstruck and temperamental yearning. It is a sinister thing, indeed, that the music which is nowadays popularly associated with the love of the sexes has in it so much smartness, so much glamour, so much streamlined extravagance, and (when it is compared with its counterparts of, say, the sixteenth and seventeenth centuries) so little courage and integrity.

Courage is necessary to any virtue as soon as that virtue is brought down from the general to the particular, from the ideal to the practical. Courage is necessary for the preserving and the purifying and the defending of all virtues against those forces which, in this life and in the course of time, seek to pervert and destroy them. Courage is the necessity of the pilgrim. This must be what caused John Bunyan to add the lines beginning ' Who would true valour see ' to the second edition of *The Pilgrim's Progress* as a generalization of the allegory, a summary of what the reader will just have read concerning Mr Valiant-for-Truth. They are not Mr Valiant-for-Truth's song, but the reader's song, Everyman's song.

This poem, which has now by popular consent been accepted as a congregational hymn, is so human and valuable because it mentions with graphic boldness the enemies of courage. What are the lions and giants, the ' dismal stories ' and hobgoblins and fiends, but all those things which modern psychology classifies under general head of ' anxieties ' ?

Now it happens that recently a great and illuminating book has been written on the very subject of this hymn. It is Dr Tillich's *The Courage to Be*.[1] I believe we do this author no injustice if we summarize the chief contention of the earlier part of his book in some such way as here follows. Courage, let us say, is ' Courage to *be* '. This initial proposition may borrow some light from what we ventured

[1] Paul Tillich, *The Courage to Be* (Nisbet, 1952), chapter II.

to say under ' Our God, our help in ages past ' (7) concerning the remarkable treatment by the Most High of the
verb ' to be '.   Courage, we will here say, is what makes a
man a real person, the person he was meant to be.   Without
it he will be a shadow, a blurred outline, without dimensions
and without decisiveness.   He will be, so to speak, full of
possibility and even of promise, but without any fulfilment.
It will be difficult to say that he does more than ' exist '.
He will not in any positive sense ' be ' at all.   That is
familiar enough :   feelings, ambitions and promises *are*
nothing until fulfilment be added in time and in life.   Virtue
has no ' being ' at all until it has come down to the particular.   Courage is needed to give it ' being ' in life and
time.

Now there are (Dr Tillich goes on) three great enemies of
courage, three archetypal anxieties, which affect not only
men but whole nations.   They are the anxiety of death, the
anxiety of meaninglessness, and the anxiety of condemnation.
The familiar questions which gather up these anxieties are
' What is going to become of me ? '   ' What is the point of
life ? ' and ' What have I *done* ? '   Fear of fate, fear of
emptiness, fear of guilt produce the ' anxiety states ' that
dissipate men's courage and (precisely) un-man them.
Whole civilizations have been ruined by accepting a bondage
to such anxieties, the Roman civilization with its degenerate
religion of Luck, the medieval church with its corruption
of forgiveness, the modern technical society with its dangerous drift to aimlessness and nihilism.   The answer to all
this is ' Courage to *be* ', something God-given which enables
a man (and therefore a society) not merely to exist but to
be, not merely to drift but to move purposefully.   In a
sense Courage is the road by which men and societies may
partake of that incandescent and vital ' being ' which is
God's being.

So says Dr Tillich.   He says more, and the next hymn
will provide opportunity of referring to another part of his
argument.   But so far we can confirm his diagnosis from
normal experience.   What is rather remarkable, however,
is that the acute and self-analytical mind of Bunyan seems

to have come to just the same conclusions, if this hymn be evidence.

> Whoso beset him round
> With dismal stories :

There is, precisely, ' meaninglessness ' ; there are the people who say to the traveller ' There is no purpose in your journey, and the further you go the worse it gets.'

> No lion can him fright :

That is fate and death ; that is the dark question, ' How can I keep alive at all with the universe so powerfully ranged against me ? '

> Hobgoblin nor foul fiend
> Can doubt his spirit :

it needs little imagination to hear the voices of the hobgoblins and the fiends speaking in terms of guilt, ' Your past is your bondage ; there is no forgiveness ; God is dead ; God is cold ; God will not forgive, for the love of God is only a legend.' Between them these three brigades of the devil's army can surround a man and throw him into a whirlpool of grievance and self-centred misery. The worst they will do is to rob the traveller of his courage, and even of his identity.

In contrast to this the Gospel says that Christ ' calls all his sheep by name '. Before Christ a man has identity. He is somebody. Before God a man may have courage to be : ' Son of man, stand upon thy feet, and I will speak with thee ' (*Ezekiel* ii. 2). And this raising up of the mortal man to identity, to clarity of being, is directly the result of the courage of the Crucified, who is the Good Shepherd. The Good Shepherd is tough and shrewd and alert, as well as gentle. And the Good Shepherd lays down his life for his sheep. And he expressly says in that very same passage, ' I lay down my life, that I may take it again. It is not that man taketh it from me, but I lay it down of myself. I have power to lay it down, and I have power to take it again.' ' I *am* the Good Shepherd '—even in death Christ reigns,

Christ *is*. When men crucified Christ they did not make away with his identity and his courage. Those remained. It is the Shepherd who *is*, the Shepherd who is in command, who reigns, who calls his sheep by name, and passes on to them his courage, his power to *be*.

It is just possible that those who defend the rewritten version of this poem, an hortatory hymn beginning ' He who would valiant be 'gainst all disaster ', find the bold and brazen expression of courage here given to be offensive and crude. But such force and power is needed to balance the Christian life. And if the reader glances back at the hymns which immediately precede this one in our collection, it will perhaps be clear that in order to deliver from sentimentality and a supine resignation the aspirations of, say ' Abide with me ', or ' Jesu, lover of my soul ', or ' Lead, kindly light ', the prayer for courage to stand and to *be* is the very thing that must come next.

33

C. Wesley (1707–88)

Soldiers of Christ, arise,
And put your armour on ;
Strong in the strength which God supplies,
Through his eternal son ;

Strong in the Lord of Hosts,
And in his mighty power ;
Who in the strength of Jesus trusts
Is more than conqueror.

Stand then in his great might,
With all his strength endued ;
And take, to arm you for the fight,
The panoply of God.

From strength to strength go on,
Wrestle, and fight, and pray ;
Tread all the powers of darkness down,
And win the well-fought day.

That having all things done,
And all your conflicts past,
Ye may o'ercome, through Christ alone,
And stand entire at last.

H.H.L. 67–72

Courage—II : The Soldier

THE Apostle Paul, as we must suppose, was not a man of military or athletic habit ; but he was fond of military and athletic metaphors. He loved to talk of life as a battle or as a race, and of the Christian as a soldier or a runner. Nowhere does he more completely commit himself to this way of thinking than in the sixth chapter of *Ephesians*, in that passage which begins ' Put on the whole armour of God '. The hymn, ' Soldiers of Christ, arise ' is part of a very long hymn (originally of 128 lines) built on that passage.

It is, like the preceding, a hymn about courage ; but here we have a different picture. In ' Who would true valour see ' the central figure is a solitary traveller. Here it is a soldier, himself a brave man, but part of a great army. He will not himself win or lose the battle, but he will be involved in its issue. He will give as much towards its prosperous outcome as though he were personally responsible for victory ; but he will all the time be part of the greater whole.

This hymn then felicitously balances and complements the other. Life is not wholly a matter of individual actions and reactions ; and life's technique is not wholly a matter of individual courage, of courage to *be* in an individual and separate way. It is also a matter of *being* as part of a greater whole. A sentence from a later part of Dr Tillich's *The Courage to Be* puts this very point. ' The self ', he writes, ' is self only because it has a world, a structured universe, to which it belongs and from which it is separated at the same time.' That is the primary tension. But the tension is diversified at other levels. A man is himself, and must in that positive sense *be* himself, but he is also part of a family, a nation, a church ; and his relation to those larger communities has had much to do with the fact that he is a ' self ' at all. Therefore, if he must have courage in order to *be* himself, there must also be a corresponding sort of courage which will make him able to *be* an effective member of the communities with which he is associated. Politics is one theatre in which this tension is seen in operation, and in which too much emphasis this way or that produces familiar distortions like collectivism on the one hand and anarchy on the other. The life of the church, another theatre of tension, is what concerns us here.

G. K. Chesterton puts this point excellently in these words : ' There are some things that are greater than greatness ; there are some things that no man with blood in his body would sell for the throne of Dante, and one of them is to fire the feeblest shot in a war that really awaits decision, or carry the meanest musket in an army that is really marching by.' [1] That is, in its way, a remarkably Pauline comment, and it throws light on this very passage that has here come under review.

The Christian life cannot be lived apart from the church. Man was not made to be alone ; he cannot apprehend the truth of God without the help of his fellow-men (as we said at the end of No. 13). That is the axiom of the Church, which is the City of God and the Body of Christ. But the Church living in time, the Church operating and contending with the temptations of its calling and the assaults of secularism, is with great exactness called ' the Church Militant '. It is like an army. Just as the individual needs courage in order to live as God means him to live, so the Church needs courage in order that it may do the work God means it to do ; and the courage of the individual member of the Church is not merely courage to the end that he may live, but also courage to the end that the Church may live and work.

This is very much what the Apostle is saying in the letter which contains the passage about the Christian's armoury. He is writing all the time of the nature of the Church. The letter provides, at an earlier stage, the classic use of the expression, ' the body of Christ ' (*Ephesians* i. 23) ; and if

[1] G. K. Chesterton, *A Handful of Authors* (Sheed & Ward, 1953), p. 99.

we may presume that the letter had some reference to the situation at Ephesus (which it may well have, even though it is thought that the Apostle meant all, or some, of the churches in that area to share in the counsels he there sets down), then point is given to the argument by the special condemnation of the Ephesian Church which may be read in *Revelation* ii. 1–7. The iniquity of the Church for which it is there (that is, a generation later) castigated is that it has ' left its first love ', which places it in danger of ' having its candlestick removed '—that is, losing its identity, falling apart, and ceasing to *be* a church. Suppose that there were the signs of this in Paul's time—unreliable enthusiasm and demonstrative but shaky faith ; suppose that the vested interests of Diana of the Ephesians were always a danger ; suppose that Alexander the Coppersmith (*Acts* xix. 33 and *II Timothy* iv. 14) was already showing signs of being a traitor to the faith, why then that would provide reason enough for Paul's ending his mystical and profound treatise on church-manship with this exhortation to common courage.

But as it is transmitted in the hymn, the advice is to the Church member as part of the Church, that he put on his armour and attend to it constantly. In a verse which is not in all the hymn-books we have this, which enjoins attention to all the small details of life :

> To keep your armour bright
> Attend with constant care,
> Still walking in your Captain's sight
> And watching unto prayer.

' Soldiers of Christ ', then, adds humility to courage ; it makes courage not merely a lonely virtue but also a sociable virtue, a resourceful neighbourliness, a zeal which leaves room for charity.

But there is one respect, we must now say, in which the hymn has a slightly remote and romantic sound. The least touch of the antiquated in the imagery of a hymn, and it can then be easily disconnected from common life and made into a legend or a fantasy. We must not overlook the point at which this danger is beginning to overtake this hymn and

others like it.   The danger is, of course, in the whole business
of armour.   Armour suggests chivalry and medieval heroism
and the Tower of London.   It is just possible for a man
mentally to dismiss the armour, and with it to dismiss the
war.

Modern warfare does not demand armour.   It demands
technical skill.   Machines take the place of the helmet and
the breastplate and the coat of mail.   Psychological warfare
has to some extent superseded the spear and the sword,
and what is not achieved thus is completed with high
explosive and the application of nuclear fission.   Modern
war is so hideous that no modern apologist would dream of
using its details as an allegory of the Christian warfare.   The
romance of the voluntary gentleman-soldier is now long
dead, a thing of history and of the historical novel.

But perhaps we can rescue the hymn if we attempt a
certain exercise in imagination.   If ever there was a warfare
in which there was great courage and no malice, intrepid
endurance and no bitterness, it was surely in the conquest of
Mount Everest.   The pictures, now so familiar, of the later
stages of that enterprise show the climbers wearing what is
obviously the nearest thing the twentieth century can offer to
medieval armour.   From the point of view of English style
we shall not get very felicitous results by attempting to
rewrite the hymn in terms of the climber's equipment.
But suppose, in imagination, in reading the original passage
in *Ephesians*, we take out the antique units of armour and
put in the climber's boots, his helmet, his wind-jacket, his
ice-axe, his oxygen-apparatus, his food-rations.   It is more
than probable that the Apostle, had he been writing that
passage in 1954, would have written along these lines—
' Put on the whole equipment of the Christian enterprise,
let honour be your wind-jacket, let the gospel of peace be
your climbing boots, salvation your helmet, the Word of
God your ice-axe, faith your breathing-apparatus. . . . '
If ever there was courage to *be* as part of a greater whole,
personal valour welded into a common enterprise, courage
of a kind that is never eradicated from the horrors even of
modern war but which is irretrievably tarnished by the

associations of modern war's hideous immortality, surely such courage is exemplified in the men who climbed that mountain. That is the texture of the courage and the victory which are part of the equipment and part of the promise of the Christian life.

34

John Samuel Bewley Monsell (1811-75)

Fight the good fight with all thy might ;
Christ is thy strength, and Christ thy right ;
Lay hold on life, and it shall be
Thy joy and crown eternally.

Run the straight race through God's good grace ;
Lift up thine eyes, and seek his face ;
Life with its way before us lies ;
Christ is the path, and Christ the prize.

Cast care aside, lean on thy guide ;
Lean, and his mercy will provide ;
Lean, and the trusting soul shall prove
Christ is its life, and Christ its love.

Faint not nor fear ; his arms are near ;
He changeth not, and thou art dear ;
Only believe, and thou shalt see
That Christ is all in all to thee.

H.H.L. 144

Courage—III: The Disciple

'FIGHT the good fight', so well known and popular, is one of the most mystical, even the most mysterious, of all the hymns in this small collection. It begins with a four-word phrase that sounds almost like some trifling jingle; and indeed it has long been associated with a tune of the most earthly popular kind. Yet when you read it or sing it for the fiftieth time you may suddenly find yourself being thankful that all these things have helped to make it well known.

'Fight the good fight' comes from the Apostle Paul's letters to Timothy, the young minister. He uses the expression twice, 'Fight the good fight of faith,' and 'I have fought a good fight; I have finished the course; I have kept the faith.' It is a good upstanding epigram, characteristic of the Apostle in his muscular mood; and just as Paul uncannily combined hard-headed realism with a profound and tender devotion, so this hymn combines a mystical Christ-centredness with its bold and homely injunctions.

It forms a fitting third member of our trio on Courage. We have had courage in the individual, and courage in the member. Now we have what goes beyond even the exalted reach of Dr Tillich—courage in the disciple, or courage in the member of Christ. The context in Bunyan was a pilgrimage, in Wesley an army. Here, in the lines of a decidedly second-rate hymn-writer who was a faithful and excellent minister, the context is Christ, and nothing but Christ.

Observe what is said of Christ.

> Christ is thy strength.
> Christ is thy right.
> Christ is the path.
> Christ is the prize.
> Christ is thy love.
> Christ is thy life.
> Christ is all in all.

Set out like that, the string of simple statements reminds one of the great incantation in ' St Patrick's Breastplate '— ' Christ be with me, Christ within me,' etc.   But even more it brings to mind the words, ' I am the Way, the Truth and the Life.'   For that is the real thought of the hymn—the fullness of Christ, the necessity of Christ.

Now observe the imperatives in the other lines : ' Fight : lay hold : run : lift up thine eyes : cast care aside : lean : faint not : fear not : believe '.   The two elements in the hymn, the practical and the mystical, explain each other because they need each other.   ' I am the Way,' said Jesus, but a man must walk along it.   ' I am the door,' but a man must pass through it.   ' I am the Truth,' but a man must hear it, if he can stand it.   ' I am the life,' but a man must live it, not drift along it.   ' I am the light,' but a man must choose to see it.   ' I am the bread '—but a man must eat it, and all but twelve of his admirers (we read in *St John*) chose rather to turn aside and go hungry than to accept that.

The Apostle said (as we recalled under ' Rock of Ages ', No. 25) that, all those years before, the spiritual rock which provided food and drink for the wanderers in the Exodus, *was Christ*.   Christ is the way, the truth, the prize, the life. Such advice as the hymn offers is the merest pietistic verbiage unless the context of it all is Christ.   There is a sense in which the obvious consequences of the advice are contradicted by Christ.   ' Lay hold on life,' it says, but Christ said, ' Lose your life.'   ' Run the straight race,' it says, but Christ's version of that was ' Take up your cross.'   ' Lean on thy guide,' says the hymn, but Christ says ' Follow me.' ' Faint not, nor fear '—' Fear not them that kill the body ; but rather fear Him. . . .'   Treated as human aspirations they are all commonplace enough, and could be found in a heathen or a selfish life.   Disorganized, unregulated, unregenerate courage is nothing to sing hymns about.   But with Christ as the context, human courage is lifted up and assimilated with the royal courage of the Captain of our Salvation, for God ' hath put all things under his feet, and gave him to be head over the Church which is his body, the fulness of him that filleth all in all '.

35

Anon. (*9th cent. ?*)
Trans. Bishop John Cosin (1564–1672)

VENI, CREATOR SPIRITUS

Come, Holy Ghost, our souls inspire,
And lighten with celestial fire ;

Thou the anointing Spirit art,
Who dost thy sevenfold gifts impart.

Thy blessèd unction from above
Is comfort, life, and fire of love ;

Enable with perpetual light
The dullness of our blinded sight :

Anoint and cheer our soilèd face
With the abundance of thy grace ;

Keep far our foes, give peace at home ;
Where thou art guide no ill can come.

Teach us to know the Father, Son,
And thee, of both, to be but One ;

That through the ages all along
This may be our endless song,

Praise to thy enternal merit,
Father, Son, and Holy Spirit.

H.H.L. 57, 132

The Holy Spirit—I: His Gifts

'COME, Holy Ghost' and the *Te Deum* are the only medieval hymns which have yet entered into the treasury of popular English hymnody; and to be honest we must admit that 'Come, Holy Ghost' is familiar rather through its association with august occasions than because it is very frequently sung. We associate it pre-eminently with Whitsuntide, with the Coronation service, and with the ordination of Priests and consecration of Bishops, for which it is prescribed in the Book of Common Prayer. But these associations give it sufficient title to be included here. It comes from a Latin hymn of probably the ninth century. It is not here very literally translated; indeed, several other translations exist, all of which are closer than this to the original. But this is the one which has the lyric power and the imaginative sweep.

It is a prayer to the Holy Ghost that he may work his work in us. Just as we often say, 'Come, Lord Jesus' in hymns, knowing that he has already come in history, so we pray here, 'Come, Holy Ghost' knowing that he also, and in a similar sense, has come. And the meaning of that prayer is to be found very well summarized in the last word of the first line, the word 'inspire'.

'Inspire' is a word which has suffered much debasement in the common speech of Englishmen. 'Inspire' and 'inspiration' are words which, misused as we misuse them, tend to make popular English religion the thin and diffuse thing it so often is. Nowadays any unusual kind of experience is called an 'inspiration'; the condition of the artist receiving a creative impulse is called 'inspiration'—and that kind of talk confuses the present issue by reinforcing a wrong belief about the Holy Spirit. He, whose proper office is 'inspiration' in the strict sense, is no undifferentiated cloud of divinity, nor a kind of drug that produces ecstatic experiences in people. The difficulty of believing in the Holy Spirit as a Person is great enough without allowing verbal ambiguities to mislead us.

The easiest way to clear this up is to state that in the year 1627, when this English translation was made, 'inspire' still meant 'breathe in'. 'Inspire our hearts' would mean 'breathe into our hearts'; indeed, 'inspire' contains the same verbal root that we have in the word 'Spirit' itself. But as it happens the Latin word translated 'inspire', by a coincidence which is advantageous to the continuity of these papers, is *visita*, the imperative of the word for 'visit'; and on the religious use of the word 'visit', meaning 'come for a purpose', see what was said above on 'Love divine' and 'Christ whose glory' (23, 24). 'Inspire' is here not what a pleasant feeling does to a man; it is more like what a stroke of lightning would do.

The truth is, of course, that not all 'inspiration' in the modern sense is of the Holy Spirit. That is not what the Bible says. What is there written (and we think here chiefly of such passages as the eighth chapter of *Romans* and *I Corinthians* xii. 3) leads us to believe that when the Spirit operates in a man he is enabled (*a*) to pray to God as Father, and (*b*) to say 'Jesus is Lord.' That is to say (to go no further yet), that the Spirit gives a man friendship with God and the sanctified reason which makes him gear his whole life to the truth that Jesus is Lord of it. Consider the state of the man who can claim neither of these privileges; the change in his condition when the Spirit has answered the prayer in this hymn we might well compare with the activity of 'fire'; but he is not likely to think of it as resembling the breathing of a pleasant June breeze or the feeling he gets when he heard the second Piano Concerto of Tchaikovsky.

The Holy Spirit is primarily, as the Bible tells us, the author of wisdom and the strengthener of the spiritual man. As you look over the titles he is given, you find that many of them are bold and powerful words suggesting great strength. 'The Comforter' (which means 'the Fortifier'), 'the Spirit of Wisdom', 'the Spirit of Power' are such, and even

' the Spirit of Adoption ', the title associated with the Holy
Spirit's activity of making us as it were sons who can speak
to God as Father, is hardly a sentimental thought ; it
brings to mind the adoption of an orphan child, in which
enterprise there is more of heroism than of vague senti-
ment.

The hymn goes on to speak of ' the anointing spirit '.
Anointing, as Englishmen have recently been dramatically
reminded, is associated with royalty. A special revelation
of the Holy Spirit accompanied, we are told, that occasion
when Jesus set himself aside for his ministry. The Holy
Spirit at his Baptism is referred to in *The Acts* as the Spirit
' by whom God anointed Jesus '—proclaimed his royalty
and his Messiahship. Indeed the Hebrew word ' Messiah '
and the Greek ' Christ ' mean ' the Anointed One '. The
' anointing Spirit ' is now promised to us, that by him we
may be made ' kings and priests ' (see 37)—placed in this
new relation with God and with life which Jesus made
known in his humanity.

' Inspiration ' and ' anointing ' then are specific acts, and
acts which have formidable consequences. But if anything
more is required to give point and precision to this hymn
of the Holy Spirit, it will be found in that expression ' sevenfold gifts ' in the fourth line. In this traditional expression
we have the consequence of a very curious development of
ideas, which, for a reason which will make itself plain, we
will here briefly trace.

The ' sevenfold gifts ' of which the medieval author was
thinking are not, as might at first be supposed, the ' fruits of
the Spirit ' in *Galatians* v. 22 (of which, anyhow, there are
twelve). They are the seven gifts as they were classified by
the medieval men of learning in the course of that exhaustive
mapping of the Christian pilgrimage which was their special
contribution to the universal Church. From such sources
come the three theological virtues, the three evangelical
counsels, the seven deadly sins, the seven cardinal virtues,
and so on. The seven gifts of the Spirit are these : Wisdom,
Understanding, Counsel, Ghostly Strength, Knowledge,
True Godliness, and Holy Fear. These are derived not

from the New Testament, but from the Old. They come from this passage in *Isaiah* xi :

> And there shall come forth a rod out of the stem of Jesse, and a Branch shall grow out of his roots. And the spirit of the Lord shall rest upon him, the spirit of wisdom and understanding, the Spirit of counsel and might, the spirit of knowledge and of the fear of the Lord.

Since the Hebrews liked things to come in pairs, and the medieval monks, influenced by some dark mysticism that originates several hundred miles east of Israel, liked them in threes, sevens, and twelves, the six gifts here mentioned are expanded into seven by the addition of ' The Spirit of Jehovah ' which ushers in the list.

Now let us press the origin of the ' sevenfold gifts '. What was Isaiah really saying there ? It is, of course, the famous Christmas Day Lesson, the most familiar of all those prophecies that prefigure the Messiah. But the immediate occasion that caused Isaiah to utter the words was to make it clear that after the confused and degenerate reign of King Ahaz, his successor, Hezekiah (who happened to be Isaiah's pupil), would need to have all these qualities in exceptional measure if he was to save the nation from disaster. As a fact, he only just managed to do so.

To realize that the ' sevenfold gifts ' are the kind of gifts one associated with royalty, and with royalty under challenge, adds a yet stronger colour to this hymn. The ' sevenfold gifts ' recall the prayer of King Solomon, ' Give thy servant an understanding heart, to judge thy people, that I may discern between good and bad ' (*I Kings* iii. 9), and the shrewd comment of Paul, ' He that is spiritual judgeth all things ' (*I Corinthians* ii. 15). It may be said, indeed, that all the sevenfold gifts are in a sense variations of the same gift. They are primarily gifts of the mind. The hymn as it goes on introduces the New Testament note, but this initial reference to the ' sevenfold gifts ' gives it a mental emphasis which makes it peculiarly relevant to a technical and intellectual age. We are dealing here with power and wisdom and skill, the kind of wisdom that would see a man like Hezekiah, or a man like King Henry V, or a man like Winston Churchill, through a national crisis. It is not to say that this particular form of wisdom is the whole effect of the Holy Spirit in a man ; but it is to say that such inspired insight is an indication of the kind of wisdom the Spirit does give a man.

The end to which that wisdom is given is, of course, not the resolution of national crises or the composition of symphonies, but what this hymn says it is—' Teach us to know the Father, Son, and Thee (of both) to be but one.' Give us, that is, clear sight and knowledge and understanding of the nature of God. Open the blind man's eyes and then let him see Jesus as his Saviour and follow him in the way ; cheer our downcast spirits that we may rejoice, not in all things indiscriminately, but in Christ and in God's truth. Keep away our enemies and give us peace and freedom of the spirit—freedom not for self-indulgence but that we may voluntarily obey and serve Christ, and praise him.

Directed, sanctified wisdom, not haphazard cleverness ; directed and disciplined inspiration, not vague ecstasy ; directed and articulate praise, not sentimental *bonhomie* : these are the things for which we properly ask the Holy Spirit. And, considering the problems which confront the mind of man to-day, considering the grave necessity under which he lives of distinguishing between truth and fiction in the newspapers, between truth and half-truth in rumours, between information and propaganda, between leadership and demagogy, between Christ and anti-Christ, this is a very proper and urgent content for that modern man to give to his prayers.

36

Harriet Auber (1773–1862)

Our blest Redeemer, ere he breathed
  His tender last farewell,
A Guide, a Comforter, bequeathed
  With us to dwell.

He came in tongues of living flame,
  To teach, convince, subdue ;
All-powerful as the wind he came,
  As viewless too.

He came sweet influence to impart,
  A gracious, willing Guest,
While he can find one humble heart
  Wherein to rest.

And his that gentle voice we hear,
  Soft as the breath of even,
That checks each fault, that calms each fear,
  And speaks of heaven.

And every virtue we possess,
  And every victory won,
And every thought of holiness,
  Are his alone.

Spirit of purity and grace,
  Our weakness, pitying, see :
O make our hearts thy dwelling-place,
  And worthier thee.

H.H.L. 85, 206–7

The Holy Spirit—II: His Work

THERE is no hymn on the Holy Spirit which stands in relation to 'Come, Holy Ghost' as 'There is a green hill' stands to 'When I survey'; no hymn, that is, among popular hymns. No dogmatic hymn on the Holy Spirit has found its way to universal public favour, though to be sure there are many great hymns of the kind in the treasury of Charles Wesley. Perhaps the nearest to a popular dogmatic hymn on this subject is John Keble's 'When God of old came down from heaven'; but if we seek to combine true universal popularity with a certain amount of direct statement about our Lord the Spirit, our choice must surely fall on 'Our blest Redeemer'.

But we must be quite frank about this. This collection of papers is not designed to draw attention to the defects of the hymns which have been taken as the texts for the observations we are making. I do not want to draw attention to the defects of 'Our blest Redeemer'. But the fact is that just at this point in our series we have to confess that there is more, and more of vital importance, in the Christian doctrine of the Holy Spirit than any popular hymn betrays in its lines. Under 'Come, Holy Ghost' we observed certain marks of the presence of the Spirit. 'Our blest Redeemer' must be the occasion for answering one or two even more fundamental questions, the chief of which will be 'Who is the Holy Spirit?'

In its first two verses the hymn refers to the historic 'coming' of the Holy Ghost which we celebrate at the festival of Whitsun. The basis of the first verse is the passage in *St John* xiv in which our Lord promises that 'the Comforter' will come after he has left the physical world; that of the second is the very curious story of Pentecost in *Acts* ii.

Now perhaps the great popular error about the Holy Spirit is this, that we are always tempted to think of him as something sent by God to us. Some*thing*—something in the neuter gender, something without a personality. That is very nearly the truth ; it is, in a way, what everybody believed, the best that anybody could believe, in the days before Christ came. But it is not the real story. The truth is that the Holy Spirit is God. He is not ' the Spirit ' but our Lord the Spirit. We may only safely talk of the Holy Spirit as the ' Breath of God ' or even ' the Spirit of God ' when we have firmly established and built into our living and working faith the truth that the Holy Spirit is the Lord, just as Jesus Christ is the Lord and God the Father is the Lord.

To assert the existence and the personality and the God-head of the Holy Spirit is to answer finally a deep question, a primitive need of men which appears (as do all the deep questions and primitive needs) in the Old Testament. It appears also in the natural man before he has any religion or after he has renounced religion. For to lack religion or to renounce it is not to do away with the questions ; it is only to be content that they should remain unanswered. The question and the need emerge from the following problem. ' I can understand ', an innocent but ignorant man might say, ' that there must be a Creator. I can understand that at some point or points that Creator will make himself known to his creation, become intelligible to it, speak to it if you like. Yes, I can understand a Creator and I can understand a Word. But now—I am still not persuaded that that Creator, speaking that Word, is really interested in his creation all the time ; is he really involved in it, or does he simply send messages to it and run it from a distance ? ' That is an intelligent expression of the question we are unearthing. Primitive religion was content to say that all creation shared the soul of its creator—that is known as pantheism ; you can believe in one God and believe that the one God is incomplete in himself, and that part of him is to be found in all things he has made. But can you claim any such involvement with creation of the mighty and remote and august God who made himself known to the Hebrew religious consciousness ? Can the God of Israel, than whom no more richly, zealously, power-fully august deity has ever been approached in any other religion, be worshipped and adored and still held to be

involved with his creation ?   Has not the purity and power
of such worship thrust him out of his universe altogether ?

In fact the root question is—the more I come to know about
the honour and might of God, the less I am able to believe
that God cares for me and wants me.   What am I to do ?

In the Old Testament there was a settled belief in ' the
spirit of God ', which amounted to the real presence, within
his creation, of God.   When a man notably distinguished
himself among his fellows, it would be said that ' the Lord
was with him ' ;   and when such a man fell from grace or
suffered defeat, it would be said that ' the Lord had departed
from him '.   ' The Lord departed,' it was said, from Samson
when his almost supernatural strength left him.   The Lord
was personally present in those prophets and kings who had
special insight into the reality of things.   ' The Spirit of the
Lord God is upon me,' says the prophet (*Isaiah* lxi) who
wishes to authenticate the truth and urgency of his message.
And when the whole nation suffered that great disaster at
the hands of the Philistines, they said ' Ichabod ', which
means ' the glory has departed '—the Lord has left his
people, and is no longer living in them or among them.

That was the characteristic of life in those days.   It was
universally held by men of the Israelite faith that the ' spirit
of God ', or ' God the spirit ', was present only now and
again, only in specially chosen people ;   that not only was
he not present in everybody, but he was just not available
to everybody.   The writer of the books of Samuel puts his
finger on a greater truth than he fully knows when he writes
that ' the word of God was precious in those days :   there
was no open vision '.

The Lord, then, *could* be present with his people, but just
on what terms he would make himself available, men did not
fully know.   There remained in the most enlightened and
informed religious practices and religious consciousness of
the pre-Christian Hebrews an area of mystery, a touch of
the old blind propitiation of an unknown and perhaps
capricious deity.   They were not yet wholly free of the
truth about God and the world.   There was an undertone
of fear and ignorance.

When Jesus came, he said certain things about the coming of the Spirit which came back to his disciples after he had gone, but which probably seemed difficult enough at the time. But the record of St John suggests that our Lord laid great emphasis on the teaching and fortifying office of the Holy Spirit. Nothing could be more natural or appropriate. *That* was what still remained to be done—the teaching of men's ignorance and the fortifying of their timid minds and wills. The work of Jesus Christ was pre-eminently the defeat of sin, the casting down of the powers of moral and spiritual darkness, the declaration to men that they were forgiven men, rescued men, loved and cherished by God. (Of that we have written already.) The work of the Holy Spirit, as he puts it in those discourses in St John, is to illuminate that area of darkness in men's religion, to take away that primitive fear, to enlighten that ignorance, to show men just what it *meant* that God was their Father and Jesus their Saviour. ' If ye love me, keep my commandments '—there is the experience of Christ, the loyalty to Christ which follows that experience ; Christ confronts a man and makes his demand, and a man answers. That is of the will and the affections. But there is more—' and I will pray the Father, and he will give you another Comforter, that he may abide with you for ever, even the Spirit of truth '. The harvest of the cross of Christ is the coming of the Spirit of truth, the true and honourable Spirit, our Lord the Spirit. To grow up in Christ a man must first be converted and become as a little child, but thereafter he must learn to use his new freedom of the truth ; he cannot do this of himself. He cannot do this without the heavenly confidence of God. And indeed it comes to this—and this will do very well as a summary of the Christian doctrine of the Holy Spirit—that in Christ we know God forgiving us, and in the Holy Spirit we know God taking us into his confidence and talking to us in language we may understand. Experience of forgiveness is wholly necessary. A man must know himself to be a sinner and must know that God knows he is a sinner and still respects him and loves him ; but then a man must know that God is prepared to take him into his confidence.

Now we can put the primitive question more clearly and specifically. The light of Christ shows what the old question really was (as it always does). In the light of what Christ is and has done, we now know that this is what we were really pining for all the time, that this question is the yearning of every intelligent and responsible man who was ever born—'Will God take me into his confidence?' Without this, a man who knows himself redeemed may still think himself patronized; a man may sink under the burden of forgiveness.

What happened at Pentecost, then, was parallel to what happened at Bethlehem. The nativity of Jesus provided the answer to the solemn and at times almost desperate hope of those who had waited for the Messiah. Men of far sight knew of what kind their Messiah would be; they knew in what terms their God would speak to them. (Look at *Isaiah* liii for the most obvious example of that.) Jesus, born at Bethlehem, was God taking flesh and finally answering all the questions in that field. The coming of the Holy Ghost at Pentecost was God entering history once again, on a different plane and for the purpose of answering the remaining questions. A little more of the inexpressible truth will show through if we put it again this way; that in the Incarnation of the Word, we see the gathering into one, for a time, of all things heavenly and earthly. God took flesh for a limited time and for a special purpose—to show men the Way and the Truth and the Life, to turn men back to the way of Life by showing them that the gate was standing wide open when they had thought it closed. In the coming of the Spirit, God entered history permanently. What took place there was never brought to a period, as the incarnation was brought to a period at the Ascension.

The experience was more than the author of *Acts* (who probably was not there) could very clearly describe. But primarily it was an experience of understanding. The general conviction, shared by a large number of people, was that for a minute or two even the curse of Babel was lifted, and the whole story of God's action and design was made plain to everybody present, Parthians and Medes and

Elamites and the dwellers in Mesopotamia and in Judæa and all the rest. It really seems that for a moment a large assembly of people, their thoughts guided by men who had been waiting for it but themselves probably not prepared for it, saw the whole design of God as Mozart saw (as he said) in a moment of time the whole design of an opera or a symphony. Something astonishing happened to the minds of these folk, and the strangers caught the infection from the Apostles. As for the Apostles themselves, Peter pre-eminently, they saw it all and were able to speak about it. The content of their sermons (preserved in *Acts*) shows that they now grasped the design, where before they had been groping. They were free and wholly converted men who knew that their freedom of the truth, though it would be extended, and though they might misuse it, would never be taken from them. And if they talked of this in terms of a rushing wind and fire from heaven, we may say that they were describing it in uncommonly moderate terms. It is only surprising that we do not hear anything of earthquakes, or of a volcanic eruption then and there. Nothing in nature could be more explosive than what happened in that moment when the truth was spoken for the first time by men, and everybody, everybody *understood*.

The new dimension that this introduced into religious experience involved, of course, the gathering at once of the believers into a Church, the community of saved and enlightened and free men. It involved also the conviction that God was (and always had been) at work in the world, using the minds and the bodies of men for his work; that God was fully and continuously and unremittingly involved in the world; that God would never leave the people he had taken into his confidence. But Pentecost was not the conversion of the world, any more than Calvary was. Pentecost was a miraculous demonstration of what conversion essentially is; but it was not the conversion by force or by miracle of everybody present, let alone of the whole world.

All we now know is that the gate is open; that God not only wants to rescue and forgive us, but that he wants to take every man into his confidence, that he wants to guide and teach men not by rote but by conversation ; that he wants not to issue orders to men but to hear men's prayers.

Dr Karl Barth (in the same source we quoted under No. 2) has this :

> If we wish to paraphrase the mystery of the Holy Spirit it is best to choose this concept of freedom. To receive the Spirit, to have the Spirit, to live in the Spirit means being set free and being permitted to live in freedom. Not all men are free. Freedom is not a matter of course and is not simply a predicate of human existence. All men are destined to freedom, but not all are in this freedom. . . . It is indeed not a natural condition of man to have the Spirit ; it will always be a distinction, a gift of God. What matters here is, quite simply, belonging to Jesus Christ. . . . The Holy Spirit is the Spirit of Jesus Christ. . . . What is involved is the participation of man in the word and work of Christ.[1]

And the greatest man of letters among the Puritans, Thomas Goodwin, near the end of his treatise on *The Work of the Holy Ghost in Our Regeneration*, has this dramatic and penetrating passage :

> Consider, you live in times and places in which the unsearchable riches of Christ are shovelled up to your hands, every day offered, tendered, yes, put (as it were) into your hands. The word . . . is nigh thee ; and yet (*Proverbs* xvii. 16) ' A fool hath a price (i.e. a treasure) in his hand, only wants a heart towards it.' Go home and consider with thyself : these things— and not yet *my* treasure, nor hath as yet God given me a heart to make them such ! [2]

This, the richness and freedom of the Spirit, is what is being celebrated in the simple lines of ' Our blest Redeemer ' ; we have at least suggested in those lines the power, the friendliness, the confidence of the Spirit, the Spirit in a good conscience, a clear mind, a pure and undivided will, the Spirit in the man who has now begun his free progress in the Way, and who is waiting to be taught by the God whom he now knows to be his Father and his Friend.

---

[1] Barth, *Dogmatics in Outline* (S.C.M., 1949), p. 138.

[2] Thomas Goodwin, *The Work of the Holy Ghost in Our Regeneration*, in Collected Works (Edinburgh, 1863), VI. 483.

37

John Newton (1725–1807)

Glorious things of thee are spoken,
  Zion, city of our God ;
He, whose word cannot be broken,
  Formed thee for his own abode :
On the Rock of Ages founded,
  What can shake thy sure repose ?
With salvation's walls surrounded,
  Thou mayst smile at all thy foes.

See, the streams of living waters,
  Springing from eternal love,
Well supply thy sons and daughters,
  And all fear of want remove :
Who can faint, while such a river
  Ever flows their thirst to assuage—
Grace, which, like the Lord the giver,
  Never fails from age to age ?

Blest inhabitants of Zion,
  Washed in the Redeemer's blood ;
Jesus, whom their souls rely on,
  Makes them kings and priests to God.
'Tis his love his people raises
  Over self to reign as kings ;
And as priests, his solemn praises
  Each for a thankoffering brings.

Saviour, if of Zion's city
  I, through grace, a member am,
Let the world deride or pity,
  I will glory in thy name :
Fading is the worldling's pleasure,
  All his boasted pomp and show ;
Solid joys and lasting treasure
  None but Zion's children know.

H.H.L. 75–8, 143

Homeland

IF ever a hymn gathered to itself all the best in the English eighteenth century, that hymn is ' Glorious things of thee are spoken '. Professor Basil Willey, in his famous series of studies called *The Eighteenth Century Background*,[1] recalls to us a word which expresses this special quality—the word ' chearfulness ' ; it is a good word, and if we spell it in the eighteenth-century way we shall be on our guard against misunderstanding it. 'Glorious things ' is essentially a hymn of Christian ' chearfulness '.

There is much eighteenth-century literature which might be called formal, or poised, or witty, or salty before you would think of calling it ' cheerful ' in the modern sense of hilarious. Eighteenth-century architecture you might want to call urbane or symmetrical, eighteenth-century painting and society, courtly ; and even though one is almost bound to say that eighteenth-century English music is uniformly cheerful in the most obvious sense, it might be replied that much of it is not English at all but foreign. ' Chearfulness ' as we are going to use the word here is a quality at the heart, not a superficial quality ; it is associated with a settled confidence in the ultimate certainties ; it is a poise of the mind rather than a manner of speaking or acting. At its worst it petrifies into a philistine complacency in social and artistic matters against which the romantics and revolutionaries of the later years reacted with indignation. At its best it is a fine thing, one of the notable qualities in John Newton, who wrote these lines ; Newton, Curate of Olney, had been in his time the owner of a slave-ship, and had encountered most of the ugly and gruesome aspects of eighteenth-century life —indeed, he had consented to them. When he put these things behind him he exchanged what might have become

[1] Basil Willey, *The Eighteenth Century Background* (Chatto & Windus, 1940), chapter III.

a brutal acceptance of evil for a buoyant and infectious faith. And faith of this particular texture is the product of Calvinism.

The faith of John Calvin is the most ' chearful ' of all Christian ways. To describe it as stern or gloomy is to mistake the superficial for the central. For the central thing in Calvinism is confidence in the goodness and faithfulness of God, confidence in the promises, confidence in the sovereignty of God, and confidence (for the individual) in the reality and relevance of the work God has called a man to do. Only a man who takes this high ground and takes it boldly will be able to contemplate the dark things as fearlessly as Calvin and the best of his followers contemplated them. Calvin, with all his talk of doom and discipline, was the great optimist of the Reformation, and this optimism, in its theological form too strong for some English Christians, is made friendly and humanized in the hymns of the English Calvinists ; among these the author of this present hymn, a full-blooded sinner converted into a full-blooded saint, is perhaps the most characteristic of all. In his hymn he has given us Calvinism at its most colourful—high churchmanship and pride in high churchmanship.

The text written over the hymn in the original is from *Isaiah* xxxiii : ' Look upon Zion, the city of our solemnities ; thine eyes shall see Jerusalem a quiet habitation, a tabernacle that shall not be taken down ; not one of the stakes thereof shall ever be removed, neither shall any of the cords thereof be broken ; but there the glorious Lord shall be unto us a place of broad rivers and streams ; wherein shall go no galley with oars, neither shall gallant ship pass by ' (the galleys and gallant ships being, of course, battleships and destroyers). This is the essence of high churchmanship, not that a man believes in this or that form of religious practice, but that he is proud and glad to be a member of the Church, and cannot think of a religious life without that membership. But *Isaiah* xxxiii is only the starting-point of the hymn. In the very first words we have a reminiscence of Psalm 87. 3, ' Glorious things are spoken of thee, thou city of

God,' and a line or two later of Psalm 132. 14 : ' This is
my rest for ever : here will I dwell, for I have desired it.'
Then we have, once again, the ' Rock of Ages ' (see 25),
which in this context brings together the associations of
the Rock who is Christ, the Rock on which the Church
was founded in history (the spirit of Christ in the Apostles—
St Matthew xvi. 18), and the rock which kept from destruction the house that was built on it (*St Matthew* vii. 24).

All this mosaic of Scriptural thought is laid together to
form a pattern ; and from that pattern we gather the
ground of the Christian's pride in being a member of the
Church. Jerusalem is (see 48) the type of the Church, and
membership of the Church is in a sense citizenship. Pride
in that membership is a kind of spiritual patriotism ; and
just as the noble impulse of patriotism is so easily perverted
into imperialism or jingoism, so, of course, there will always
be some Christians who stridently advertise the honours,
and secretly avoid the responsibilities and tensions, of their
calling. Our author leaves us no grounds for accusing
him of preaching religious jingoism. See what he goes on
to say.

First he tells us very clearly (verse 2) what is the source
of all that in which the Christian takes pride. It is not in
his own goodness, not, ultimately, in the heroisms and
precious martyrdoms which make church history glorious.
Ultimately it is in the Love of God. So again he plunges
into his Bible, and in a couple of lines about ' living waters '
suggests to us the 46th Psalm, ' There is a river, the streams
whereof make glad the city of God,' *Ezekiel* xlvii, where
the prophet shares with us his vision of a stream issuing
' for the healing of the nations ' from the gate of the house
of God, and *Revelation* xxii, where Ezekiel's image is used
to show us that this is the shape of things as, in the ultimate
purpose of God, they will be. There is, along with all
this, the thought of the clear and refreshing water which
issued from the rock in the wilderness when Moses struck
it (*Exodus* xvii. 6).

This again is Calvinism, and essential Christianity. No
Christian can seriously believe that the security and joy

of the faith are his because he has deserved them.   They are his, he might say in modern speech, by his extraordinary good fortune.   If a man denies this, and says that in the fellowship of the Church he enjoys what he has earned and is entitled to enjoy, the only answer is that he has not yet had any experience at all of the measure of the joy that can come from God through the Church ;   he has, in fact, only had pleasure on the scale of what human effort can earn.   We are just not talking about that kind of pleasure.   What man in love ever ascribed that heavenly grace to his own attractiveness or goodness ?   What man, taken up into heaven by the music of Palestrina or Mozart, gave his first thought to his own remarkable degree of musical culture ?   Similarly we ask, what man who has really come to know Christ wants to talk about his own meritoriousness ?   ' Ye have not chosen me ;   I have chosen you,' said Christ, and the Christian wants to say nothing beyond that.   The central thing in the Christian's response to the Gospel is gratitude, not personal claim ;   for gratitude is precisely the answer to grace, and grace is the fabric of the Church.   Grace is the texture of God's dealings with men.   The ' water ' here and in all Biblical symbolism means grace, and in the practical life of the Church the water of baptism signifies the grace of God which is renewed for us from the beginning of each life, the grace which ' well supplies ' the sons and daughters of the King.

The third verse turns to the obligations of the Christian. Towards God, his central thought is gratitude.   Towards men, his central thought is humility, and humility is gathered up in the thought of ' priesthood '.   Peter (if we may assume it was he), writing to the Church at large, coined the famous phrase, ' a royal priesthood ' (*I Peter* ii. 9), and in the *Revelation* we hear twice that Christ has made his friends ' priests and kings to God ' (i. 6 and v. 10). All men who covenant with Christ become kings and priests responsible to God ;   and if anybody ever wanted an exposition of that famous dictum, why here it is in the hymn :

'Tis his love his people raises
Over self to reign as kings,
And, as priests, his solemn praises
Each for a thankoffering brings.

A king is one who rules, and the ruler in the Kingdom
of God is one who serves ; characteristic of such a responsible attitude to life is self-discipline, an harmonious and
integrated manner of living, wise and prudent, gentle in
season, and, when the occasion demands, inflexible and loyal.
That is the royalty of Christian living. As for priesthood,
which in ancient times was very closely associated with
royalty, it is that in virtue of which a man makes sacrifice ;
the primitive priest lays the suffering and the loss on another
(a bull or a goat or a lamb), but he who is allowed to share
in the priesthood of Christ takes the suffering and loss on
himself ; the ' priest ' of the City, the ' priest ' of modern
life is he who will go anywhere, do anything, give up anything, endure anything, risk anything that the good of his
neighbour may be served. Paul wrote once, ' I could wish
myself accursed from Christ for my brethren ' (*Romans* ix.
3) ; even that he would risk and tolerate in order that the
people whom he so highly regarded might share his knowledge of Christ. That is priesthood. The scientist who risks
his health or his life in experiments designed for the advance
of medicine is a priest. The citizen who casts his reputation
to the winds and invites the contempt of his fellow-citizens in
the cause of some great social reform is a priest. Wherever
rights are foregone, innocent things are given up, comfort
is exchanged for hardship, for the sake of men's good,
there is priesthood, and that, says the hymn, is the texture
of the Church's life—service and sacrifice. Writing of the
City of God in different language but with the same thought,
F. T. Palgrave puts it thus :

Thou art where'er the proud in humbleness melts down ;
Where self itself yields up and martyrs wear their crown ;
Where faithful souls possess themselves in perfect peace.

For in these details of life there may be reflected, through
membership of the Church, that high-priesthood in which

Jesus took to himself all the sorrow and forsakenness of
the world. That is the pattern of all priesthood.

The last verse of the hymn sets out the consequences of
this kind of living. ' If I am a member of this community—
if, that is, I have the great good fortune to be a member
of it—the keynote of my life will be praise, and the way
will be attended by great joy.' The great value of this
last verse is its high-spirited repudiation of a gloomy
religiosity or a fugitive other-worldliness. There is no
high-mindedness here, not much high-toned Hollywood
religion. ' Solid joys and lasting pleasures ' : while the
man of the world builds bigger and bigger storehouses for
his accumulating property, while he pursues a happiness
which is always round the next corner, the Christian will
show him how to live, for he knows what sort of pleasure
is really solid and lasting, and how to find it. And if a
man believes that that is the truth about the Christian life,
why pretend otherwise ?

The great thing about ' Glorious things ' is that it communicates the gaiety and toughness of Christianity. No
hymn more jubilantly disposes of the legend that the
Christian faith puts a premium on vagueness, ineffectiveness,
other-worldliness and the accent of the stage parson. There
is something in the best and most full-blooded sense vulgar
about it all, vulgar in the sense in which the eighteenth
century was vulgar. But then the disciples of Jesus were
thought very vulgar by the mincing and inhibited ecclesi-
astics of the day. John Wesley was far from being thought
respectable in his earlier days because of the enthusiasm
he imparted to his followers.

' Christianity ', said William Temple, ' is the most
materialistic of religions.' Solid joys and lasting pleasures,
together with living sacrifices and the royalty of service—
that is the Christian manifesto. That is what this hymn
teaches men to expect from the Church.

38

Bernhart Severin Ingemann (1789–1862)
Trans. Sabine Baring-Gould (1834–1924)

IGJENNEM NAT OG TRÆNGSEL

Through the night of doubt and sorrow
  Onward goes the pilgrim band,
Singing songs of expectation,
  Marching to the promised land.
Clear before us through the darkness
  Gleams and burns the guiding light ;
Brother clasps the hand of brother,
  Stepping fearless through the night.

One the light of God's own presence
  O'er his ransomed people shed,
Chasing far the gloom and terror,
  Brightening all the path we tread :
One the object of our journey,
  One the faith which never tires,
One the earnest looking forward,
  One the hope our God inspires :

One the strain that lips of thousands
  Lift as from the heart of one ;
One the conflict, one the peril,
  One the march in God begun :
One the gladness of rejoicing
  On the far eternal shore,
Where the one almighty Father
  Reigns in love for evermore.

Onward, therefore, pilgrim brothers,
  Onward with the cross our aid ;
Bear its shame, and fight its battle,
  Till we rest beneath its shade.
Soon shall come the great awakening,
  Soon the rending of the tomb ;
Then the scattering of all shadows,
  And the end of toil and gloom.

H.H.L. 281, 295

Travelling

GLANCING through one of our well-known modern hymn-books, I find that hymns translated from other languages are distributed among ten languages ; of these, four may be called 'dead languages' (ancient Greek, Latin, Syriac and medieval Erse), and among the other six, German accounts for all but seven hymns. Seven hymns are left, and five languages —it is remarkable how little traffic there is between the Protestant nations, let alone the Christian nations, in hymnody. But 'Through the night of doubt and sorrow' is a song translated from the Danish by the author of 'Onward, Christian soldiers', and is the only Danish hymn in common use in this country. The translation is bracing enough in places, but the original is a powerful battle song, full of great words that ring and rattle like armour.

> Igjennem Nat og Traengsel
> Gaaer Sjoelens Valfartsgang
> Med stille Haab og Loengsel,
> Med dyb Forventningssang.

You need not be intimate with the Danish language to be captivated by the zest and energy of that.

'Through the night', as we know it, is a song of hope. It is a song rather than a hymn, for it is not addressed to God, and its subject matter is human hope and aspiration. It is one of the 'Tipperaries' of the Christian army—not profound or searching, like 'The Church's one foundation', not scripturally jubilant, like 'Glorious things', but simply a series of familiar and simple thoughts that clamour to be sung to some rousing tune.

The *motif* is hope, rather than (as one might perhaps think at first) unity. What the hymn has to say about unity is, when you look at it, largely beside the point.

The overall impression it creates is one of movement and pilgrimage, and in doing that it does good service.

True, there is more than a hint of a famous passage in *Ephesians* iv in its central verses. ' There is one body and one spirit, even as ye are called in one hope of your calling ; one Lord, one faith, one baptism, one God and Father of all, who is above all, and through all, and in you all.' But that is not really what the hymn is saying. Paul is dogmatic ; the hymn is experimental. It may be called an expansion of ' One hope ', but no more.

The principle of unity here, then, is hope. ' One object, one faith (here meaning loyalty), one looking-forward, one hope, one song, one conflict, one peril, one march, one final rejoicing.' It is one thing to say, as Paul says, ' As the Godhead is many and also one, so the church is many and also one,' and another to say, as the hymn says, ' We are all in this together.' But this is not to say that the hymn is trivial or unnecessary to faith. No Church member can be anything but profited by being reminded that he is a traveller, and that his journey is not a fruitless one.

There is a great temptation to believe that the journey is fruitless, that the figure of a journey is an illusion, that the goal is like the end of the rainbow, and that the proper course for a prudent man is to dig himself in. This temptation is very clearly exposed in the story of the Exodus ; at every point the people who were moving from Egypt to Palestine were subject to almost invincible inertia, even to a positive urge to turn back and pretend that the journey had never started, and give themselves up again to slavery. But Moses said (as we understand from *Deuteronomy* i. 5), ' Turn, and take your journey.' Peter, voicing the thoughts of the two other disciples at the Transfiguration, wanted to establish a camp there on the hill, away from the world, and stay there for ever. But Jesus, with no further words, hurried his friends back into the troubled and muddy stream of life.

This applies equally to men and to the Church as a whole. In its present context we must apply it to the Church, as the hymn does. Oddly enough, we find Biblical

authority for this in that very passage in *I Peter* from which
'Glorious things' (37) takes its thought about the royal
priesthood.   As soon as he has called his people a royal
priesthood, the Apostle goes on, ' I beseech you as strangers
and pilgrims '—as if he could see the good folk misunderstanding his ' royal priesthood ' and rushing off then and
there to get themselves measured for crowns and cassocks.
Strangers and pilgrims, travelling light, ' abstain from
fleshly lusts '.   'Strangers and pilgrims', echoes the *Epistle
to the Hebrews*, saying that the great quality common to all
the real heroes of history was that they admitted themselves to be ' strangers and pilgrims on the earth '.   The
men who make history and do the will of God are those
who are content to keep moving, to travel light, not looking
back with regrets for the pleasures and satisfactions that
are past, and not encumbering themselves with heavy loads
of rights, honours, and ambitions.   When our Lord sent
out his disciples on their first experimental campaign of
evangelism, he emphasized this same necessity of travelling
light, of not staying anywhere too long, of being un-
encumbered with preconceived thoughts and prepared
speeches.   And it is interesting to observe that in a document
a little later than the Gospels (known as the *Didache*), which
is by way of being a tract for the times for the Church of
about A.D. 150, it is roundly asserted that if an itinerant
preacher stays more than two days in the same place you
can write him off as an impostor.   The danger of digging
in, material and spiritual, was, and remains (in our different
context) a very real one.

The special truth which we may associate with this
hymn is that all people who live like that, who love the
scenery of the Way without insisting that the first pleasant
valley is the end of the road, all who taste but do not cling
to the joys of life, all who steer between blind, fanatical
and proud asceticism and spineless and unenterprising
sloth—all these are bound into a community of faith.
To put it at its lowest, such people are men of like mind,
men of humour and peace, men with leisure to be gracious
because they spend no time worrying about themselves,

men with strength to rise to the world's needs because they are not weighed down with pomp. They are efficient soldiers of Christ, good disciples, faithful apostles. It is of these that the hymn speaks so eloquently—men who are strangers and sojourners.

Here and there you will find a Church that can measure up to this. Two questions may be put to any local community. One is, ' Are you strangers and travellers in the world, alert for every special and crying need of your own generation, or are you entrenched in a dug-out which you prepared in the year 1860 ? ' ; and then, if that question be well answered, there is this further, ' Have you so lively a faith in the eternal Christ who is Head of the Church that you will remain through the coming years as alert and unfettered as you are now ? Or will that for which you are now respected and loved become an anachronism ? ' Where this question can also be answered with confidence, there you have a Church which is relevant, adaptable in its practices to a changing situation at a moment's notice, in bondage neither to buildings nor to worries nor to customs, sober, vigilant, effective, wise, obedient, and faithful.

39

S. J. Stone (1839–1908)

The Church's one foundation
  Is Jesus Christ her Lord ;
She is his new creation
  By water and the word :
From Heav'n he came and sought her
  To be his holy bride ;
With his own blood he bought her,
  And for her life he died.

Elect from every nation,
  Yet one o'er all the earth,
Her charter of salvation
  One Lord, one faith, one birth,
One holy name she blesses,
  Partakes one holy food,
And to one hope she presses
  With every grace endued.

Though with a scornful wonder
  Men see her sore opprest,
By schisms rent asunder,
  By heresies distrest,
Yet Saints their watch are keeping,
  Their cry goes up, ' How long ? '
And soon the night of weeping
  Shall be the morn of song.

Mid toil, and tribulation,
  And tumult of her war,
She waits the consummation
  Of peace for evermore ;
Till with the vision glorious
  Her longing eyes are blest,
And the great Church victorious
  Shall be the Church at rest.

Yet she on earth hath union
  With God the Three in One,
And mystic sweet communion
  With those whose rest is won :
O happy ones and holy !
  Lord, give us grace that we,
Like them the meek and lowly,
  On high may dwell with thee.

H.H.L. 113–5, 247

How Long?

WE have travelled far enough now in the course of these papers to hazard some kind of judgment on the constituents of a great hymn. Perhaps the quality of greatness (which is not precisely the same as the quality of ' goodness ') is the product of two cardinal virtues—that of having plenty to say, and that of saying it in a manner which will at once transfer the message of the hymn to the mind and the will and the imagination of the singer. What is said must be true, and faithful to the thought of Scripture and to the teaching of the Church ; but the ordinary Christian singer demands also that there be in his favourite hymns a certain thrust of energy which will not merely commend the hymn to his attention but write it on his memory. Well, if all this be anywhere near the truth, then ' The Church's one foundation ' is one of the dozen greatest hymns in English, one of the two or three greatest on the subject of the Church, and beyond question the greatest on that subject to be written within the last hundred years. The first time you sing it, you realize that it is saying something of importance and saying it with authority ; the fiftieth time you sing it you begin to realize what a depth of doctrine and truth there is in it.

This hymn was a direct consequence of a grievous controversy in the Church of England (as I have recorded in *Hymns and Human Life*, pp. 113 ff.). In the year when it was written (1864) Englishmen were undergoing great heart-searching concerning the nature of the Church and of its authority. It has four things to say, of which three are derived from Scripture. The fourth has nothing to do with Scripture and is the boldest and most moving of all the things the hymn has to say. These four propositions are these.

First : the Church is directly derived from Jesus Christ, and has a duty to Jesus Christ.

Second : the Church directly emerges from history, and has a duty to history.

Third : Jesus Christ loved and loves the Church.

Fourth : the Church is in schism.

(We might add for completeness a fifth proposition : that the Church is a company of travellers in time, but we have already said enough about that to enable us to omit it here.)

1. 'The Church's one foundation is Jesus Christ, her Lord.' At once the hymn takes the highest ground. Indeed, the sheer dogmatic force of this opening sweeps us through the second and most difficult couplet before we have time to realize what we have said. This is a thoroughly Scriptural opening—' Other foundation can no man lay than that is laid, even Jesus Christ,' wrote the Apostle (*I Corinthians* iii. 11) echoing what had stood written in the Psalter, ' The stone which the builders rejected is become the head stone of the corner ' (Psalm 118. 22). This at once contradicts the notion that the Church is a kind of social contract, and the not uncommon error that Jesus Christ never meant to found a Church.

No good will come to anybody from taking the line that what Jesus had to say was essentially simple and obvious, and that certain people have deliberately obscured it all and made it difficult in order to ensure for themselves (who alone understand it) a kind of superiority or sense of election. There are some, for example, who say that the Apostle Paul has overlaid the simple Gospel with a great deal of academic theology, and confounded the humble believer. The versatile Mr Robert Graves is just now taking even higher ground, and attributing this learned and unscrupulous perversion of Gospel truth to the Evangelists themselves. There have been many, too, in the generation just past, who have taken the view that the Church itself is an unnecessary complication of the Gospel.

Human nature, in a way, makes such views plausible. It is just *like* people, you would say, to make the Gospel difficult in order to gain credit for their skill in interpreting it ; it is just *like* people to turn the company of believers into a clique or an aristocracy. It is only too probable that it happened just as these critics say it happened. But it has not happened so. History is against it. The Bible (if you care to take any of it seriously) is against it. Experience, which must include the grace of Christ as well as the perversity of nature, is against it.

We may not claim too much for the Church. We may not claim that, as it stands at present, the visible Church is identical with the Kingdom of heaven—though we may indeed claim that the politics of the Kingdom are more relevant to the Church's daily life than the politics of the secular world. We may not claim that the Church as it stands, the visible Church, is as Jesus meant it to be. But scripture and experience insist that we admit the Church to be part of the purpose of Christ ; we assume, if we say no more than this, that Christ had in mind a community of men in God's confidence which should do for the world at large (and do better and more completely) what the ancient people of Israel had been called to do for the world in their day. If we admit that for the setting forth of God's truth about life and about the world, a community is needed, that for such a purpose a series of individuals who take no notice of each other and prophesy in a vacuum is insufficient, then from that alone we are led straight to the proposition that Jesus founded the Church.

2. But the second couplet brings this picture out into the round. ' She is his new creation ', it says, ' by water and the word.' This is a compendious and technical way of saying that the Church is involved with history—not merely with history since the birth of Jesus, but with all history. We must expand this.

' By water and the word ' means by baptism and by preaching. To say that Jesus new-created the Church by water and the word means that Jesus new-created it by *his* baptism and *his* preaching ; with the additional thought that Jesus not merely spoke the Word but *was* the Word—that his preaching and his life were one.

Now the baptism of Jesus was the public authentication of his Messiahship. John the Baptist was a prophet of the old-fashioned kind ; that is how his contemporaries thought of him. He had revived a technique they thought was quite dead. The prophet's technique was to interpret events and show people their religious consequences. (A prophet is not primarily a man who foretells the future ; he is a man who interprets the present in terms of its consequences.) A prophet would always base his observations on what, by his obedient insight, he knew to be the purpose of God ; and he always implied (you can find this all the way from Elijah to Daniel) that God had a purpose which he was going to bring to a consummation in sending a Messiah, an ' anointed one ', an authentic and absolutely unquestionable bearer of his full message or Word to the world. John the Baptist revived this way of speaking ; but with a difference. Whereas Isaiah and Jeremiah and the rest of them had had to be content to say, ' The Lord will send his Messiah in his good time,' John the Baptist was able, one day, to say, ' Here is the Messiah coming along the road now : Behold the Lamb of God, that taketh away the sins of the world.'

The baptism which Jesus then underwent was a gesture in which Jesus accepted the whole of history ; he involved himself with all the hopes of his race. The ceremony itself symbolized a new beginning, a washing clean of the slate of history, and yet at the same time it symbolized his going down into history and accepting it and committing himself to it. Thereafter Jesus followed out the responsibility which he had taken on himself ; and in the course of his ministry he made it as plain as he could make it that he had come to bring into focus all the hopes of the religious men who had gone before ; that he was going, you might say, to act out history himself ; that he has something to say to every aspect of human nature that appears in history. In his words and acts he confirmed all the good and judged all the evil that ordinary men and women had known and done and been involved in.

There is a mysterious verse in *St John* which will throw light where we most want it here. ' Abraham ', said Jesus, ' rejoiced to see my day.' You might put that truth by saying that if Abraham, Jacob, Moses, Isaiah, Jeremiah, the Psalmists, and all the other heroes had been present when Jesus came on the earth, every one of them would have said, ' Yes ! This is what I meant.' The best in every faithful man of history would say ' Amen ' to Jesus. If we follow out the details of the Gospel narratives, we find that in many cases Jesus deliberately seems to have said things and done things just in the manner that would bring to the popular mind some great event in their history —like the feeding of the multitude in a lonely and desert place and the penetrating manner in which he would quote their scriptures (the Old Testament), especially those they knew best from their worship, the Psalms, to confirm his Messiahship, and show them that this really is what they had all been looking for. In sum, the life of Jesus is nailed down to history at every point. In its consummation, the life of Jesus was precisely, and in the most dreadful sense, nailed down to history.

Jesus, then, is historic not only in having been a real person but in the special responsibility and saving ministry he took on himself in relation to history. He is Everyman's saviour, and history is Everyman's story.

The Church is historic in just that sense. The new kingdom, the new outlook, the new life which Jesus brought to the world is expressed in a community bound together not by regulations but by a common loyalty to the love of Christ, and a common sense of being in God's confidence. And being historic the Church carries on the rite of baptism in order that for every new child brought into the world the ancient and eternal truth may be repeated. The Church, new-created by *that* Baptism, is new-created by each repeated baptism. Similarly, the Church, new-created in time by that Word, is new-created by the preaching of the word that makes effective in contemporary minds the ancient truth. In the Church it is not act alone nor speech alone, but speech and act, Word and Sacrament.

The besetting temptation of Christians is to let slip the belief that the Church is in this sense historic ; for if one can believe that the Church is not historic, not bound up with the story of Everyman, then one can also believe that the Church has no obligations to history now. It can then become a society of people who are interested in the same thing, a society separated from history and from life. To the eyes of the profane that is just what it appears to be—a pious society. There is little consciousness in the popular mind that the Church is as much a part of life as food, drink, the weather, birth, marriage, and death are part of it. There is little in the conduct of the Church that impresses on men of the world that the Church is integrally built into life and history in exactly the same sense, and by the same Creator, that the mountains and the sea and the sun are built into it. But it is the truth, ' She is his new creation, by water and the word ' ; by those historic acts in the ministry of Jesus, and by their repetition and re-enactment in the Church's liturgies, the Church was re-created, and continually is re-created.

3. Now the Biblical text which suggested this form of words is to be found in *Ephesians* v. 26, where the Apostle writes, ' Christ loved the Church, and gave himself for it, that he might sanctify and cleanse it with the washing of water by the word.' The truth on which all the rest hangs is that Christ loved, and loves, the Church. Not only is the Church built into history as a chimney or a heating-system is built into a house. We have also the organic image that tells us that the Church is built into the life and purpose of Christ as a bride is built into the life of her husband, or a bridegroom into the life of his wife, and for reasons not dissimilar. How pale is all the doctrine we have so far rehearsed, compared with this, that ' From heaven he came and sought her to be his holy bride.' Christ founded the church ; the Church is built into history. Yes, we have now had a picture, and then a sculpture in the round. But now the whole thing is brought to life. It was all because God loved the world. The Church is no foundation made simply to the commemorating of a founder now dead ; it is not simply a society which human history cannot do without. It is those things, but this as well—the ' bride of Christ '.

Experience confirms this too. The more we look at the Church the more we are likely to criticize it ; and the more we find fault with it, the more astounding it is that Christ should have troubled with it at all. The Old Testament tells how God had patience with disgruntled and inefficient and stupid people of our own sort ; the New Testament and all subsequent history tells how Christ loves and bears with the Church. In spite of the Church's faithlessness so often repeated, Christ still shares with it an intimacy and a love which the Bible does not shrink from comparing with the love of man and woman. It is still true that in the Church (in its fellowship and its worship and its sacrificial social activity and all the rest) a man may come to know the mind of Christ, and may be enabled to make known his own mind to Christ, more completely than he could know and be known through the most devout life outside the Church. The metaphor of marriage is pressed to the uttermost. Christ's relation with the Church is one of utter self-giving. In this world of time Christ so trusts the Church, and so commits himself to the Church, that his continuing ministry is incomplete without it. The Church is founded in the self-giving and self-surrender of Christ.

4. And with all this, the Church is in schism. What, then, is ' the Church ' of which we have written, and of which this hymn is bidding us sing ? The Church is the whole company of men who believe in Christ and are, through the operation of the Holy Spirit, in the confidence of God. Men cannot make covenant with God without making covenant with one another ; men cannot need God and not need one another ; men cannot (as it is written in *I John* iv) claim to love God and hate one another. And yet we have with us the sorrow of schism.

Now ' The Church's one foundation ' says much about the grounds of the Church's unity. ' Elect from every nation, yet one o'er all the earth '—that is the classic principle of catholicity. When the word ' catholic ' was first coined it was used to contradict those who thought

that men of different races and nations might, because of
that difference, go out of communion with the Mother
Church. ' One Lord, one faith, one birth ' is very much
what the Apostle writes in *Ephesians* iv, ' One Lord, one
faith, one baptism '. In the worship of the one God,
Father, Son, and Holy Ghost, and in the celebration of
the Lord's Supper, the Church is one throughout the world.
And yet there is schism.

Schism and heresy are the two things that divide the
Church. Technically, to embrace heresy is to deny some
Biblical or credal doctrine (whether or not another be
substituted for it) while to go into schism is to separate
from the Church on a point of discipline or practical
procedure. But technicalities are of little use just here.
Controversial matter is even more impertinent at this
point.

Let this, then, be enough for the present. ' The Church's
one foundation ', in that brave verse which few modern
editors dare print in their hymn-books, states the fact of
schism, and calls the Church to repentance. All Christians
are bound to acknowledge schism as a fact and to be sorry
for it. Men have made various attempts to come to terms
with the grievous fact of disunity. It has long been clear
that it is not enough for all who dissent at any point from
a given interpretation of the mind of Christ to be *eo ipso*
unchurched. No better sense can be made of the opinion
that each man must be entirely his own guide to orthodoxy.
One thing, then, we venture to say here with all circum-
spection, and another we will say with every possible
dogmatic emphasis.

First, it is probably more conducive to a neighbourly
and penitential attitude concerning those divisions which
frustrate the Church's witness that all Christians regard
themselves as in a sense ' in schism '. That proposition will
be interpreted by some in one sense and by some in another ;
that perhaps is all we can expect. But suppose a man
takes the view that there is, here and now, an orthodoxy
from which some have lapsed, and to which all would
conform but for the sin and confusion that history and

the world have produced in us ; to such a man the dissenting or unorthodox or non-Catholic bodies will be as a lapsed or defaulting member under discipline—excommunicate, perhaps, and separated from the fellowship, but the object of constant prayer and penitence and fasting within the fellowship from which he has separated. If, on the other hand, another wishes to be associated with the view of Martin Luther that there is an ' invisible ' Church of faithful men, whose membership is known only to God, and which is by definition indivisible, while the visible Church continues to suffer from the sorrows of disunity, his hope will be in looking to the time when the invisible Church and the visible are one. Both views are held, and the hymn gives guidance to men of either persuasion. ' Their cry goes up, " How long ? " '—all men of goodwill share in that.

But while we may not here go further nor be more dogmatic on that matter, on this other we can be quite firm. The seeds of that disunity which is wholly displeasing to God and which continues the sufferings of the Crucified are not organizational difficulties or technical disputes, but the ancient sins to which all men are heirs, pride, wrath, greed, fear of the truth, fear of losing face, self-love, and all the rest. We wrestle not with flesh and blood but with spiritual wickedness and the powers of darkness. These are the powers of darkness, the commonplace and dreary sins of common life. They assault the Church. They are the source of its distresses. None is free from them ; none dare say that in respect of these he stands in no need of the judgment and teaching of God the Holy Spirit.

What no Christian can ever deny is what this hymn positively urges, that the present divisions of the Church have much of deliberate sin in them, and that the prayers and the work of Christians must be devoted to the forgiving and the eradication of that.

Where is disunity and sinful division ? Is it in the fact that members of one communion cannot meet at the Lord's Table with members of another ? That is not sin—that is.a sorry consequence, but it is not sin. Here is sin exposed —when at the Armistice Day service in the parish church the Methodist minister is invited to read the Lesson and the Congregationalist is offended because he was not invited. The real prayer is not ' Take away our divisions ' but ' Forgive us our trespasses.'

40

Sabine Bering-Gould (1834–1924)

Onward, Christian soldiers,
  Marching as to war,
With the Cross of Jesus
  Going on before.
Christ, the royal master,
  Leads against the foe ;
Forward into battle
  See his banners go.
  Onward, Christian soldiers,
    Marching as to war,
  With the Cross of Jesus
    Going on before.

At the sign of triumph
  Satan's host doth flee ;
On then, Christian soldiers,
  On to victory !
Hell's foundations quiver
  At the shout of praise ;
Brothers, lift your voices,
  Loud your anthems raise.

Like a mighty army
  Moves the Church of God ;
Brothers, we are treading
  Where the saints have trod.
We are not divided,
  All one body we,
One in hope and doctrine,
  One in charity.

                    H.H.L. 6, 279

The Army

THERE is no more colourful or cheerful moment in the worship of the Church than that at which the Church, or its representatives, set out in procession. Whether it be a procession of witness in a Lancashire mill-town or a solemn procession in church before the Eucharist or after Evensong, the procession is essentially a great moment in the Church's life. And ' Onward, Christian soldiers ' is the simplest and the most inspiriting of processional hymns. It was written for just such an occasion—a children's festival at Horbury Bridge, Yorkshire, in 1864—and it has all the colour and humanity, together with the cheerful tune, that is wanted for it.

It is no use looking for profundity in such lines as these ; but then the procession—especially the open-air one—is not a profound occasion. It is one of the more creaturely and childlike things that the Church does. Indeed, neither of the two reasons for holding a procession—special celebration of one's own Church's prowess or prestige, and special celebration of some great event in the Church's year, is a very recondite reason, even if one seems, on the face of it, to be somewhat more creditable than the other. But ' Onward, Christian soldiers ', though it does not go deep into things, has this special quality in good measure, that it provides a good, memorable, spirited march, and small children usually love it.

The military image of the Church is, of course, the whole content of the hymn, and there are some who do not care for it for that reason. ' Like a mighty army moves the Church of God ', many who can accept the Pauline picture of the Christian as soldier (for which see 34) find the image of the Church as an army a little crude. The trouble is that the days in which processional pomp and discipline are especially associated with the Queen's Forces have in this latter age overlapped with the days in which the whole business of the Forces has become in the eyes of many (in a sense, in the eyes of most) immoral and ugly. The horror of war has wholly overshadowed its glamour for most of us, and that has put ' Onward, Christian soldiers ' under an eclipse.

But in these present days the matter is not even as simple as that. In a sense, of course, we have left behind the days of military glamour ; its appearance on ceremonial occasions like the Coronation is, to some, little more than a pleasant archaism. ' The army ' means, to modern Englishmen, Korea and Malaya, not some civic procession. We have even left behind the days of the army's war. Conscription and civil defence have done much in that process ; war became, in 1940, a matter of the indiscriminate slaughter and dispossession of civilians as well as soldiers. Nobody is outside the immediate war-situation ; the only distinctions are between men and women who give their whole time to the business of warfare (or ' defence '), men and women who give part of their time to it, and men and women who are dragged into it. Nobody is outside it.

All this has obscured that aspect of the soldier which forms the inspiration of this hymn. The old-fashioned virtues of the soldier tend to be forgotten or ascribed to people of some other walk of life. But there have been two striking cases in these last years in which precisely those virtues, resource, discipline and courage, have been made over to the necessities of peace-time emergencies. The American Air Force at Harrow in October 1952, and the men of the Services in the East Anglian floods in February 1953, provide examples, not yet faded from the public mind, which have done much towards rescuing the military from those associations which two world wars had brought. Emergencies of this kind, of course, together with many other less spectacular modes of serving the human race at large, provide a rational future for the military, and thoughts of this kind make Christians able to think of the ' Christian soldier ' once more without cynicism and without censure.

The truth is that international war is a perverse parody of that natural and supernatural warfare which is the

business of every living and intelligent man.   Suffering and
disease have to be fought ; sin and its consequences have
to be fought.   Courage as well as charity is part of the
Christian's equipment.   This we have said before, but now
we add, it is part of the Church's equipment.   ' Onward,
Christian soldiers ' is a simple hymn of the Church's courage,
that courage in virtue of which it may, in every generation,
be a Church.   The processional associations of the hymn
give it also the sense of *purpose* ; for to sing it presupposes
the conviction that the Church is, or ought to be, going
somewhere, making headway, claiming conquests in the
holy war.

There are men alive who will tell you, if you press them
to such intimate confessions, that in time of war (either of
the two World Wars) they *lived* more fully than they ever
had a chance to live in time of peace.   There are men who
' found themselves ' in the Battle of Britain or the Ypres
Salient ; for they found in such days that somebody needed
them, that there was something they could do and do well.
They found that life had shape and purpose, and on their
return to civilian life they found that it paled again into
a mere ' existence ' (a distinction which we drew, in another
connection, under No. 7).   There are many who have had
their vitality drained off by the triviality and aimlessness of
what they found peace-time life to be.   It is a sorry thing
that those who profess the ' calling ' of Christianity (and a
' calling ' is a faith that gives shape and purpose to life)
have managed to avoid communicating this spiritual thrust
and challenge to such as these.   It has meant a wicked
waste of human virtue.   ' Onward, Christian soldiers ',
simple and naïve though it may be, communicates just that
purposefulness which is at the heart of the Christian calling.
The Church is on the move here, carrying the truth into the
world.

And the Church on the move is the Church asking for
trouble.   The Church on the move is the Church prepared
to fight, to fight ignorance with the artillery of theology and
want with the air-lift of charity.   There is something to be
said, once in a while, for a battle-song, a ' Tipperary ',

which heartens the Church and makes it say, ' Woe to anybody who stands in the way of this, for we mean business.'
This, rather than the lack of comprehensiveness in such an
expression as ' We are not divided,' is the thing to value in
this hymn.   There is a place in an honest man's religion for
vulgar enthusiasm and crude courage.   The rest of the faith
will temper their asperities.

And behind the rattle and tramp of the military images
there stands he whom medieval poetry and carol have so
often compared to a soldier, or a knight of chivalry.   Intro-
ducing the great pageant of the Crucifixion, Langland wrote
in *Piers Plowman*, ' This gentle Jesus will *joust.*'   The springing imagination that could think of Jesus as a knight could
also think of the drama of our Redemption as a dance.
There is more than modern battledress and bombs in the
military image.

> I have a Captain, and the heart
>   Of every private man
> Has drunk in valour from his eyes
>   Since first the war began.
> He is most merciful in fight,
> And of his scars a single sight
> The embers of our failing might
>   Into a flame can fan.[1]

---

[1] From T. T. Lynch's hymn, ' My faith it is an oaken staff ', *C.P.* 518.

41

Samuel Johnson (1822–82)

City of God, how broad and far
  Outspread thy walls sublime !
The true thy chartered freemen are,
  Of every age and clime.

One holy Church, one army strong,
  One steadfast high intent,
One voice to raise one triumph-song,
  One king omnipotent.

How purely hath thy speech come down
  From man's primeval youth !
How grandly hath thine empire grown
  Of freedom, love, and truth !

How gleam thy watch-fires through the night
  With never-fainting ray !
How rise thy towers, serene and bright,
  To meet the dawning day !

In vain the surges' angry shock,
  In vain the drifting sands ;
Unharmed upon the eternal rock
  The eternal city stands.

H.H.L. 115, 225-6, 242

The City

EDMUND CRISPIN, near the end of his detective story, *The Case of the Gilded Fly*, allows one of his characters to offer the judgment that the hymn, ' City of God ' (which at that point in the story is being performed in an Oxford college chapel) is one of the best pieces of religious verse in the language. There you have an epitome of the astonishing story of this hymn's popularity.

When Edmund Crispin (whom most people know to be a distinguished church musician in disguise) wrote his book the hymn had been in currency in this country hardly forty years. It is without doubt as indispensable a part of the English religious landscape now as ' Praise, my soul '. But it has achieved that eminence in little more than a generation. It is by a long way the ' youngest ' of the hymns in this collection, if the measure of its age be taken to be the length of its currency in England.

But that strange context of hymnological criticism which we quoted above tells us more. ' City of God ' is particularly popular in college chapels, cathedrals, and places of academic and ceremonious worship. It has a particular appeal to the lettered and critical who find the crudities of evangelical hymnody harsh and tiresome. It is, indeed, the theme-song of intelligent Anglican Christianity. It is, as Mr Crispin's character says it is, a first-rate piece of writing, lyrical and imaginative, wedded to a fine tune that makes the most of just those qualities.

At one or two points it makes contact with a hymn of such very different style as ' Glorious things of thee are spoken '. Those, to be sure, are the one or two points at which it makes contact with Scripture. The most obvious of these is in the thought that the Church is founded on a rock and therefore unshakable. But it is rather to be contrasted than compared with all the other well-known hymns on the Church ; for whereas they are all to some extent hymns of the biblical tradition, this is, first and last, a meditation written by a poet who rejoiced in the young, vigorous, and successful culture of America in the year 1864. The romanticism of ' Glorious things ' is biblical ; so in the end is the romanticism of ' Onward, Christian soldiers '. But the romanticism here is unashamedly literary, and nineteenth-century literary at that. The city has walls, indeed, but it is the walled city not of the Old Testament but of the historical novel. The city has unity, all its citizens are freemen, all rally to its defence, all live and work for the same ideals, all sing the same song (this one, as it has turned out), all wait for the ' dawning day ' ; and those who move towards the city are guided to it by the ' watch-fires ' (perhaps the richest imaginative touch in the whole hymn).

These are high and inspiriting thoughts, to be sure. On the strength of them this American hymn has pervaded the English singing Church to such an extent that it finds its way into a detective story written for men of literary culture and initiating the fictional career of a detective who is a Professor of English.

It is something of a coincidence, a coincidence that certainly provokes speculations into which we must not enter here, that this hymn was written in the same year (1864) as both ' Onward, Christian soldiers ' and ' The Church's one foundation '. It is, without doubt, more widely sung in the present time than either.

Now here is a matter which tends to the confusion of those who vilify contemporary popular taste in hymns. Looking over any list of popular hymns among English people such as that which forms the basis of this collection, one is bound to say that there is hardly one which does not stand up to careful scrutiny, whose obscurities or even inconsistencies cannot be illuminated by reference to Scripture. The popular English hymn is an eminently sensible (as well as often a highly pleasing) piece of writing, in which the words mean what they say. The popular English hymn is not, normally, impressionistic, however

strong may be the general tendency to sing and interpret
it impressionistically.

But ' City of God ' is an exception to all that, and a
triumphant exception. It is entirely ' impressionistic '.
It is freely imaginative. Nothing in the Bible, very little
in common life, corresponds to those ' watch-fires '. It will
profit little to try to harmonize that third verse with the
third verse of ' The Church's one foundation ', with the
lamentable history of schism and the drama and the pains
of scholarship. Nothing here corresponds to the rock-like
honesty or the innocent high spirits of the usual popular
English hymn. The object of ' City of God ' always was,
and remains, a propagandist object pure and simple. It
creates an impression, it releases a feeling of confidence, it
baptizes and tames for the service of the Church all the
nineteenth-century American rough-and-tumble, with its
shameless optimism, its popular heroics, its industrial and
political chivalry. It is as much a ' Tipperary ' of the
cultured as ' Onward, Christian soldiers ' is a ' Tipperary '
of the simple.

In consequence the hymn has its detractors. But the
remarkable and thankworthy fact is that the attempt to
bring the charge of sub-Christian impressionism that is
sometimes brought in this case has hardly ever been made
in the case of any other popular hymn. Even so, ' City of
God ' has great craftsmanship and masterly technique in
its favour, and a generous breadth of thought. It is the
point of contact between traditional public worship and
the highly cultivated detective-story reader, perhaps a
unique point of sympathy between many educated seekers
after truth and the felicity of congregational Christian
praise. It is not the one hymn a mature Christian would
care to take with him to a desert island ; but in that rich
context which the other popular hymns provide, it shines
like the attractive jewel it is ; and the Englishman's treasury
would be much the poorer without a hymn whose purpose
is, admittedly, largely ornamental, but whose power over
the wayward mind is, by the testimony of common experience, so penetrating.

42

John Ellerton (1826–93)

The day thou gavest, Lord, is ended,
  The darkness falls at thy behest ;
To thee our morning hymns ascended,
  Thy praise shall hallow now our rest.

We thank thee that thy Church unsleeping,
  While earth rolls onward into light,
Through all the world her watch is keeping,
  And rests not now by day or night.

As o'er each continent and island
  The dawn leads on another day,
The voice of prayer is never silent,
  Nor dies the strain of praise away.

The sun that bids us rest is waking
  Our brethren 'neath the western sky,
And hour by hour fresh lips are making
  Thy wondrous doings heard on high.

So be it, Lord ; thy throne shall never,
  Like earth's proud empires, pass away,
But stand and rule and grow for ever,
  Till all thy creatures own thy sway.

H.H.L. 84, 145

Empire

I DO not know of any other hymn which to me recalls so vividly the atmosphere of evensong in a country parish church as does 'The day thou gavest'. No doubt that is partly due to personal accidents ; and yet I set down the scrap of autobiography with the suspicion that many readers will find they agree. It breathes the very spirit of *Hymns Ancient and Modern*, of settled, orderly, decent family worship in a well-rooted society. People who know hardly half a dozen hymns by their number will be found quoting this as ' four-seven-seven ', which honourable number it has borne in *Hymns A. & M.* since the year 1875.

If this be not mere fantasy but, as I suspect it to be, part of the truth about 'The day thou gavest', it contrasts rather abruptly with two other facts about the hymn, one of which concerns its content and the other its history.

It is a hymn of the world-wide Church. It was written as a missionary hymn, and it celebrates the bright and heroic story of missionary expansion during the nineteenth century. The remarkable thing about it, of course, is that it does so in just the same terms that you would have used, at that date, to celebrate the expansion of the British Empire. ' An empire on which the sun never sets ' is precisely the thought that is here adapted to Christian use. The whole setting is geographical ; each verse invites the singer to contemplate the territorial extent of Christendom. That is almost certainly what has made the hymn so attractive in the remotest hamlets of the country—that and its boldly attractive tune. To stand up in your local church, whether it be a medieval treasure in the depths of Herefordshire or a down-town chapel in the slums of Bradford, and sing about the far-flung empire of Christ is a heartening and comforting experience. To be reminded of the vastness of the distances and achievements within the Christian fold is as good for the ordinary urban or rural Christian as it was

for Abraham (*Genesis* xv) to come out of his stuffy tent,
when he was feeling depressed and doubtful, and look at
the stars. But the danger, of course, is that that contemplation of the Christian empire may encourage a cosy
detachment like that with which a man in a cinema gazes
at a picture of the climbing of Mount Everest.

That brings us to the second point, the historical one.
It appears that the great popularity of ' The day thou
gavest ' dates from the year 1897, in which Queen Victoria
chose it for the Diamond Jubilee. That, we gather, was
what established it as an inseparable property of the English
singing congregation. The Diamond Jubilee was a pro-
digious festival of thanksgiving for all that Victorian England
had meant, and justly and rightly was that thanksgiving
decreed by the Queen. But that same occasion drew
another hymn from a very different author—it caused
Rudyard Kipling to write his *Recessional*. What penitence,
and power, and prophecy there were in these lines,

> Lo, all our pomp of yesterday
> Is one with Nineveh and Tyre
> Judge of the nations, spare us yet,
> Lest we forget. . . .

Nobody is going seriously to say that Kipling wrote in that
strain because he was feeling depressed that day. He wrote
that way because he had seen to the heart of that which he
had loved so much and sung with such zest. That day,
still a young man not far past thirty, Kipling had seen that
the heart of empire is ' Thine ancient sacrifice : a humble
and a contrite heart '. I take him for a prophet here, not
in that he foresaw the recession of English imperialism, but
in that he saw, at that moment, the difference between
responsible and irresponsible power.

We need not pursue that politically ; but in our missionary hymns that sing with triumph of the expanding church
as though it were a territorial Empire which ' belongs to us '
we shall all be led badly astray unless the note of penitence
and reverence be strongly sounded. For we are now presented with all the evidence required to persuade us, if we

had believed otherwise, that the Kingdom of God is not the same as the territorial extent of the Church administered by European missionaries. Any man who has been a missionary in China, and has now returned home, finds it difficult to sing 'The day thou gavest' without some reservations.

There are two things which, if they be entertained as living ideas among Christians, will ensure that 'The day thou gavest' will not contribute to the imperialistic error in respect of missions. The first of these can best be put in words which P. T. Forsyth used when preaching a sermon on behalf of the London Missionary Society a year or two after that Diamond Jubilee.

> The missions of a universal Father rest on a gospel of Father-hood sovereign by death. Is it a strange thing, then, that missionaries should daily die as other men do not? They minister at that world-altar of the Father. They are specially delivered unto death. You cannot separate the mission and the Passion in a universal Christianity. There is no world crown without the cross. . . . Let us go back from our social impatience to the effective way of faith—back from our exacting socialism, our moral rigorism, our critical severity, and the impotence of them all, to the holy, tender sacrifices of the Father's Cross, and the contagious obedience of the beloved Son.[1]

That is the heart of missionary work. Forsyth went on to give a cool and pitiless catalogue of numbers, so many dead here from fever, so many murdered there by savages. 'The percentage of premature loss,' he says gratingly, referring to the Central African Mission of that Society, 'is fifty-three.' Then he bursts out, 'I think my life a piece of disheartening self-indulgence when I read missionary biography and track its quavering red line of apostolic succession from the beginning till now.' That story, written in life and loss, is the story of the missionary work of the Church; that sacrifice is the mainspring of its empire.

The other thought is this, that the universal Church is

[1] P. T. Forsyth, *Missions in State and Church* (Hodder & Stoughton, 1908), pp. 35 and 41.

part of God's design, as it always was.   The empire of
Christ is already claimed, and the title-deeds of the universal
Church are already made out.   Men live in ignorance of it,
or in defiance of it ; but the fact is there.   The basic fact
is the empire, not the ignorance.   Men seek to coerce each
other into knowledge, to open other men's eyes by prestige
or by violence or by arts of which Christ takes no knowledge ; and the result is bitterness and suspicion.   The best
of us are but unskilled labour in a concern where the wisdom
of Christ is the only skill.   But this is right—this emendation
made in the last verse of the hymn, no doubt for mere
euphony, but with great justice all the same—' Thy kingdom stands, and grows for ever.'   The kingdom stands.
We may sing of a kingdom upon which the sun never sets,
for there has always been a kingdom on which the sun
never sets.

These considerations are enough to banish any imperialistic complacency from the missionary thought of the
Church.   Let the hymn be sung always at the foot of the
Cross, the Cross which is *the* mission from God to man, and
all will be well.

43

Lewis Hensley (1827–1905)

Thy kingdom come, O God ;
  Thy rule, O Christ, begin ;
Break with thine iron rod
  The tyrannies of sin.

Where is thy reign of peace,
  And purity, and love ?
When shall all hatred cease,
  As in the realms above ?

When comes the promised time
  That war shall be no more,
Oppression, lust, and crime
  Shall flee thy face before ?

We pray thee, Lord, arise,
  And come in thy great might ;
Revive our longing eyes,
  Which languish for thy sight.

Men scorn thy sacred name,
  And wolves devour thy fold ;
By many deeds of shame
  We learn that love grows cold.

O'er heathen lands afar
  Thick darkness broodeth yet ;
Arise, O morning Star,
  Arise, and never set.

H.H.L. 96, 145

Kingdom

THOSE excellent but dangerous people who would remove from all common life, and from all worship, everything that is not immediately comprehensible to the careless would, no doubt, make short work of the Lord's Prayer. Seldom has so much depth and mystery been packed into a few sentences as it is there ; and yet neither the depth of mystery nor the fact that ancient authorities never managed to agree on the true Greek text of it have prevented the Lord's Prayer from being and remaining the family prayer of the Church of Christ. Nor is the Prayer a kind of incantation, which men utter without any notion of its meaning. It is never that. To the child as he first learns it, it presents a very clear and definite sense of talking to God. It makes sense to that very considerable extent. For the great paradox of communication, when you are dealing with the real and deep things, is that at any point you can understand fully, and yet every day your understanding grows. Most of us find the power of the Prayer in its verbs—' Hallowed, come, give, forgive, lead, deliver '. We all mean something by those from the first. But if we are really alive, not merely passing the time, we mean more by each as each day passes.

' Thy kingdom come ' is one of the phrases in the Prayer that goes deep. What does the child mean by it ? He means, of course, ' I hope you will win, and I am on your side.' Children have, when their parents do not stifle it, a lively sense of God. Dozens of stories are told about the childish consciousness of God in picture or word, like the child who was heard, during a thunderstorm, calling out in the tone we associate with the touch-line, ' Go it, God ! ' This is one of the great and colourful things in life. It comes of simple and vital faith that says, ' There is a God ; then of course God is interesting ! ' By the same token, when the child says ' Give ', he means, simply, ' Give ', and expects the daily bread to be given.

This hymn begins from the phrase, ' Thy kingdom come '. As childhood gives way to the scepticism of youth and the criticism of maturity every sentence of the Prayer comes under scrutiny. A man begins to say ' What does it mean ? ', and he goes on to say ' Does it mean anything ? ' He is right to ask these questions ; he is right to let the hidden paradox have its way with him, to let himself be tugged and torn by it. He is bound to ask, some time, ' How do you reconcile " Thy kingdom come " with " The kingdom of God is within you " ? '

Let us begin with a comment which St Jerome made in the fourth century on this very phrase in the Prayer, as it is recorded in *St Matthew*. *Grandis audaciæ*, said he, *et puræ conscientiæ, regnum Dei postulari et iudicium non timere*. ' He is a man of enormous courage and a man of pure conscience who can demand the coming of the Kingdom without fear of the Judgment.' To say ' Thy kingdom come ' is to make a proud boast of loyalty. Who dare pray for the coming of a kingdom of pure righteousness and justice and love ?

But then, is not the kingdom already come ? The answer is precisely, Yes and No. For in regard to the Kingdom of God there are three different propositions which God puts to man. One is this, that God has always been King, that there was never a time when he was not King, that the ' rule ' of God stands and endures as the most durable and unshakable thing that exists. This has the corollary for Christians that Jesus Christ is King, and the Holy Spirit is King.

The second proposition is this : that not everybody has realized this, not everybody has accepted it, not everybody lives as though this were true. Taking the whole population of the world and the whole of history under review, hardly anybody does. This means that there is a tension between the reign of God and the rebellion of men, a tension that has to be resolved in each individual case over which God and the devil fight their battle, and that tension is reflected in world history.

The third proposition is this, that though not everybody yet accepts the reign of God, there will be a time (or a state of things) when everybody does ; whether this means that in this world as we physically know it that consummation will be achieved, or whether it means (as many now think) that history will in the end, and precisely because of this achieved harmony with the divine will, be gathered up into eternity, nobody can say. There is much that remains dark to us. But here is the matter which concerns us at the present point : that all these propositions are true. The human reaction to the first is faith, which accepts the established rule of God and makes it the axiom of life ; to the second, work, which seeks to clear the way for its establishment in those places where it is not accepted ; to the third, hope, which confidently expects its overt accept- ance by all men.

The whole idea of the kingdom present yet unfulfilled is luminously illustrated in an analogy that originates from Bishop Berggrav of Oslo, and which has been established as a classic religious parable by Dr John Marsh in his book, *The Fulness of Time*.[1] Suppose a village in Norway, suffer- ing under the Nazi occupation of the late war. Suppose then that the news of liberation had been brought to the capital, and had spread to the important towns, but, for some considerable time, had not penetrated to this remote village. The inhabitants of that village would be living as though under occupation when in reality the occupation had been defeated by the liberators ; conversely (here Dr Marsh extends the original analogy), suppose in that village it had been possible for a revolution to have been engineered by emissaries of the liberating power, and the village to have been ' liberated ' in advance of the country at large, then they would be living under the new dispensation even though the country at large was not. Let us venture a third clause, a bitter but not unbiblical one : suppose that, given the news of liberation, a substantial part of the villagers decided that actually they were happier under the occu- pation ; then you would be bound to say that they had

[1] John Marsh, *The Fulness of Time* (Nisbet, 1952), p. 152.

chosen voluntarily a servitude for whose imposition they were not to blame in the first place ; and it would be some-body's business, presumably, to persuade them morally of the benefits of liberation.

The Kingdom of God is there well presented. The king-dom is established as surely as the liberation of Norway was established ; but there are many wide tracts of ignorance—people living under the Old Dispensation, people not made free by Christ. (Conversely you can say that many people in the Old Testament who came temporally before the revelation of Christ none the less lived under a kind of pro-leptic or anticipated liberation : what else explains *Isaiah* liii ?) But the grievous thing is that many people positively prefer the *Old* way of living after the *New* way has been presented to them.

This last sorry truth is embodied in the second of the three propositions about the kingdom that we set out above, and the hymn ' Thy kingdom come ' is geared particularly to it. ' When comes the reign of peace ? ' it pleads, and ' When comes the promised time ? ' It echoes the old Advent prayer, ' O Lord, raise up (we pray thee) thy power, and come among us. . . . ' and the 130th Psalm, ' My soul waiteth for the Lord, more than they that watch for the morning.' It is so simple in its language, so honest, that at least one eminent authority has written it off as ' depres-sing '. But it was written for the advent season, the season in which the Church looks forward to the fullness of Time, to Christmas, to the Liberation and the Gift upon which a man can hardly dare to look. Advent is not a time for depression ; but, says the Church, it is a time for penitence, for an honest facing of the unspeakable folly that makes man prefer not to expect the kingdom or to accept liber-ation. It is a dark hymn, for gross darkness covers the earth ; but it has a flash of brightness in it that comes from the love of God, the Sun of Righteousness. It is well that men should stretch out their hands and strain their eyes towards the bringing-in of the kingdom, each in that sphere of life in which he is personally concerned.

These lines were written in 1867 ; there seems to have

been little sign since then of the dispersion of war and lust
and oppression and crime.   There is plenty of additional
evidence, these eighty and more years, of the coldness of
men's love and the shame of men's ambition.   Who among
the well-informed can be anything but a pessimist?   Who
among those who knock about the world or write for the
papers or edit features for the B.B.C. or conduct chaplaincies
in the Glasgow docks can hope for anything at all?   Only
he who is persuaded that the liberation has come.   Only he
who has seen that nothing but those truths about the Rule
of God fits the facts of life and gives ground for hope.   In
that faith men can yet pray, ' Thy kingdom come '.

44

Isaac Watts (1674–1748)

Jesus shall reign where'er the sun
Doth his successive journeys run ;
His kingdom stretch from shore to shore,
Till moons shall wax and wane no more.

For him shall endless prayer be made,
And praises throng to crown his head ;
His name like sweet perfume shall rise
With every morning sacrifice.

People and realms of every tongue
Dwell on his love with sweetest song ;
And infant voices shall proclaim
Their early blessings on his name.

Blessings abound where'er he reigns ;
The prisoner leaps to lose his chains,
The weary find eternal rest,
And all the sons of want are blest.

Let every creature rise and bring
Peculiar honours to our king ;
Angels descend with songs again,
And earth repeat the loud Amen.

H.H.L. 13, 14, 63–6

Victory

HE shall have dominion also from sea to sea, and from
the river unto the ends of the earth. . . .
He shall deliver the needy when he crieth; the poor
also, and him that hath no helper. . . .
And he shall live, and unto him shall be given of the gold of
Sheba : prayer also shall be made for him continually, and
daily shall he be praised.
Blessed be his glorious name for ever ; and let the whole earth
be filled with his glory ; Amen and Amen.

Those are the verses of the 72nd Psalm which Isaac Watts
has paraphrased in the most famous and the oldest of
missionary hymns. The story of the emergence of this
hymn from that very ancient source is so remarkable, and
such an excellent illustration of the deep roots which our
hymns have in human experience, that it will serve as an
exposition of it.

In the early days of the Jewish kingdom (say eight centuries and more before Christ) there was a popular hymn
which was always used at the coronation of the new King.
That hymn, containing prayers that God will save the King,
and that the King may bless his people with just and
righteous government, may well have been to the Jewish
people as sacred as our own ' God save the Queen '—not
perhaps so frequently heard but as solemn in its intention.

Now the Psalter as we have it is a hymn-book which, we
must suppose, passed through the hands of an editor, and
probably of several editors at different stages, before it
reached the form in which it is familiar to us. It seems
that it occurred to one of these editors that this venerable
and beautiful coronation hymn would form a great enrich-
ment to the worship of the people if it were discreetly edited
in such a manner that its special intention could be generalized. By this time, indeed, it might well have lost all its
relevance in its original form, for after the seventh century

there was no king to be crowned. Now, what would an editor of those days do to universalize a hymn whose local associations had disappeared and made it an anachronism ? He would, perhaps by the insertion of a verse or two, perhaps by the recalling of some other Scripture passage, perhaps by a discreet alteration here and there, assimilate the hymn to the general trend of popular religion. (A reasonable parallel is what the Scottish revisers did with ' O God of Bethel ', No. 9.) The dominant note in popular religion was, by now, distinctly forward-looking ; men were more and more (in, say, three or four hundred B.C.) looking for the day when the King would come. The Lord's Anointed, the Messiah, was the focus of religious attention—even to the exclusion of certain social and practical matters which ought to have had part of the people's attention and for whose neglect they were castigated by Nehemiah and Ezra and men of that age. So the coronation hymn was rescued for public worship by being referred not to a particular king, but to *the* King, *the* Messiah ; this was done by inserting a verse or two strongly reminiscent of the greatest of the Messianic books, *Isaiah* xl–lxvi. The chapter specially recalled here is chapter 60. A doxology was added at the end (quoted above, ' Blessed be his glorious name for ever . . .') for the merely practical purpose of signifying that this psalm brought to an end Part II of the complete hymn-book ; the doxology is addressed, of course, not to the Messiah but to God the Father.

What resulted was our 72nd Psalm. Now observe what Isaac Watts did. He in turn quite deliberately seeks to rescue the psalm from the Old Testament, from its reminiscences of tribal Jewish rites, and by translating the hope of the Messiah into the Christian hope to make it a Christian hymn. He has taken it as he finds it in the last and canonical edition of the Psalter. Some of his verses go back to the original coronation hymn, some are from the revision in the Psalter, and the last is from the impressive but quite accidental doxology. No matter—the whole is thrown into the melting-pot and emerges as a triumphant hymn on the victory of Christ.

Now where in hymns will one find a better example than
this of the thrusting forward of particular and specialized
human experience towards the universal and eternal truth
of life ?   For the ordinary believer, if we may distinguish
him from the professional scholar, it matters little to discern
the difference between the way hymns were used in the
Temple and the synagogue, and the way they are used
at the parish church ; it matters not much whether the
editors of the Psalter, or whether Isaac Watts, would have
described their intentions just as we have here described
them.   What matters much more is the use to which men,
under God, have come to put these ancient thoughts and
words.

The hymn carries all this weight of pedigree very lightly.
It needs very little direct comment, save upon this one
point, that its special subject, like that of the original, is the
tribute which the nations bring to their king.   The psalm
spoke of the King receiving the gifts of all the neighbouring
civilizations—Persia, Arabia, Assyria and the rest.   A great
procession, this, of all the choice and distinguished people
in all the Great Powers bringing the King a symbol of
respect.   In the original context this does not rise higher
than international courtesy and formality.   But Watts has
used the figure for the spread of the Church under missionary
enterprise, and he has left us with the astonishing statement
that Jesus not only brings light and freedom and healing
to those to whom he comes, but that he receives their gifts,
their ' peculiar honours '.   He receives, and delights in,
the gifts which best express the character and enterprise of
all the peoples over whom he reigns.   This is a triumphant
refutation of the old ' white man's burden ' view of missionary
work.

Everybody knows, and the enemies of missionary enterprise are not slow to say, that missionary expansion during
the last hundred and fifty years has become inextricably
entangled with commercial expansion, and the self-interest
of the Western powers.   Of course it has been.   You may
well say that the trader has followed the missionary, and
that had it not been for the missionary his nemesis would

have fallen years before it has done. P. T. Forsyth once said in a missionary sermon (not the one quoted under No. 42), ' It was a gross mistake to make the free entrance of missionaries one of the concessions extorted after the Chinese war. And I shall never forget a reason given in my youth by Bishop Ellicott for voting for the Afghan War. He said it might be a means of getting Christianity and the Bible into Afghanistan. Nothing in truth has so much hampered our missionary success as the fact that we are a conquering people.' [1]

Well and rightly was that said—and prophetically, for it was said at least fifty years ago. But the whole theme of conquest is transformed by Jesus Christ. When he conquers it is not so much that he exacts tribute as that men and women rush to offer him of their best, as the Magi offered their gifts to the Holy Child. Jesus wants just what men of all races and colours have to offer him. Missionaries may patronize, ministers may be insensitive and ignorant. Jesus does not patronize. Jesus is a wise and courteous Lord. It is for that wisdom and courtesy that Christians sing, and sing with pleasure, ' Jesus shall reign '.

[1] P. T. Forsyth, *Missions in State and Church* (Hodder & Stoughton, 1908), p. 117.

45

Edward Perronet (1726–92)

All hail the power of Jesus' name ;
  Let angels prostrate fall ;
Bring forth the royal diadem
  To crown him Lord of all.

Crown him, ye morning stars of light,
  Who fixed this floating ball ;
Now hail the strength of Israel's might,
  And crown him Lord of all.

Crown him, ye martyrs of your God,
  Who from his altar call ;
Extol the Stem-of-Jesse's Rod,
  And crown him Lord of all.

Ye seed of Israel's chosen race,
  Ye ransomed of the fall,
Hail him who saves you by his grace,
  And crown him Lord of all.

Hail him, ye heirs of David's line,
  Whom David Lord did call,
The God incarnate, Man divine,
  And crown him Lord of all.

Sinners, whose love can ne'er forget
  The wormwood and the gall,
Go, spread your trophies at his feet,
  And crown him Lord of all.

Let every tribe and every tongue
  That bound creation's call,
Now shout in universal song
  The crowned Lord of all.

H.H.L. 267, 293

Coronation

'ALL hail the power' is pre-eminently the hymn of the coronation of Christ the King. It has been a favourite with English-speaking Protestants ever since it was written towards the end of the eighteenth century. But now, while we can still remember the coronation of Queen Elizabeth II, these familiar home-spun lines take on a new illumination for Englishmen. For although many hymns have been written about the crowning of the King of kings, never was a hymn written which looked and sounded so much like a coronation as does this one.

To go no further for a moment, the very literary texture of the hymn suggests pageantry and procession. It thunders along on its majestic ground-bass, 'Crown him Lord of all'; each verse says the same thing but with a variation, each verse brings in a new sacred community and urges it to praise. All these cohorts of cheering and praising people suggest irresistibly the many-coloured regiments and orders who gathered for that coronation in June 1953. Even the crude heraldry of the words, 'the strength of Israel's might', 'the stem-of-Jesse's Rod', 'Israel's chosen race', 'heirs of David's line', suggest all those historic and august associations which the coronation carries, the banners and flags and coats-of-arms and the lords of heraldry. Just as in its own fashion an English coronation brings up all English history into the present, so that you cannot examine its ceremonies or explain its pageantry without rehearsing most of English history and even some history that goes back beyond England, so 'All hail the power', by its mysterious blazons and ornaments, gathers up all sacred history in its praise of Christ the King. Let us first explore it in this way.

'Crown him,' it begins, 'ye morning stars': let all creation crown its creator. Then, 'Crown him, ye martyrs': men who have died for the faith and know now that your death was not in vain, because He is the goal of history.

' There shall come forth a rod out of the stem of Jesse,' the prophet had said : and the promise was fulfilled in Christ. He promises and does not betray those to whom he has promised; let all who bring him the precious allegiances of sacrifice and suffering and poverty remember that.   Then, ' Ye seed of Israel's chosen race ' :   that is, simply, the whole Church of God, the New Israel.   The old Israel was bounded by heredity and law ;   the new Israel is called to its duty by the grace of Christ, but the two Israels understand one another, for both know what duty is and what vocation is.   Then another device, ' Ye heirs of David's line ' :   Jesus, says the tradition, was descended from David according to the course of nature.   All men and women who have confessed faith in Christ are descended from Christ in the succession of grace, they are, as we saw (No. 37), ' Kings and priests ', ordained and made royal in their service to the Kingdom.   And then finally, all who recall the royalty that suffered on the Cross, the obedience and the glory of that precious Passion, cannot help regarding their own human achievements as of singularly trivial value when they think of what He has done.

Now that kind of exposition is of the same kind as the explanation one might coax out of some coat-of-arms in medieval heraldry.   I set it down here merely to preserve up to this point the heraldic atmosphere of the whole. These things are intricate and perhaps obscure, and at a coronation a certain mystery and intricacy are not at all out of place.

But if we draw away from the details and survey the scene as a whole, there will be more to see.   Recall again the scene of the English Coronation.   May we not say, when we have swept off all the froth of journalistic sentimentality, that that occasion left a deep religious impression on English people ?   The origin of that impression was surely this, that what the people saw was something that genuinely surprised them.   We had all expected pomp and ceremony and colour.   What took us all by surprise, I suspect, was to realize that this coronation was not a declaration of power so much as a conversation of allegiances.   All coronations in

H.F.—T

the English tradition are so designed in theory, of course ; there was something about the small details of this one that brought out this truth more clearly than it had been brought out before, that was all.   At one point the Sovereign casts aside her crimson robe ; at another she takes the cloth of gold and the crown.   Here the Queen knelt before the priest ; there the priest knelt before the Queen.   Here the Queen took the Coronation Oath, there the people shouted, ' God save the Queen '.   The whole was a majestic counter-point of loyalties, the whole counterpoint (like Bach's Giant Fugue) erected over a ground-bass of loyalty to the King of kings and Lord of lords.

Reference to the printed orders of service and memories of the occasion will, I believe, confirm these judgments. But even that is seen at its true value when it is thought of as a pointer to the coronation of Christ.   It would have no enduring value at all beyond the value of a first-rate drama-tic performance if it failed to be such a pointer.   Had it been so ordered, or so conducted, as to obscure this central truth, it could have been a tawdry and wasteful demon-stration of ponderous pomp.   It was that strong, moving note of humility mixed with the splendour that really went home that day.

What then does it mean to enthrone Christ as King ?   It means not to ascribe to him irresponsible and dictatorial powers.   It means not to ' make him a king ' in the sense in which some people, while he was yet on earth, wanted to make him a king.   ' Again, the devil taketh him up into an exceeding high mountain, and sheweth him all the kingdoms of the world and the glory of them, and saith unto him, All these things will I give thee, if thou wilt fall down and worship me.'   To enthrone Christ means to make him the focal point of thought, action and hope ; to regard nothing as complete without him.   It means accepting the fact that Christ is faithful to men as well as demanding their faith.   Christ placed himself at men's disposal, suffered and died even in the moment of his coronation.   Jesus is faithful : he will not go back on his Oath.   The justice of Christ is mercy, and his law is love, and his sword is truth.   To be his soldier is to be his friend, to be his subject is to be his son. For he defends his realm, and he saves his people.

'Hallelujah, for the Lord God omnipotent reigneth ! The Kingdoms of this world are become the Kingdoms of our God, and of His Christ, and He shall reign for ever and ever.' What human truth, what human achievement, what human hope can be complete or even sane without taking account of that ?

46

John Henry Newman (1801–90)

Praise to the holiest in the height,
And in the depth be praise,
In all his words most wonderful,
Most sure in all his ways.

Oh loving wisdom of our God !
When all was sin and shame,
A second Adam to the fight
And to the rescue came.

Oh wisest love ! that flesh and blood,
Which did in Adam fail,
Should strive afresh against the foe,
Should strive and should prevail ;

And that a higher gift than grace
Should flesh and blood refine,
God's presence and his very self,
And essence all-divine.

Oh generous love ! that he who smote
In man for man the foe,
The double agony in man
For man should undergo ;

And in the garden secretly,
And on the cross on high,
Should teach his brethren, and inspire
To suffer and to die.

Praise to the holiest in the height,
And in the depth be praise,
In all his words most wonderful,
Most sure in all his ways.

H.H.L. 85, 110–11, 138, 160

Death

'PRAISE to the holiest in the height' is a remarkable hymn in most ways; in the present collection it provides the only exception to what may have already been inferred as a rule, namely, that popular hymns are either self-explanatory, or readily to be explained through the Scriptures, Christian doctrine, or common life. We have managed to get along pretty well so far without that kind of literary criticism and examination of sources which is a familiar part of hymnology. But 'Praise to the holiest' demands that we abandon this technique, because it positively requires explaining through its original context. It is, of course, the most conspicuous and best loved of those hymns which were not intended by their authors for congregational use. It is part of a larger poem, John Henry Newman's *The Dream of Gerontius*; and although that poem is familiar to many in association with Elgar's music, it is yet possible that by attending for a while to its words apart from that august association we shall the better understand the purpose of 'Praise to the holiest'. Concerning that general purpose, then, we shall say no more, until we have made some observations on the place of the hymn in the longer poem, than that its chief subject is *death*.

THE DREAM OF GERONTIUS AND THE CHOIRS
OF ANGELICALS

Gerontius is Greek for 'little old man'; you might almost say, in this place, for 'humble, or plain, or defenceless old man', or Everyman about to die. The 'dream' is a dream of what takes place at the moment of death.

The poem is in seven cantos, cast in dramatic form. The speakers-in-chief are the soul of 'Gerontius', angels, demons, a priest reading the burial service, and certain shadowy figures called 'assistants'. These build up a dramatic picture of the struggle, or (in the strict and ancient

sense) the ' agony ' of death, and the message of the poem is
that which Christ, in being crucified and rising from death,
has done in respect of each man's personal death.

In the course of the fifth canto a long hymn, sung in five
sections, is put in the mouths of a series of ' choirs of angelicals '.   It is this long hymn with which we are more
immediately concerned.   The fourth canto ends with these
words, spoken by the Angel :

> There was a mortal, who is now above
> In the mid glory ; he, when near to die,
> Was given communion with the Crucified,
> Such, that the Master's very wounds were stamp'd
> Upon his flesh ; and from the agony
> Which thrilled through body and soul in that embrace,
> Learn that the flame of the Everlasting Love
> Doth burn ere it transform. . . .

The angel's voice, speaking to ' Gerontius ', fades out half-
way through the line.   The emphatic word in that passage
is ' agony ', again in the sense of the great battle in the soul
that takes place at the hour of death.   On this the fifth
canto opens, completing the unfinished line :

> Hark to those sounds,
> They come of tender beings angelical,
> Least and most childlike of the sons of God.

Then, immediately :

FIRST CHOIR OF ANGELICALS

Praise to the holiest in the height . . .

What follows begins with the familiar first verse, but the
rest is not our ' Praise to the holiest '—not yet.   ' Praise to
the holiest ' is originally a hymn of thirty-five verses divided
into five sections, one for each of five ' choirs of angelicals ',
each section beginning with the same first verse.   The
sections are divided from each other by dialogue of varying
length ; but read straight through they provide a rehearsal
of the whole story of the Fall and of the processes of Redemption.   It is like a modern version of the old medieval hymn,

' Sing, my tongue, the glorious battle ', setting the Cross in the context of all life.

The first choir of angelicals sings of the first chapter in creation. (Remember that they are *angels*, for which see further under No. 49) :

> To us his elder race he gave
> To battle and to win,
> Without the chastisement of pain,
> Without the soil of sin.

> The younger son he will'd to be
> A marvel in his birth :
> Spirit and flesh his parents were :
> His home was heaven and earth.

(This ' younger son ', is, of course, mankind)

> The Eternal bless'd his child, and arm'd,
> And sent him hence afar,
> To serve as champion in the field
> Of elemental war.

The ' elemental war ' is the conflict between the principles of Good and Evil, between God and Satan, which exists in principle before man exists ; the thought here is of the conflict being waged by those ' pure intellects ' which are angels, and which live outside the categories of pain, time and sin ; and then of its being passed to the hands of the ' younger child ', man, who has a new technique of waging war, based on his ability to love and to suffer. What will be the issue ?

The ' second choir ', after the opening verse, ' Praise to the holiest ' again, tells of primitive man and the emergence of the old Israel, through whom God's truth was first to be made known.

> Woe to thee, man ! for he was found
> A recreant in the fight ;
> And lost his heritage of heaven
> And fellowship with light.

> Above him now the angry sky,
> Around the tempest's din ;
> Who once had angels for his friends
> Has but the brutes for kin. . . .

> Glory to him who from the mire
> In patient length of days
> Elaborated into life
> A people to his praise !

But, says the ' third choir ', though the relevation of God begins to break through, and holiness begins to leaven brute life, there remains the ' agony ' :

> Yet still between that earth and heaven—
> His journey and his goal—
> A double agony awaits
> His body and his soul.

It is a ' double agony ', a compound and complex struggle, because death is physical dissolution, repulsive in itself, and bringing keen regret for the physical life that must be surrendered.

From the ' fourth choir ' we hear of the laughter of Satan over the confounding of the plan of God.   In this we have something of Milton's cosmic vision of the failure of ' flesh and blood '.

> The foe blasphemed the Holy Lord,
> As if he reckoned ill
> In that he placed his puppet man
> The frontier-place to fill.

> For even in his best estate,
> With amplest gifts endued,
> A sorry sentinel was he,
> A thing of flesh and blood. . . .

> And when, by blandishment of Eve,
> That earth-born Adam fell,
> He shrieked in triumph, and he cried
> ' A sorry sentinel ! '

> ' The Maker by his word is bound,
> Escape or cure is none ;
> He must abandon to his doom,
> And slay his darling son.'

There is the contempt of Evil for Good, that charges Good

with being gullible and impotent, that pours contempt on
flesh and blood for being flesh and blood. So well has the
Devil done his work that even good and classic Christians
have found this the worst stumbling-block in the way of
faith, that God should use flesh and blood to redeem flesh
and blood, that the physical and material should be deemed
by him worthy of redemption. It is far easier to believe
that matter is eternally under condemnation and that it is
the whole duty of man to leave the material world as far
behind him as he can. ' Praise to the holiest ' takes up
precisely this point. For now the ' fifth choir ' comes in
with the closing verses of the long hymn, which are those
that we know. The opening verse once more, and then,

> O loving wisdom of our God !
> When all was sin and shame
> A second Adam to the fight
> And to the rescue came.

The second Adam is Christ ; he comes to the rescue of *flesh
and blood*, to undergo the *double agony*,

> To teach his brethren, and inspire
> To suffer and to die.

At that point the hymn ends. It does not finish, in *The
Dream*, with a repetition of the opening verse. That is most
important. It shows that the whole accumulating force of
the simple lines is directed to that final verb, to the subject of
The Dream, which is the Christian technique of death.

GOD, MAN AND DEATH

' A second Adam '—that is one of the phrases in the hymn
to which the earlier sections of the poem provide a clue.
It is the language used by the Apostle in *Romans* and *I Corinthians*, ' For as by one man's disobedience many were made
sinners, so by the disobedience of one shall many be made
righteous ' (*Romans* v. 19), ' For as in Adam all die, so in
Christ shall all be made alive ', ' The first man is of the
earth, earthy ; the second man is the Lord from heaven '
(*I Corinthians* xv. 22, 47 : and observe that in the *Romans*

quotation the sense of being ' made ' sinners is to be taken in the manner which we noticed under No. 21, where we had to deal with the expression, ' He died to make us good ').

It is still fashionable to think that one must choose between treating the opening chapters of Genesis as history and treating them as a fairy-tale. Some put it more truculently and say they are a lie. Either approach is frivolous and out of tune with the subject. All that is required is that a man trust the Genesis story about Adam as being *true* ; and nobody of any mental development at all is likely to think that the only way of writing truth is writing history.

In a way it is unfortunate that one great branch of modern symbolic writing is called ' fiction ' when, in his everyday use of the word, a man understands ' fiction ' to mean ' deliberate lies '. This makes some honest and high-principled people contemptuous of the art of reading and writing novels. I dare not say, because I know I should be misunderstood, that the Adam story is a novel ; and actually the expression is not so accurate that it is fair to challenge a reader with it. But this at least we may press, that novels, from *Pride and Prejudice* to *No Highway*, are not lies. They are not ' untrue '. At their heart there may well be something that is vitally true, there may well be even some pure Christian doctrine. There are bad novels and trivial novels —and there are bad and trivial imitations of religion. What is here required of the man of faith is that he shall look at the Adam story and confess that it is as *true to life* as *The Pilgrim's Progress*. There, anyhow, is a good respectable book that nobody calls a novel and that carries the imprimatur of conventional religion. But I do not see why we should shrink from saying this, that if there be some modern man who does not know his *Pilgrim's Progress*, and finds his means of grace and truth somewhere else, then let him by all means think of the Adam story as being as true to life as *No Highway*, for that will be better than thinking it is a diabolical and ugly lie—which is the only other thing it can be.

The Adam story is part of the story of primitive religious

experience. Adam is Hebrew for 'man' in the most general sense, for the Latin *homo* and the German *Mensch*. What Adam is portrayed as doing in *Genesis* iii is not, if you like, exactly what every man does ; it may not be precisely (down to the smallest details of biology and of the study of snakes) what any historic man did. But it is the kind of thing, exactly the kind of thing, that every man does. I know that this is right and that is wrong ; I resent the limitation on my freedom imposed on me by any suggestion that I ought to do the right ; acting on the impulse to do wrong, I blame the nearest person for the consequences. If the Adam story had been true merely as the story of Magna Carta is true I might well have locked it up in history and said ' That has nothing to do with me.' The Adam story is searching because it is in an uncanny way about *me*. That kind of truth brings me to a decision ; I am bound to choose between ignoring and pretending I had never heard it, and adjusting my life at this or that point under its influence.

Every moment of impatience with the divine command, every act done against conscience, every human claim to self-sufficiency, every cynical disregard of consequences or of truth, every intention of erecting efficiency or reputation or wealth or prestige above the divine command when that command is well known, is gathered up in the Adam story. What can ever be done about the prevalence of this disobedience and the obvious gravitation of men away from the familiar divine law of love ?

The Christian faith says that the decisive thing was done by Christ ; and this hymn makes a special application of that conviction. In Christ, says our Faith, the good, the purely and innocently and boldly good, defied all the iniquity, the delight in scandal, the double-dealing, the hatred, and all that makes man lower than the beasts that perish. What man was responsible for, *a man* redressed, not to remove all tension or heroism from the world, but to remove despair and aimlessness. We may not now say that the battle is bound to go to the enemy in the end. We may not despair of human nature. We may never grow so superior that we can treat mankind, or any single man or woman, as wholly lost and sinful beyond recovery ; we can never ourselves go beyond the reach of God's reclaiming zeal. The only way in which this truth can be so put to mankind that mankind not only can understand it but cannot possibly evade it, was for *flesh and blood* to do what Jesus did. And among all those evasions of Christianity which are invented by and for the benefit of people who have not the grace to receive this inestimable benefit from God, you will find very few that do not begin by removing the true humanity of Christ from the faith.

For what Christ did, and its effects on us, is indeed a benefit that a man can hardly bear to receive. At every point where flesh and blood went wrong in Adam, and ever goes wrong in anybody, Jesus went right, and went right by honest, willing, free decision. Just those things which flesh and blood' saddle us with, the temptations and ignorances and despairs which seem to have no other origin, flesh and blood in Jesus subdued to the will of God. As a result, all things physical, including his own physical body and every department of life which is in contact with man's physical nature, were in him not the origin of confusion but the willing collaborators with the mind of God. Rightly then does the hymn say, ' O wisest love '. There is wisdom in this as well as love. There is hard, efficient, down-to-earth reality in every line of the Gospel story. The light came into the world, the light of God's wisdom, and the world could not put it out. But it tried its best to put it out. The victory of the light over the darkness is so blessed a gift to men that the writer of the hymn is driven into an almost impossible paradox—' A higher gift than grace '. Can there be a higher gift than grace ? There cannot, of course : all this is precisely the operation of grace. But this is the kind of thing you find yourself saying when you want to find words to describe the love of God.

And all this weight of truth is invoked by John Henry Newman in order to show a little old man how to die.

Modern Milton scholars incline to the view that in *Paradise Lost* Milton assumes that death, like sexuality and other

major events of physical existence, was not itself created by
the Fall (the wrong decision of man) but was radically
affected by it.   It is possible to say, as Milton does, that
Adam's Fall ' brought death into the world ' ; but what
we mean by that is that the stain and sourness in man's
nature have given death all the qualities that make it so
repellent to us.   After all, it is difficult to believe that God
intended the race of man to be immortal in the sense of
never leaving the life of this world, that no *generation* of men
was really intended by God.   That interpretation of the
Adam story, with all the emphasis on the pleasant garden
in which Adam and Eve were destined to wander hand in
hand throughout eternity, is altogether too romantic to fit
into the story of God's work as the Gospel presents it.
Although on this the Church has never dogmatized, we may
safely believe that in God's plan, before man's rebellion
radically altered it, death was meant to be (as Dr C. S. Lewis
has said) simply a homecoming, a cheerful and gentle surrender of physical life.   The best evidence for this is what
happens in some choice cases—a really happy and triumphant death-bed where there is no fear and no doubting.

When you look at the ' normal, healthy ' fear of death,
it is, of course, all of a piece with the rest of the fears, healthy
or unhealthy, which beset the human race.   Few men are
so consistently atheistical that they have not at least a superstitious fear of what may lie on the other side of death.   But
whence comes any such attitude to the God into whose
presence most people agree we pass after death ?   Whence
comes a cringing or resentful attitude to him ?   It comes
from the conviction that we have given him cause to be
angry.   There it stands written into the Adam story—
resentment, hiding, fear.   The message of the last verse of
the hymn is that in the manner of his death and resurrection,
Jesus stripped this last horror of all its power to frighten.
In the Apostle's phrase, he ' drew the sting ' of death.   He
showed that all the wrath and ugliness are on man's side,
all the love on God's side ;   that however mountainous our
burden of sin, however insistent the clamour of a dreary or
guilty past, the God to whom we go at death is not **what**

we have made him out to be ; that we can yet, even at that stage, decide to love him and honour him and treat him as a friend. None of it ever happens automatically : decision is required in a way decision is never required of slaves or prisoners. But the decision can yet be made—that is the good news. It is not too late.

Dr C. S. Lewis has written many moving and many edifying pages ; but I believe I would give them all for the last paragraph or two of his Preface to the volume of *Essays Presented to Charles Williams* (1947), in which he writes of the effect on himself of the sudden and (by human computations) premature death of Charles Williams, his friend. The last few lines of these run as follows :

No event has so corroborated my faith in the next world as Williams did simply by dying. When the idea of death and the idea of Williams thus met in my mind, it was the idea of death that was changed.

' The idea of death was changed.' That, superficially understood, may have some connection with the fact that anybody who ever met or even saw Charles Williams always found himself describing the poet as ' vital '. It is true that he had the ' gift of life ' in unusually abundant measure. But the real value of this (as you may read a little earlier in that place, is that it points to the great historic and cosmic fact, that when the idea of death and the idea of Jesus meet, it is death that is changed ; indeed, it is death that is defeated.

Man's sense of superiority to God brings death into the world—we say that because the death consequent on that is so different from what God meant death to be as to be unrecognizable. The obedience and the wisdom of Christ in precisely the same sense took death out of the world, not by infinitely extending the mortal span of his followers, but by so transforming it that it has nothing but outward signs in common with what we ' normally and healthily ' fear. The death of Jesus was not corrupting, it was positively fruitful. It was the necessary preliminary to the revelation of God the Holy Spirit and the sealing of God's confidence in men.   It is just this fruitful, patient, gentle technique of death that he has bequeathed to us.   ' O loving wisdom ! O wisest love !   O generous love ! '   By Christ we are simply taught how to deal with this most intractable of the world's terrors—death.

' It was the idea of death that was changed.'

47

Bernard of Morlaix (1091–1153)
T. J. M. Neale (1818–66)

URBS SION AUREA

Jerusalem the golden,
  With milk and honey blest,
Beneath thy contemplation
  Sink heart and voice oppressed ;
I know not, oh I know not,
  What social joys are there,
What radiancy of glory,
  What light beyond compare !

They stand, those halls of Syon,
  Conjubilant with song,
And bright with many an angel,
  And all the martyr throng ;
The Prince is ever in them ;
  The daylight is serene ;
The pastures of the blessèd
  Are decked in glorious sheen.

There is the throne of David,
  And there, from care released,
The song of them that triumph,
  The shout of them that feast ;
And they who, with their Leader,
  Have conquered in the fight,
For ever and for ever
  Are clad in robes of white !

O sweet and blessèd country,
  Shall I ever see thy face ?
O sweet and blessèd country,
  Shall I ever win thy grace ?
Exult, O dust and ashes,
  The Lord shall be thy part ;
His only, his for ever,
  Thou shalt be, and thou art !

H.H.L. 28, 81–5, 195

Heaven

OTHER people's follies and iniquities have often drawn from the pens of men of letters tracts and satires and exhortations. In our own day the two commonest literary forms which emerge from this cause are satires like George Orwell's *1984*, and social surveys or Government reports on specified aspects of contemporary life. On the whole, the best way to approach 'Jerusalem the golden' is to recall that it is a translated excerpt from a medieval poem written by a French monk for precisely the same reasons that bring out the social survey and the satire, and the full value and extravagance and incandescent truth and absurdity of the whole scheme of the hymn is best appreciated when it is laid alongside the Government Report on Gambling, or the first chapter of *English Life and Leisure*, by B. Seebohm Rowntree and G. R. Lavers.

The critics of Christianity sometimes call it unworldly. They say that there is an unhealthy preoccupation with the world to come. An eminent scientist said not long ago to an eminent ecclesiastic, when they were both returning from a funeral at which this hymn had been sung, that that kind of thing is what empties the churches. Your healthy and sensible fellow has enough on his hands in this life without troubling his head about 'eternity'.

English Life and Leisure provides, in its first chapter, an adequate comment on that view. The first chapter, which I here mention because it is probable that most of my readers will have read it, consists of two hundred case-histories; these are summaries of two hundred people's view of life as it was elicited from them in conversations conducted by investigators with the appearance of casualness but with a concealed object of finding out each person's views on certain homely issues of life and death.

Three disconnected and almost contradictory impressions are to be gathered from these two hundred cameos of popular life. One is the abysmal folly, the sour stupidity, the rank hatred, the downright sinful corruption that disfigures many of the minds here presented. The second is of the great and grievous travail of the Church—for on analysis you find that three in eight of these people claim some connection, however distant, with the Church or offer its teaching some kind of respect, and some of these are among the most disagreeable characters here reported. The third impression is the curious desperate insistence with which so many of those who are obviously ignorant of religion and of life cling to some hope concerning the future life.

You cannot, in fact, avoid being struck very forcibly, reading this chapter, by the contradiction and the relevance of the Christian teaching about heaven.

Reporters on English life and leisure react in this objective and (so far as they can make it) full report on the mind of the man in the street. St Bernard of Cluny reacted by writing a poem about heaven under the title ' On the contempt of the world '. At bottom, St Bernard and Rowntree and Lavers are writing about the same thing. They differ only in one matter of importance. Rowntree and Lavers leave the reader to form his own conclusions. Bernard is dogmatic on the vital point.

The vital issue on which a responsible person must at some point decide is this : what is reality ? Is it the squalor or is it the love ? Do we say that the ugly is a perversion of the noble or that the noble is an illusory escape from the ugly ? Bernard is perfectly clear about it. He says, in the plain indicative mood, that the beautiful, the desirable, the happy and the noble are the real things. He had written a little earlier lines that are thus translated :

> Brief life is here our portion,
>   Brief sorrow, short-lived care ;
> The life that knows no ending,
>   The tearless life is *there*. [His italics.]

And again—

> The miserable pleasures
>   Of the body shall decay ;
> The bland and flattering struggles
>   Of the flesh shall pass away :
> And none shall there be jealous ;
>   And none shall there contend :
> Fraud, clamour, guile—what say I ?
>   All ill, all ill shall end !

Broaden and universalize these sentiments (if indeed they need any broadening) and they chime with the thought and desire of any man of any age.   Everybody *wants* a condition of things where you can distinguish the passing pleasure from the enduring, where there is no more of the bitterness of common life, only its graces.   But it is the Christian's view that that condition of things is not merely desirable, but real.   It is his view that God meant the world to be like that, and that any and every divergence from that plan can be attributed to man's preference of his own plan before God's.   Moreover, says the Christian, just because man has decided that the kind of life we are here accustomed to is best for him, that need not be supposed to have caused God to conduct his own life any differently.

But let us not go too fast.   It is natural that men shall have often expressed their feelings on these matters in terms of a certain nostalgia ;   this good condition of things, we tend to say, is not so much a condition towards which we must strive to progress as a condition we ought never to have left.   To achieve or experience this undiluted goodness and truth of things is more like going home than reaching a strange destination.   Men have often written as though they were actually exiles, men separated from their true home.   And exiles are sometimes sad men, but often they are angry men.

It is, indeed, the Christian doctrine of heaven that forms the best basis for that wrath and indignation which a Christian is bound, from time to time, to feel as he looks at the condition of the world.   The psalmist in exile cried out in grief and wrath, ' If I forget thee, O Jerusalem, let my right hand forget her cunning ' (Psalm 137. 5), and indeed that whole psalm, so full of black anger and hatred, is best used for edification by being taken as the inspiration for the Christian's anger against hypocrisy and hatred and malice and all the other burdens of the world. ' Jerusalem ' is his home, the place where he has left his family, and the place where (by an accident of religious history) he almost feels he has left his God. His wrath spurts out of him against the people who have separated him from these things, and the wrath of a Christian should be implacably directed against the social and spiritual things that separate the world from the felicity that God designed for it. William Blake, in that mysterious poem *Jerusalem*, whose prologue is so familiar, has exactly the ambiguity of the Christian's battle. There are ' dark satanic mills ' of a kind, a physical and obvious kind, which he hardly knew of, and redemption must be preached and worked out there. But there are the ' dark satanic mills ' of the mind and spirit, the hatred of truth, the abuse of beauty, the disparagement of goodness, the deliberate poisoning of mind and soul by evil habits of thought, which were certainly his concern and are equally the Christian's. They are well set out in *English Life and Leisure*. ' Heaven ' then, in that sense of the presence of God's love, is the root of Christian social action. You will not find many effective Christian reformers in any field who had not a very clear doctrine of heaven.

But Christians have come to mean something else by ' Jerusalem ' and by ' heaven '. They are persuaded that felicity and beauty of the kind naïvely suggested by the golden streets and the jewelled towers are the essential quality of the life after death which is offered to the faithful. ' Jerusalem the golden ' may properly be interpreted as a hymn of hope and confidence in that life.

We said under No. 46 that Jesus in dying ' changed the idea of death '. We can now go on to say that by his Resurrection Jesus made known a whole new area of truth about death. The events that followed the Resurrection (in whose light many of the things said by Jesus before his death became clear in retrospect) placed certain facts beyond doubt ; for example, that it was possible after death to be alive. There was never any question of Jesus simply having ' come back from the dead '. That was the mistake Mary made in the garden, and Jesus at once corrected it by saying, ' Do not cling to me : I am on my way to the Father.' The Resurrection was not a return to the old life and the old dimensions. As a matter of fact, people to whom Jesus appeared after the Resurrection did not at first recognize him until he gave some personal proof of his identity. The indications were that there is life, and a new kind of life, beyond death ; and this, the disciples came to see (and John the Evangelist set it down on paper) had the very important corollary that there was a clear identity between this life after death and that ' eternal life ' which Jesus said could, on conditions, be experienced here and now.

No sooner had this truth begun to emerge than the old picture re-formed itself, and was seen to be part of a larger picture. The old picture was of a home to which men were returning, like the Promised Land of the Exodus or the coming Kingdom of the Messiah of which the prophets spoke. The Resurrection puts this to men, that the ' otherness ' of this promised land, the distance of it and remoteness of it, can hardly be better explained than by saying that it lies on the other side of death. But were Christians then to say that the whole concern had resolved itself into a very simple matter after all—here is life, and after death, new life ? Not at all, for Jesus has said that the Kingdom of heaven is among us, now, and that eternal life could be known, now. The vital point is not that death automatically opens the gate to the resolution of all doubts and the freedom of all pleasures ; it is that *a certain kind of death* does so.

A certain kind of death : that is to say, a faithful death. All men must physically die. Considered as mere physical extinction, death is the great leveller. Man cannot choose when or whether to die ; he can, in respect of this death, only choose in what state of mind he will die (if he is allowed time for such preparation). But physical death is only one species of death. The Apostle Paul talks of being dead to sin and rising in Christ. Jesus talked about losing life and finding it. This implies that the dissolution which marks the end of physical life is not the only kind of natural barrier between us and the full understanding and love of God. There is a natural barrier in another plane which has nothing to do with physical extinction. It separates us just as effectively—but to pass through it enables a man to enjoy that from which he was separated before. We have no word for this kind of death. A simple word expresses the technique of undergoing it—self-denial. But the point is this, that this kind of death can be willingly undergone, undergone by choice, at any time. The other side of it is God waiting with all the generosity of his mercy and truth, and the kind of life that people live when they have surrendered to it is explained in all those parables which our Lord begins with the phrase, ' The Kingdom of heaven is like . . .'

We may then briefly state three consequences of the Christian belief in these two kinds of death and heaven. The first is that heaven and all its appurtenances are desirable and essentially good, and that everything that separates men from it is the object of the wrath of Christ and the wrath of the Christian. The whole conspiracy of the forces of darkness is directed towards turning away a man's mind from the sane and level contemplation of the ' natural barrier '. Men desire anything rather than the truth about surrender, either in physical death or in self-surrender. *There* are the ' dark satanic mills ' against which the Christian must bring his artillery, the false social values, the lying books, the evil suggestions of perverse art, the folly of idle speech, the sentimentality and cruelty and ineptitude that crucified Christ and would crucify him again.

The second consequence concerns those who have physically died ; we may be confident that the only difference between a man in this life and the same man after he has passed into that other is that then he will become more vividly *himself* than he was before. Recall what the being of God has done to the verb *to be* (Nos. 6 and 32) ; by analogy consider what the life of God does to life. The man

who is in God's presence *is* himself, free from the blurring
and tarnishing agents of life.   Our friends, whom we last
knew perhaps as elderly, infirm, battered by the world, we
may now think of as wholly gracious and energetic and
happy, as God meant them to be and as the world would
not allow them to be.

> They come with shining faces to the house of the Lord ;
> The broken hearts and weary, that life has racked and scored :
> They come hurrying and singing, to sit down at his board,
> They are young and they are joyful in the House of the Lord.[1]

Thirdly, heaven is sociable.   This particular aspect of
heaven is foreshadowed in intercourse between friends.
There are few more felicitous experiences in life than free,
frank and friendly conversation.   It is perhaps God's
greatest gift to mankind.   Jealousy, ignorance and suspicion
and all the rest of the devil's armoury do their best to make
it impossible.   There are few indeed who can carry on
a rational conversation, free of hurt feelings or deliberate
misunderstandings for the space of half an hour.   But when
it happens it is in the strict sense heavenly.   In that life
which God has prepared and for which he made us, one of
the brightest things is the free converse between men and
men, men rejoicing in each other and in God.

It is no wonder that the Bible, and the medieval monk
following it, talk so much of a banquet ; or that heaven
sometimes appears in the Bible to be like a great choral-
society.   It is all owed to the Crucified.   Truth and felicity
are the legacy of the bitterness of Calvary.   ' He hath
washed them and made them white in his blood.'   Precisely
—the very horror and wickedness of the world, concentrated
in the Cross, have become under his hands the agents of
blessedness.   Through life and death a man may learn to
live, to *be*, by the grace of Christ.   Heaven is *there*, but it is
God's will that heaven, in exactly the same sense, heaven
bought by cheerful and charitable death and the denial of
all dark things, shall be here also.

[1] From ' I would rather be a doorkeeper ', by Katharine Tynan
Hinkson, from *Enlarged Songs of Praise* (1932), No. 196, verse 3.

48

Bishop W. W. How (1823–97)

For all the saints who from their labours rest,
Who thee by faith before the world confest,
Thy name, O Jesus, be for ever blest.

Alleluya !

Thou wast their rock, their fortress, and their might ;
Thou Lord, their captain in the well-fought fight ;
Thou in the darkness drear their one true light.

O may thy soldiers, faithful, true, and bold,
Fight as the saints who nobly fought of old,
And win, with them, the victor's crown of gold.

O blest communion ! fellowship divine !
We feebly struggle, they in glory shine ;
Yet all are one in thee, for all are thine.

And when the strife is fierce, the warfare long,
Steals on the ear the distant triumph-song,
And hearts are brave again, and arms are strong.

The golden evening brightens in the west ;
Soon, soon to faithful warriors cometh rest :
Sweet is the calm of Paradise the blest.

But lo ! there breaks a yet more glorious day ;
The saints triumphant rise in bright array :
The King of glory passes on his way.

From earth's wide bounds, from ocean's farthest coast,
Through gates of pearl streams in the countless host,
Singing to Father, Son, and Holy Ghost.

H.H.L. 81–4, 122, 133

Saints

IN an unguarded moment I once said to a friend, speaking of a third person we both admired, ' There's a saint ! ' My friend replied, ' No, no. Much too nice to be a saint.' That scrap of conversation convicts us both of error ; for according to the Church's use of the word, based on the Bible, it is neither true to say that a saint is by definition a nice person nor that a saint is a dull person.

' For all the saints ', not by a long way the most profound of hymns on the saints of the Church, has this great advantage over most of its fellows, that at its very beginning it draws attention to the quality essential to sainthood—faith. ' Who thee by faith before the world confessed '—that is the most important line in the hymn ; the rest is background and scenery.

The truth about the saints is told in the eleventh chapter of *Hebrews*, where we have that famous catalogue of heroes of Old Testament history. If anybody wants to know just what a ' saint ' is, and just how a saint can be expected to help him, it is all there.

Just before the opening of this chapter the author of the tract has said, ' You have need of patience '. He is writing especially at this point to Christians who are in danger of persecution, and he is saying, ' This is no time to lose heart.' Casting round for some word of comfort that will not sound cheap and facile, he fastens on this word, ' faith ', in the celebrated phrase, ' The just shall live by faith . . . (and) we are of them that believe to the saving of the soul.' Faith, then, is the source of comfort for men who are up against the world at its most truculent. What is faith ?

' Faith,' he goes on, ' faith (my brothers who may be taken off to the labour camp or the salt mines any day) is the substance of things hoped for, the evidence of things not seen.' The man of faith (that is) is in the position of the man who holds the title-deed to a property which he knows will, in the course of time, be his absolutely to use and enjoy. The man of faith is he who lives on the assumption that God's promises are true. The man without faith is he who orders his life in the assumption that God's promises are lies and God's character is the character of a confidence-man.

Of this he proceeds to give all the examples he has space for. Abel, Enoch, Noah, Abraham, Isaac, Jacob, Joseph, Moses and (of all people) Rahab. These, he says, will do for the present, but there are many more where they came from. The list goes right down through history. The character that they all share is not goodness in a diffused sense, nor spectacular and sustained spiritual power. The character they share is faith. Understand that, and the problem of Jacob's character sorts itself out ; it is no longer so incomprehensible that a swindler like Jacob, a drunkard like Noah, or the prostitute Rahab all have their place in the procession. Samson and David and Samuel are there too, and none of them come very near moral perfection. Samson and Gideon, indeed, were sorry failures in the end. But they all share this, that at some time in their lives, when they were given the opportunity for choosing in a matter of crucial importance, they chose a course that was in line with the purpose of God. They all share faith.

For faith in all these cases is the act of mental and spiritual submission by which each one of these allowed himself to be built into the plan which God had for the world. Each of them put that before his own desires, before his own reputation. The Bible is the most morally daring and shocking book in the world. It is prepared to justify Abraham who was ready to kill his son, Jephtha who actually killed his daughter, Jacob who deceived his father, Samuel who told Saul he ought to have hewn Agag in pieces ; crises like these, which in themselves use up all the moral energy of most people, the Bible brushes aside as less important than the great story of which they form part. The only ultimate question concerning any man, according to that mysterious but quite unambiguous common mind of the Bible, is whether or not he is at God's disposal ; and whether he lives on the assumption that God is honest.

Other books tell other stories ; another book will take longer to tell a shorter story ; and upon its own scale it will justly condemn this or that sinner for his sin. But this issue alone is the concern of the Bible, and it is, according to that scale of values, less important that this or that man was a sinner on this or that occasion than that God used him and saved him and forgave him.

It is important to be reminded that none of these heroes knew he was being a hero. We must allow this much to Jacob, that he nowhere appears as a vain man. Abraham and David, men of about as different character as men can well have, share this, that they take little credit to themselves for what they achieve ; they do not build themselves up in the public eye as holy men. As for Rahab, a person who took a single decision on the calculation that the invading army was going to win and she might as well show friendliness to them, you could not safely apply the adjective ' saintly ' to a single action of her life—not even to that which turned out to be of such importance.

Faith seems to be a virtue in some of these cases, but in many of them it looks more like good fortune or backing the winner. And the truth to which this points is that faith is not primarily a virtue in men at all ; it cannot be more than partially described if you put its focus at the human level. Faith is primarily a gift of God ; it is the fact of being used by God and the acceptance of that fact through submission to God. Secular and trivial standards and ways of thinking are likely to make it more difficult for men to see the reality of God's goodness and power, and therefore more difficult for men to be ready to be used. A special enemy of faith is the desire, here and now, to be secure and in command of the situation. Material security is a familiar enough idol, but moral security is perhaps the worse of the two. ' I like to know where I am ', and ' I don't care what anybody says ; this is what I think ' are remarks you will not hear from a saint of any age. You are likely to be able to say of any saint that in some sense ' he went out not knowing whither he went ', that he had a queer gift of being ready for anything without ever being stupidly imprudent.

Your saint is likely to be difficult to shock, because he has a firm hold on essentials and can afford a resilient mind. Your saint is likely to have a sense of humour, because you cannot have that and at the same time be wooden with pride.   Your saint will take himself lightly, because a man takes himself seriously only in as much as he is proud or a coward.   Your saint will travel light because only a man who is frightened of how he will appear to other people carries an enormous portmanteau wherever he goes.   Your saint will be an *interested* person because he spends so little time thinking about himself that he has long practice in thinking about things outside himself.

So we could go on, for what is more agreeable than to write about the amiable and lovely qualities of good people ? But none of this is fundamental.   An American or a Spaniard would have written that paragraph above differently ;   there is something limited about it, perhaps even something insular.   It is just as well that we do not have to claim finality for such judgments.   The fundamental thing is that the ready and alert person is in fact used by God ;   that the story that makes sense of his life is the great story of history and of God's salvation.   Saintly *qualities* are outward signs of that quality of mind and will which makes a man ready for the signal, and able when it comes to interpret it and act on it without a second's delay.

Either you are helping or you are not.   Either you are on duty or you are a passenger.   That is how it looked to the author to the Hebrews.   The same thing which binds the saints together in a community is the one thing that is going to help in the crisis which is the immediate occasion for his writing.   There is faith in example and in history ;   what will now be wanted is the practice of that same faith in the situation that has produced so much panic in the Church. Here, in fact, in this persecution, is the signal.

That is at bottom what a saint is and how a saint helps. What applied to the saints of the Old Testament applies also to those of the New.   Take any saint you like from the Christian calendar—it is important, by the way, that you should like him and be able to imagine his being a man of like mind with yours ; take any such saint, and it will be found that he helps by showing clearly what is the quality of the successful life and death. You see what he did and why he did it, and you realize that this problem of yours is not after all either new or unanswerable. Certain Christian traditions speak much of many saints ; other traditions give most of their attention to the great figures of Scripture. In ancient times there were patron saints for all the guilds of trade, for the good reason, as Chesterton said somewhere, that it helps plumbers to know that there was once a perfect being who really did plumb. There have been many variations on this theme of the faith of the saints, and most of them are gracious and creaturely ; but the variations, where they appear to be really variations, are less important than the theme. Men may choose between the variations but they may not ignore the theme, which is that the faithful mind, the childlike mind, waiting to be used by God, is the mind that knows the secret of living. He whose Rock and Fortress and Might is Christ confesses Christ in his life and in his way of speech and thought. To such it is given to see the King of glory passing on his way, and, perhaps, to hear him say, ' To-day I must abide at thy house.'

49

Richard Baxter (1615–91) *and others*

Ye holy angels bright,
  Who wait at God's right hand,
Or through the realms of light
  Fly at your Lord's command,
    Assist our song,
      For else the theme
      Too high doth seem
    For mortal tongue.

Ye blessèd souls at rest,
  Who ran this earthly race,
And now, from sin released,
  Behold the Saviour's face,
    God's praises sound,
      As in his light
      With sweet delight
    Ye do abound.

Ye saints, who toil below,
  Adore your heavenly King,
And onward as ye go
  Some joyful anthem sing ;
    Take what he gives
      And praise him still,
      Through good or ill,
    Who ever lives !

My soul, bear thou thy part,
  Triumph in God above,
And with a well-tuned heart
  Sing thou the songs of love :
    Let all thy days
      Till life shall end,
      Whate'er he send,
    Be filled with praise.

H.H.L. 58

Praise

'YE holy angels bright' seems to be the right hymn with which to bring to a close this series of papers. It brings us back to the point from which we set out, for it is a hymn of pure praise, and a hymn of cosmic praise. It has even some slight affinity with that 148th Psalm on which our No. 1 was founded ; for whereas that hymn was a paraphrase of the psalm, this one is a fresh application of its central thought— that of calling on all creation to praise the Lord, and it is written in a metre which would ensure at the time of writing (1672) that if it were ever sung it would be sung to a tune that would recall the 148th Psalm in the current metrical version.

It is founded on a hymn by Richard Baxter, but it is not now a hymn that Baxter would easily recognize ; for Baxter wrote sixteen verses, and we have here but four. Baxter's original was more like the psalm in being ample and exuberant and comprehensive ; this is more like a modern hymn in being carefully and skilfully wrought on a clearly discernible pattern.

The pattern is remarkable, and gives the hymn a great rhetorical force. Note how it goes : verse 1, angels ; verse 2, the blessed dead ; verse 3, the Church militant ; verse 4, 'my soul'. You have here a counterpoint between the diminishing scale of vision and the natural tendency of a hymn to gather momentum towards its end, and the result is a remarkably impressive and sustained utterance of praise.

Perhaps the only part of the hymn that needs any direct comment is the very first line. But since the opening phrase has so much to do with setting the tone and predetermining the impression of a hymn (or for that matter its tune), we may perhaps pause a moment on the expression, 'Ye holy angels bright'.

Angels are one of the ornaments of the Christian faith,

not part of the structure of it. They do not appear in the classic creeds, but like all the other ornaments of doctrine they often appear in hymns.

They are, of course, very far from being unbiblical. But they hover round the periphery of the story in a manner that makes many intelligent people somewhat sceptical of their importance, and somewhat confused as to what they ought to believe about them.

The word ' angel ' means ' a messenger ', and in the Bible that is the first connotation of angels ; they appear in the Old Testament, and in the New Testament up to and including the Ascension, as messengers through whom God communicates with men. From this point of view, one may well say that since the complete communication between God and men was established in Christ, this office of angels may be said virtually to have lapsed, and that a good deal of what was ascribed to angels in the Old Testament may well be attributed partly to human beings and partly to God the Holy Spirit.

But there is also the idea of *service* in the conception of the angels ; they ' wait at God's right hand ' ; they are no doubt of the same general order of being as cherubs and seraphs and the other mysterious supernatural characters in biblical mythology. They appear to have great responsibility, and to be at the same time under God's immediate control. Satan in *Job* is a kind of angel, and in a development of that kind of mythology he is a ' fallen ' or disobedient angel, comparable with the ' fallen angels ' in that very odd sixth chapter of *Genesis* (verses 1–4), where we have an explanation of the world's evil not in terms of man's wrong decision but in terms of the confusion produced by angels leaving their appointed sphere and invading the territory of this world. From this point of view, then, angels seem to have been thought of as being in charge of the great elemental movements of the universe, and they are what we might well call in our own time, ' forces '— ' forces of evil ', ' powers of darkness ', ' forces of nature ' and so forth. We hear more of this in *Revelation*.

Thirdly there is a definition of angels which is also a

significant limitation.   Scholastic philosophers define angels
as ' pure intelligences '—minds, that is, without any physical
incarnation of any sort.   (This is the thought in the ' choirs
of angelicals ' in *Gerontius*, see No. 46.)   The Bible catches
this thought in those impressive places where we read that
there are mysteries which are intelligible to flesh and blood
but hidden from the angels ;   the best example of this is
where Peter writes (*I Peter* i. 12) that the scheme of salvation
which has been planned by God is something that ' the
angels desire to look into '.   And Isaac Watts wrote of the
Lord's Supper—

> Th' Angelick Host above
> Can never taste this food ;
> They feast upon their Maker's love,
> But not a Saviour's blood.

And to tell the truth, Christians have derived more edification, on balance, from contemplating the contrast between
the angelic and the earthly state, with advantage to the
earthly, than in speculating upon the particular glories of
the angels themselves.

If then we are calling on the angels to ' assist our song ',
what are we saying ?   We are saying that our Faith entitles
us to call upon the strong, dark, impenetrable forces of the
cosmos, the supernatural messengers of the unknown, to
help us to praise God.   That means that these forces are
friendly.   We have, by faith, achieved dominion over
elemental fears, and can really say, and say with a semblance
of sense, that the whole creation *can* praise God, and wants
to praise him, and will help us to praise him, not hinder us.
Nature and Life are not a conspiracy to silence our praise,
but, as we here declare with boldness, sources from which
we can gather assistance which we entirely need for the
perfection of that praise.

It will not do to enthrone angels where Christ should be ;
nor will it do to attend to them at the expense of the great
family of the Church Triumphant.   Our praise, to be perfect, needs the assistance of all our friends, living and dead.
God's praise is a communal affair, a matter for all living
things, not an interminable series of solos but a chorus.

When a man thinks of the vastness of the universe that has been made known by the astronomers, the imponderable splendour and size of it, the heaped-up glory of galaxy and constellation, he sometimes comes near to being crushed by the weight of what he contemplates. If God has all this to look after, can he then hear my prayers ? If the universe is so unthinkably enormous and full of power, am not I, a man, small and feeble, and is not even my universe but a detail in the whole great picture ? Are not all the choir of heaven and the furniture of earth but stray thoughts in the mind of God ?

The psalmist was a good scientist when he wrote, ' When I consider thy heavens, the work of thy fingers, the moon and the stars which thou hast ordained ; what is man, that thou art mindful of him, and the son of man that thou visitest him ? ' That was well spoken, for it is full of wonder and full of humility, but there is no servility in it. There is none of the attitude of ' Of course I'm not interesting enough for you '. The assumption is that God *is* mindful, that God *does* visit (in the sense of *visit* in No. 23), and in that is the wonder.

It is then proper for a Christian man to see life according to the pattern so skilfully worked out in this hymn. Priority of power, if you like, to the angels. Priority of wonder to the fact that God has demanded the praise of ' my soul '. My praise is offered in the context of all life, common life and cosmic life. In it there need be no artificiality or unreality ; no contempt of the common or shyness in the presence of the cosmic. In the performance of praise common life will rise up to heaven, and the Kingdom will be in the midst of those who love God.

Therefore with angels and archangels, and with all the company of heaven, we laud and magnify thy glorious name, evermore praising thee and saying, Holy, Holy, Holy, Lord God of hosts ; heaven and earth are full of thy glory ; Glory be to thee, O Lord most high.